CRUEL
AND
USUAL

CRUEL
AND
USUAL

OUR CRIMINAL INJUSTICE SYSTEM

Rudolph J. Gerber, Judge
Arizona Court of Appeals

Foreword by Patrick M. Brennan

Westport, Connecticut
London

Library of Congress Cataloging-in-Publication Data

Gerber, Rudolph Joseph, 1938–
    Cruel and usual : our criminal injustice system / Rudolph J.
  Gerber ; foreword by Patrick M. Brennan.
      p.   cm.
    Includes bibliographical references.
    ISBN 0–275–96475–2 (alk. paper)
    1. Criminal justice, Administration of—Moral and ethical aspects—
  United States.   2. Imprisonment—Moral and ethical aspects—United
  States.   3. Criminal law—United States.   4. Judicial ethics—United
  States.   I. Title.
  HV9950.G47   1999
  364.973—dc21   99–14853

British Library Cataloguing in Publication Data is available.

Library of Congress Catalog Card Number: 99–14853
ISBN: 0–275–96475–2

First published in 1999

Praeger Publishers, 88 Post Road West, Westport, CT 06881
An imprint of Greenwood Publishing Group, Inc.
www.praeger.com

Printed in the United States of America

The paper used in this book complies with the
Permanent Paper Standard issued by the National
Information Standards Organization (Z39.48–1984).

10 9 8 7 6 5 4 3 2 1

Copyright Acknowledgments

The author and publisher gratefully acknowledge permission for use of the following material:

Portions of Chapters 2 and 4 were first published as "Felony Murder Rule" by Rudolph J.
Gerber in substantially similar form in the *Arizona State Law Journal*; and as "A Judicial
View of Plea Bargaining" by Rudolph J. Gerber in *The Criminal Law Bulletin*. This article is
reprinted from *The Criminal Law Bulletin* of Jan.-Feb. 1998, pp. 16–31 with the permission
of The West Group.

Dedication to my daughter
Kristin Elizabeth Gerber

Nunc scio quid sit amor
—Virgil

CONTENTS

FOREWORD

Hypocrisy is the tribute vice pays to virtue. The wisdom of La Rochefoucauld's remark is the insight that there is a condition worse than hypocrisy. The hypocrite acknowledges virtue for what it is but fails to make it his or her own. Worse than the hypocrite is the rationalizer, who, making vice to be virtue, vaporizes every chance to be virtuous or even hypocritical. For virtue to be a possibility, we must neither forget nor falsify it; we must acknowledge virtue for what it is, even in the face of the persistent hypocrisy that verges upon decline. Even to be capable of choosing to be virtuous, we must know virtue, and to know it we must be not only teachable but taught. There must, therefore, be a teacher. Enter Rudolph J. Gerber.

Cruel and Usual is a book about the hypocrisy of our criminal justice system. Judge Gerber thus compliments his readers by treating them as women and men capable of recognizing the gap between our ideals and achievements. As he chastens and hastens us toward our ideals, Judge Gerber proves himself a worthy teacher. *Cruel and Usual* is at once monitory and hopeful, a stalwart, intelligent, and humane refusal to let the garden-variety vices of our criminal justice system leech the last seeds of its virtue.

Though a call to virtue in our criminal justice system, *Cruel and Usual* is not the precious product of the ivory tower. Bringing to bear long, personal experience in our criminal justice system, first as a prosecutor, then as a trial judge, and finally as an appellate judge, in each of eight successive chapters Judge Gerber presents massive empirical data to describe some practices current in our criminal justice system. Each of these eight includes a section entitled "The Injustice," in which Judge Gerber argues that the chosen practice is vice, not virtue—a failure to achieve our ideals. The result is a thorough description and efficient thrashing of sentencing guidelines, the bargaining of pleas, the drug war, and a handful of other practices, some timely and some classic but all formative of—and, in Judge Gerber's judgment, destructive of—the lives of more and more people each year. Even readers not persuaded of "the injustice" of this or that practice will have before them both the facts that must inform intelligent analysis and a worthy case for why in ever-expanding aspects of our system of justice, it is injustice that is going forward.

Though *Cruel and Usual* is a résumé of injustices worked by our criminal justice system, Judge Gerber does not begin the book with a theory of justice. Though the book is a summons to a virtuous criminal justice system, he does not begin with an account of virtue. The book does not set forth a sweeping architectonics and then proceed to show how specific practices deviate from it. Rather, each of the eight practices is criticized without explicit appeal to a comprehensive theory of justice or virtue. The arguments, though replete with the language of principle and justice, have a commonsensical quality tailored to win adherents piecemeal. Time after time the reader can agree with Judge Gerber without ever having to swallow a system.

In the ninth and final chapter, however, Judge Gerber lays out his theory of criminal law and then, in light of it, offers specific recommendations for the overhaul of each of the eight offending practices. The recommendations are worthy of consideration; all are carefully calibrated, and some are bold. Judge Gerber urges a modification of rigid sentencing practices to allow judges to take account of the particularities of the persons before them, the use of sentences that not only punish but potentially rehabilitate persons, the decriminalization of marijuana for personal use, and the elimination of the felony murder rule on the ground that it punishes not because of anything about the culpability of the person but instead because of that person's bad luck during the commission of a felony. These are just a few examples. A criminal justice system reshaped along Judge Gerber's lines would look very different.

Nor should this surprise. In *Cruel and Usual* Judge Gerber is not only teaching virtue in the sense that he is reminding us of the ideals of our criminal justice system and exhorting us to rededicate ourselves to their achievement. He also is insisting that the ideal of our criminal justice system itself is, or ought to be, the teaching of virtue in the Aristotelian sense. This theory of the criminal law Judge Gerber denominates the *magisterial* view. The term has liabilities. For some readers magisterial may call to mind *magisterium*, a term that itself bears abundant baggage. But *magister*, teacher, the linguistic source of both terms, contains the root idea. Whereas the contrasting positivist view makes modification of conduct through threat of force the apogee of our criminal justice apparatus, the magisterial view holds that the primary purpose of the criminal justice system is to teach human virtue. On the magisterial view, by the example of its principled treatment of its participants and by the specific demands it makes in terms of conduct, our criminal justice system is to educate citizens in virtue. The virtue and "highest function" of our criminal justice system, on the magisterial view, are its teaching virtue to the humans who live under it.

With the magisterial view's understanding of the highest purpose of the criminal law, the advocates of "morals laws" would, of course, agree. When Robert George, for example, advocates attaching criminality to consensual sodomy, his argument is that the leading purpose of the criminal law is to shape human conduct along the lines of virtue. But if traditional natural lawyers will find much to approve of in Judge Gerber's book, it should be emphasized that in *Cruel and Usual* the usual ruts of natural law analysis have been avoided. The book is a catalog of perceived injustices, but Judge Gerber rarely moralizes. Like the vision of law he champions, Judge Gerber appreciates that, on pain of irrelevance, the teacher must take his pupils as they are. Law that is out of touch, law that fails to sound in the values people hold or can understand invites its own disregard.

What this means, in a pluralistic society, is that law can hope to teach only by being part of, and instantiating, the *ongoing social dialogue*. This is not to fold virtue into vice. It is simply to apply to contemporary reality the ancient wisdom that law is for people (not the reverse) and that if ever it is to lead them to the higher places, it must go out and meet them, wherever they happen to be. It must speak all the languages they use, lest they not find themselves in their law. It must lead them bit by bit, lest they find the law a burden to be thrown off. Thus, though he disapproves of plea bargaining on the principled ground that it substitutes barter for justice, recognizing that the practice is here to stay, he offers a principled plan for increasing the practice's fairness. Thus, though Judge Gerber's principled disapproval of the death penalty might be analytically sufficient, he wisely studies the relevant empirical data to develop objections to the practice recognizable even by those with no patience for his principled objection. Thus, though Judge Gerber finds in our own American theories of criminal justice sufficient reason to retire the felony-murder rule, he adduces examples of its abandonment elsewhere in the world.

Its exacting insistence that we be a people of shared principle, rather than competitors in an unprincipled political race to be toughest on crime and cruelest to criminals, distinguishes *Cruel and Usual* as a book that manages to be moral but not moralistic. I cannot conclude this Foreword, however, without wondering whether the book and the criminal justice system it imagines are not just a little too moral for us mortals. Judge Gerber has done a masterful job of speaking the babel of languages necessary to make principled arguments in a pluralistic society; I do not suggest that his ideals are unrecognizable.

But we are, as Judge Gerber mentions time and again, people who, in fact, imprison our population at a rate six to ten times higher than that of other advanced societies. He offers an explanation: "We are engaged in a repressive experiment to test the degree to which our society, for the first time in its history, can maintain national order through punishment rather than through shared civic values."

Our repressive criminal justice system represents an attempt to occupy the space emptied by morality's involuntary exit from the public square. Judge Gerber, for his part, would call the experiment off, restore virtue talk to the public square, and rededicate our criminal justice system to the achievement of virtue. The experiment is, of course, a failure—unless one concludes that the last decade's modest reduction in violent crime is worth our locking each other in cages for ever longer periods and all out of proportion to terms of imprisonment in the rest of the West and our executing each other more often and for less serious crimes. (Judge Gerber reports that it is now a federal capital offense to interfere with a federal poultry inspector.) To ascertain whether what we have wrought is success or failure, it helps to ask the question posed by a perceptive Canadian thinker a half century ago: Is everyone to use force against everyone to convince everyone that force is beside the point?

Because he knows that law must take people as they are, I am confident that Judge Gerber's own implementation of the magisterial view would bear none of the repressive marks of certain moral forces that would claim alliance. But still I wonder whether we are ready for Judge Gerber's alternative. One consequence of making the achievement of virtue the general justifying aim of the criminal law is that *reform* becomes the system's objective when a person fails to follow the criminal law. As I think C. S. Lewis long ago observed, in the name of doing good for people we may well inflict treatments that exceed the scope of mere punishments. Institutionalized benevolence tends to become despotic. A humanitarian view of the purpose of criminal law may be the most repressive.

It depends on who's running the show. About that, realism, not optimism, is required. For every Judge Gerber, there are a dozen souls who would delight to have a socially legitimated reason to inflict treatments aimed at remaking people they don't like. This is not fanciful. In several years of teaching criminal law, I have been struck by how many students are, by their own description, thoroughgoingly indifferent to the personal integrity and dignity of the men, women, and children they see on the wrong side of the criminal justice system. Unauthentic people get themselves unauthentic leaders. The magisterial view would invest courts, legislatures, and correctional authorities with vast responsibility and power. Are our judges, legislators, and prison administrators equal to the task? So long as the bearers of power lack the stuff to show their power to be authority, a counsel of restraint may be in order.

The basic human problem, as Judge Gerber has reminded us with his magisterial theory of the criminal law, is how to make men moral. The criminal justice system willy-nilly plays a great role in the process of leading people to virtue or vice. *Cruel and Usual* calls our attention to the gap between our system's actual and potential contributions to that process; it should be the rare reader who does not wonder how we have strayed so far from virtue. But recognizing virtue does not make us moral. To be moral, we have to want it. Judge Gerber compliments his readers again by believing that they and their leaders do.

Patrick M. Brennan
Professor of Law
Arizona State University

INTRODUCTION

The stop-history systems which dominate the contemporary scene can maintain the appearance of truth only by an act of violence, i.e., by prohibiting questions concerning the premises and by making the prohibition a formal part of the system.

—Eric Voeglin, *The Ecumenic Age*

Memories of twenty years as a trial and appellate judge include more than shoveling smoke or wading with alligators. One of the most insistent recalls a lunchtime gathering of seasoned judicial colleagues, much given to humor and insight, who all somberly agreed, well before dessert, that despite our oaths and best intents, we judges do a considerable amount of harm—much of which, worse still, seems inescapable. Hence, this modest effort to surmount that futility.

That well-intentioned judges do harm undoubtedly strikes an incongruous note. After all, this is the American judiciary, not that of the former Soviet Union or of Hitler's Germany. But history is not our friend here. Justice is usually in the eyes of those who invoke it. Like the judges of almost every other country in the world, we American judges mechanically intone and apply some criminal laws and procedures that teach wrong lessons to those needing to learn opposite lessons.

Acknowledging deficits in our law does not deny its more frequent, admirable instances of justice. Indeed, that critical acknowledgment may be the first step to strengthen its claim on the ideal of justice.

What are these evils? Here is a start:

- our supposedly more careful criminal law at times uses principles repudiated by our civil law;
- to teach that human life is sacred, we kill those who take it;
- to divest criminals of their manipulative traits, we expose them to our court bazaar of plea bargaining;
- to achieve individualized justice, we impose mandatory, at times draconian, sentences set well in advance of an individual offense;
- to solve their addiction, we send nonviolent drug offenders to drug-infested prisons;
- we punish marijuana offenders with prison sentences while winking at much more lethal alcohol and tobacco usage;
- we send malleable, first-time, nonviolent offenders to share often brutal prison and jail conditions with hardened criminals; and
- to make room at the prison's front door for nonviolent offenders, we push violent offenders out its back door.

There are more. One of our greatest shortcomings is the cloak of formality hindering judges and lawmakers from frank public evaluation of the laws and practices that create these and similar harms. Indeed, popular election campaigns encourage at times the very opposite of honesty, trumpeting instead personal image at the expense of candor.

When judges and lawmakers allow our complex legal procedures to substitute for critical thinking, we diminish the acuity of our moral squint. As we faithfully oil the wheels of justice, it is easier to ask only for more oil rather than about our direction. One of the triumphs of the English common law was that its judges regularly used an inner moral compass about the justice of their rulings. Their realization of the shortcomings of the written law generated a flourishing system of equity courts to correct the excesses of legal formality. In our country at our millennium that moral compass has become skewed by simplistic "tough" solutions to crime, some judicially adopted, some legislatively mandated, that stifle candid evaluation, including practical queries about cost-benefits, tax results, effect on crime rates, and ability to deter.

These issues are both moral and practical; they invoke social science research as much as consistency of principle. They appear unique to the criminal law. In the mercenary debates of our civil law, once the finances are depleted or reallocated, the litigants go home to something approaching business as usual, without being destroyed or learning counterproductive lessons. Wrongheaded practices in criminal law, however, breed widespread public disrespect, teach wrong civic lessons, and in the process can ruin lives beyond repair.

The origins of these harms reside in both the legislative and the judicial branches of our federal and state governments but in different ways in each.

The legislative contribution to criminal injustice resides in our lawmakers' steady politicization of crime issues over the past quarter century as they have discovered that one of the surest routes to vote-getting is unnuanced toughness on crime issues. Toughness generates many more votes than smartness. That crime approaches the number one issue in public concern virtually guarantees that nothing really significant will be enacted to make our streets safer and our legal lessons truly exemplary because the goal of most politicians' crime policy is often only to polish their halos. The public is afraid of criminals, and the politicians are afraid of losing votes. As politicians vie with each other to talk toughest, good slogans take the place of good policy, toughness replaces smartness, and dramatic sound bites become laws with little debate or discussion or dissent.

Our political debate on crime rarely seems about real crime-cutting measures like gun control and mandatory education or government service during juvenile crime-prone years. Crime policy instead is about the politics of getting and staying elected. Much of the public misconstrues slogans like the "War on Drugs" as solutions. But, like war, justice itself is not self-justifying—Hitler and Stalin, after all, also invoked its name. As Karl Jaspers reminded the German people in *The Question of German Guilt* after World War II, passive acquiescence is a greater danger than questioning government policy, especially when lawmakers regularly give the public what they think it wants—tough talk and tough symbols without candid appraisal of their lessons and effects. In the end the campaign for toughness at the expense of justice puts toughness at loggerheads with justice itself.

The judiciary escapes responsibility no less than lawmakers. Our robes, formalities, and discreet silences can mask criminogenic problems that we regularly encounter but to which we easily turn our backs. Readers of François Rabelais encounter Judge Bridlegoose, who served as a judge for many years, respected for his wisdom and skill. The authorities put him on trial when they discovered his method of deciding cases: after receiving arguments and pleadings, Bridlegoose would retire to the privacy of his chambers and cast dice for each party. He would wait an extended time to announce his decision, all the while ordering and receiving elaborate and expensive pleadings. He would eventually explain his court procedures and rulings in solemn Latin malapropisms, creating an aura of profundity and insight beyond the ken of mere mortals.

Bridlegoose defended his decision-making process in several ways. First, in his view formality is necessary for court processes and results to be perceived as authoritative. Second, he needed to cast the dice for exercise in order to keep his mind sharp. Third, the passage of time allows the case to "ripen" while exhausting litigation energies, so the loser more readily acquiesces without appeal. In the end Bridlegoose receives a pardon because the judges judging him have themselves upheld all his decisions on appeal and have themselves engaged in similar conduct.

What makes this parody recognizable is not so much the travesty of judicial demeanor as Bridlegoose's devotion to unthinking formality, a professional hazard that can incubate, termitelike, in the darkness under judicial robes. His rulings gain their legitimacy precisely because of the ornaments of form, regardless of justice or fairness or principle or social consequences. Indeed, to Bridlegoose, formality is the utmost value precisely because it destroys abstractions about justice and practicality. His devotion to ornamental formalism shows that judging can succumb to the triumph of form over substance, of status quo over the candor that begins with wondering whether our laws work well.

A second example is real rather than fictional. In *Justice Accused*, Robert Cover studies judicial approval of slavery in several nineteenth-century cases. The judges in his study, all personally troubled by slavery, faced a "moral-formal" dilemma rooted in their constitutional positivism that they thought required them to uphold slavery despite their serious reservations about its morality. The judges' decisions featured protests that responsibility lay elsewhere, coupled with pleas of distress, helplessness, and even regret. Cover finds in their timidity that the authority of the robe can insulate judges from critical thinking "outside the lines" of formal subservience, leaving the antislavery judges mired in the dilemma of four unsettling choices: (1) apply slavery laws against conscience, (2) follow conscience and be faithless to the law, (3) cheat, and (4) resign.

Why did the antislavery judges almost uniformly bolster the very institution they purported to abhor? Cover sees them constrained by sanctimonious positivism, groping blindly in a forest of forms for a way to preserve impartiality but shrinking from even modest evaluation, and ending by opting unhappily for the safety of the status quo. In place of this model Cover, like Jaspers, suggests that the ideal judge is a social agent always questioning both the moral content and efficacy of the laws judges enforce: Does it work? Is it fair? What are we teaching?

A half century ago in Europe, the phenomenologist Edmund Husserl urged his philosopher colleagues to return to the "things themselves" (*zu den Sachen selbst*) to get beneath centuries of interpretive layers distorting the essence or core reality of things perceived. The more limited effort here shares with his goal the desire to address some basic criminal justice issues that judicial formalism and legislative tough-on-crime policy have repeatedly overlaid with tiresome layers of slogan instead of candor.

These pages are written the old-fashioned way, by myself, not by graduate students or law clerks, over many lunch hours and late nights. No organization inspired or funded them, and they reflect the views of no person or entity other than myself. It has been encouraging, nonetheless, to find my judicial experiences confirmed in the more eloquent writings of Norval Morris, Michael Tonry, Eric Schlosser, and many others cited in these pages. My friends at Western International University and Phoenix College and several thoughtful Jesuits stimulated some of these thoughts, which I trust are not jesuitical. Mary Davison and Kathy Harsha helped greatly with technical matters. These thoughts could germinate only in the fresh air of Arizona's merit system of selecting judges: candid discussion of the following topics or, indeed, of almost any serious crime topic would be nearly impossible these days in any popular electoral campaign. These pages hope to capture a bit of what Victor Hugo, the creator of the law-and-order prosecutor Javert, wrote in *Les Miserables*:

Will the future ever arrive? . . . Should we continue to look upwards? Is the light we see in the sky one of those which will presently be extinguished? The ideal is terrifying to behold, lost as it is in the depths, small, isolated, a pin-point, brilliant but threatened on all sides by the dark forces that surround it; nevertheless no more in danger than a star in the jaws of the clouds.

I
IGNORING PRINCIPLE

1
CRIMINAL SENTENCING POLICY AND POLITICS

The champions of law and order valued those goals in reverse order.
—John Mortimer (cited in Tonry, 13)

Two scenarios separated in place and time illustrate the subtle dilemmas plaguing our current national sentencing policy. The first is an Arizona case where a young drunken driver caused considerable personal and property damage. A jury imposed on him, in addition to compensatory penalties, a $100,000 punitive fine. The majority of my appellate colleagues affirmed the penalties. I dissented, in part, as follows:

This defendant is a young, relatively newly married man with a non-employed wife, with two children who, at trial time, were five years and one month old respectively. He had lost his job in bankruptcy proceedings. His income in the year in question was $38,000; in the prior year it was approximately $44,000. He is the sole support of his family. In addition to suffering compensatory damages of $133,000, he is now saddled with an additional $100,000 in punitive damages.

The $100,000 punitive damage award is two to two and one-half times his family's annual income. It is not speculative to envision that its effects go well beyond punishing simply this defendant. For him to pay off the $100,000 out of savings, even at the harsh rate of $500 per month, without any payment of interest, would require 17 years; when interest is added, it could take almost twice as long, possibly his entire remaining life. This punishment spreads beyond this wrongdoer; it punishes his three innocent family members as well and could readily deny or seriously impair education for the children, force the wife or husband to work second or third jobs, cause deprivation of basic family needs, and put the marriage itself to the test.

The law's deterrent desires regarding this defendant's drinking problem need to be balanced against other social values. Deterrence needs to be measured against the long term effects upon society at large when the debilitation of this family taxes all of us on the rebound. It little profits us as a society to deter so mightily as to cause greater disasters. . . . It is a narrow view to consider simply the true but worn refrain of "sending a message" of deterrence; we also need to embrace the larger view of the effects of disproportionate punitive damage assessments on a family and our larger society when its members are destroyed by poverty, debt, or even unyielding cynicism. Unfortunately, in my opinion, the arctic winter of punishment has here encroached on prudence, leaving one to ponder Clausewitz's comment that, at times, the law becomes plunder without the excuse of war.[1]

The case illustrates the need to tailor sentencing to individual circumstances.

A second scenario: before sentencing Timothy McVeigh to death, the jury in the Oklahoma City bombing case heard heart-wrenching testimony from victims' families. Some say that such testimony, no matter how moving, has no place in the courtroom. Whether a criminal defendant dies requires reasoned reflection, they argue, not victims' anger. Others maintain that juries must know the full measure of the victims' suffering. Judge Richard Matsch seemed torn between these two positions. While he allowed some victims to testify, he excluded testimony that might inflame the passions of the jury. Such emotions, he said, were inappropriate in deciding sentencing.

The judge's ambivalence reflects a conflict among competing purposes of sentencing and general criminal punishment. Those who favor giving victims a voice in sentencing rely on two arguments—one therapeutic, the other retributive. The first sees punishment as solace for the victim, a catharsis, or emotional closure. If punishment benefits the victim, the victim should have a say in it. The therapeutic theory finds expression in laws that invite victims to express their opinions of the defendant, which they sometimes do in raucous courtroom scenes resembling daytime talk shows. Texas law even allows victims and their relatives to berate the defendant in open court.

The second, more sophisticated theory—retribution or "just deserts"— primarily rests on the proposition that punishment is a moral good, a necessity for the offender. Retribution, however, can easily blend into its neighbor, vindication or revenge, where victim outrage controls.

SENTENCING JUSTIFICATIONS

These competing views introduce a deeper dilemma about penal justification. The need for justifying punishment lies in its deprivative character. The law speaks of the convicted person as paying back or satisfying a "debt

to society." Because punishment begins with condemnation and deprivation, it may seem paradoxical, if not contradictory, to inflict a pain not
easily distinguishable from that of the crime itself. This seeming reciprocity
of evils needs justification to articulate implications at work under euphe-
mistic names such as "treatment" or "just deserts."

There are four competing penal justifications for sentencing. Retribution,
in the Kantian sense described earlier, argues that society needs to punish
one who has broken the law for that reason alone. Desert lies in the fact
that the offender, like Dostoyevsky's Raskolnikov in *Crime and Punishment*, is morally responsible because of free choice to break the law. Retribution seeks to restore moral balance simply because the offender deserves it.

Deterrence, which differs sharply from retribution, maintains that punishing dissuades the criminal and others from committing future crimes
because they supposedly predict that expected costs of punishment offset
expected rewards of crime. Special deterrence addresses offenders; general
deterrence views the general populace. But in this theory who is punished
is unimportant provided punishment reaches potential wrongdoers. The
purpose here is not really to punish the past crime but rather to prevent
future crime by penal example. Deterrence thus can justify both punishing
the innocent or punishing excessively in order to improve its exemplary
threat, thus raising a moral dilemma when we punish minor crimes with
disproportionate severity, such as public flogging for parking violations.

Rehabilitation, a third attempt, justifies punishment only insofar as it
reforms the offender via social or psychological therapy. Here, punishment
yields to therapeutic reformation. The focus shifts back to the individual
and away from society and the victim. The goal of rehabilitation appears
in the term "corrections." Extreme forms of rehabilitation abolish personal
responsibility in favor of the notion that criminal behavior resides not really
in the criminal but rather in genes, environment, or illness.

Finally, incapacitation, the fourth penal justification, argues that society
needs protection against crime; its goal is to remove from society those
who are dangerous. Punishment itself is not really justified at all so much
as the identification and segregation of dangerous individuals. The shift is
away from the offender back to society's right to protect itself against an
aggressor. Incapacitation predicts that this offender, unless isolated, will
harm society by further crime. Some of incapacitation's advocates claim
great powers for advance prediction of criminal behavior.

JUSTIFICATION AND SENTENCING POLICY

Up to the 1970s, our state and federal justice systems operated under a
rehabilitative format with moral undertones, featuring indeterminate and
individualized sentencing, minimum terms, and early parole. Subject only

to rare statutory maximums and minimums, judges enjoyed broad authority to sentence defendants to open-ended probation or prison. Parole
boards decided when inmates were sufficiently corrected to be released,
which usually came after serving a third of the maximum sentence. Prison
managers typically would reduce sentences for good behavior. A moral
shell overlay this rehabilitative goal. In the traditional ritual of sentencing,
the judge pronounced not only society's Kantian need to punish but also
its right to do so. Central to that ritual was informed judicial discretion to
weigh all circumstances of the case and all purposes of punishment to acknowledge the moral personhood of the defendant and the moral dimen-
sion of the wrongdoing.

This individualized sentencing philosophy also reflected a non-Kantian
rehabilitative justification. Prisons should "correct" behavior, not just
warehouse inmates or punish them for punishment's sake alone. This goal
seemed like a humane culmination of Montesquieu's eighteenth-century
hope that scientific therapies could fix the prisoner. From the early decades
of this century to about 1970, rehabilitative sentencing accordingly featured
broad judicial discretion, individualized sentencing, and flexible release
dates.

Then a penological earthquake occurred. Support for indeterminate sentencing and its moral-rehabilitative ideal began to erode in the early 1970s,
but for differing, even contrary reasons. Reformers questioned the ethics
and efficacy of the rehabilitation model, especially after Robert Martinson's
finding that prison rarely rehabilitates offenders and that parole boards
could not accurately determine when they had been "cured."[2]

Concern with sentence disparity shaped an important book in 1972,
Criminal Sentences: Law without Order, by then–federal judge Marvin
Frankel,[3] who denounced widespread sentencing disparities. He proposed
a sentencing commission to develop uniform sentencing guidelines. But his
was not the only voice; other pressures also sought sentencing change. Civil
rights activists concerned about racial bias called for an end to sentencing
discretion. Legal scholars working for fairness and against disparity argued
that sentencing should embody uniform rules and results.[4] Political conser-
vatives, concerned about seemingly lenient judges, also pushed sentencing
reform but as a way toward harsher sentencing.[5]

By the mid-1970s, these influences, especially the last, jelled into a new
sentencing philosophy to fill the rehabilitation void, "just deserts," a movement narrowing judges' and prison officials' discretion so as to ensure
"truth in sentencing" and to make harsh prison sentences inescapable for
judges and unalterable by corrections officials. The truth-in-sentencing
movement introduced politics into sentencing and stimulated conservative
politicians to seek very severe prison sentences, less discretion, and elimination of parole release and good behavior credits and instead to advocate

pre-set legislatively circumscribed sentences, so that crimes could be punished in advance with assured severity.[6]

Assumed judicial leniency in sentencing moved legislatures; a quest for predictability in sentencing moved academic reformers. Both agreed that truth in sentencing meant the sentence proclaimed would be the sentence served. The groups had little else in common. This unlikely alliance between those favoring more condign punishment and those favoring more predictable sentencing greatly increased prison commitments as well as the severity of sentences served there. Legislatures, federal and state, moved to mandatory prison sentences for whatever "crime of the month" where judges had seemed too lenient. These mandatory-minimum sentences obliterated judicial discretion and caused substantial increases both in the numbers sent to prison and in the duration of their confinement. The great increase in our national rates of incarceration over the past two decades reflects these sentencing "reforms."

STATE SENTENCING COMMISSIONS

After his 1972 book, Judge Frankel's sentencing commission became the early model for some state sentencing reform. Uniform penal deserts replaced rehabilitation in theory and practice. Frankel recommended that each jurisdiction create a permanent "commission on sentencing," to create sentencing guidelines. His root motivation was to encourage a positive law of sentencing to replace "lawless" discretionary power, to attack irrational disparities, and to import the precept of *nulla poena sine lege* into punishment. His plan only partly succeeded.

Some benefits of state sentencing commissions over indeterminate sentencing soon appeared. In some states, guidelines inspired by Frankel did reduce some sentence disparities.[7] In states like California and Arizona, however, where sentencing policy stayed in legislative hands, and sentence lengths rapidly increased, the prison population increased by 400 percent between 1980 and 1994.[8] By 1997, twenty-two states had sentencing commissions. Guidelines are now in effect in twenty of these states.[9] All have experienced prison overcrowding. Most state sentencing guidelines involve two-dimensional tables with severity along one axis and the extent of criminal history along the other. Sentencing occurs where the criminal record column intersects the severity axis. The chart typically divides crimes into ten or twelve categories.[10] Most provide a range of presumptive sentences such as "twenty to twenty-six months."[11]

Because sentencing charts link punishments to the severity of crimes in order to treat like crimes similarly, they can disregard unique differences among offenders—their personal backgrounds, differing mental states, and the effects of punishments on their families—and thereby treat unlike cases alike. State guidelines can also affect the psychology of sentencing by making sentencing a soulless, computer-like calculus. Unlike the federal guidelines, however, some state guidelines can correct these problems to some degree when they feature a broad presumptive format with flexibility to rise above or below the normative sentence based on specified aggravating and mitigating factors. In addition, probation and some intermediate sanctions still remain realistic options in some states.

FEDERAL SENTENCING GUIDELINES

Federal sentencing is more troublesome and more bureaucratic than state systems. Under the influence of Judge Frankel, the first wave of federal sentencing reform in 1974 sought primarily to reduce unwarranted disparities by subjecting sentencing to rules and to appeal. Harshness was not his goal. By the time of the Sentencing Reform Act of 1984, however, a conservative political climate had selected goals of severity and rigidity other than the Frankel concern over disparity.[12] The Sentencing Reform Act at first seemed a triumph of equity over demagoguery, an experiment of the Progressive Era, when panels of appointed experts seemed the ideal form of penal justice. Judge William W. Wilkins, Jr., Ronald Reagan's first appointee to the federal bench, became chairman. Wilkins and his fellow commissioners devised prison sentences for about 2,000 federal crimes, each with a numerical value. To sentence, a federal judge does not look, as state judges usually do, to an intersecting axis; instead, the judge adds and subtracts points by matching an offender's total points with a range of criteria listed in a mathematical schedule with a "base offense level" adjusted upward or downward. A two-dimensional grid fixes a sentence matching the adjusted offense level and criminal history. A federal judge can depart from the guidelines only with an explanation for doing so.

Federal judges must sentence within the calculated range unless they find unusual factors not adequately considered in the guidelines. Authorized departure is very rare; the guidelines are intended to take account of most important sentencing factors. The guidelines specify fifty-two levels of offense seriousness and categorize each offense on one of these levels, reflecting money or damage loss. They create a single sentencing regime, decided in advance and in the abstract by the sentencing commission. It no longer matters which judge an offender is assigned because the sentence depends not on the judge but on the offense and the past character of the offender as revealed in preset numerical diktats. The offender becomes an inanimate variable in an equation, a cog in a sentencing machine.[13]

The Sentencing Reform Act directed its commission to ensure rigidity in sentencing. Prison is thus the normative sentence: there is little role for nonprison dispositions.[14] The guidelines cover all federal crimes, regulatory as well as "white-collar" and also drug and common-law crimes. The sentence announced, less time off for good behavior, is the sentence served. The maximum good-time credit is 15 percent of the sentence; thus, at least 8.5 years must be served of a 10-year sentence.

Unlike the moral and discretionary aspects of past sentencing, judicial sentencing under the guidelines involves mind-numbing mathematical calculations seemingly far removed from individual attention. The commission did not deduce sentencing guidelines from principles of justice or other logical penal principles. Instead, it based its sentences on mathematical averages of past sentencing practices regardless of their differing goals. As a result, no commission member or judge can give an explanation for any current sentence other than to say that it is simply and generically the mathematical average of what has been imposed in the past.[15]

Here is an actual federal sentencing:

The court finds that the base offense level is 20. Pursuant to Guidelines 2K2.1(b) (4), the offense level is increased by two levels [to 22]. . . . The Court notes that the criminal convictions . . . result in a total criminal history category score of 18. At the time of the instan[t] offense . . . the defendant was serving a parole sentenc[e] in two causes of action. And pursuant to Sentencing Guidelines 4A1.1(D), 2 points are therefore added. The total criminal history points to 20. And according to the Sentencing Guidelines Chapter 5, Part A, 20 criminal history points establish a criminal history category of 6. . . . [As a result] the guidelines range for imprisonment is 84 to 105 months.[16]

The judge doing this math must feel awkward in trying to explain a sentence that may appear more mathematical than moral. The proceeding demands no moral deliberation, little discussion of the human qualities of the victim or the defendant, and little mention of unquantifiable moral aspects of crime or of the type of sanction suited for any purpose. Sentencing in the end becomes simply compliance with numbers. Like the law in Kafka's *Trial*, federal sentencing has receded into an impenetrable mathematical maze inaccessible to the offender—and to justice itself. The judge sentences not so much an individual as a criminal *genus* defined by numbers on a chart containing 258 boxes.

Advocates of federal sentencing contend that these reforms have led to greater equality in punishment regardless of race, gender, or class because sentences treat each offender equally. True, the discretion judges once possessed to impose nonuniform sentences has been virtually eliminated. Classifications that favored wealthy majority individuals like education, employment history, and family obligations have been invalidated as considerations. These changes have helped to eliminate some discrimination and uncertainty in sentencing. But the picture is far from positive. This attempt to eliminate "interjudge disparity" by curtailing judicial discretion has meant the virtual elimination of particularized moral judgment from sentencing. As federal judges themselves have noted, reduction of interjudge disparity has created a system that ignores moral judgment, individuation, and proportionality.[17]

Relevant Conduct

Under the federal guidelines prosecutors have vast power to shape a sentence by decisions made in their offices rather than in courts. Their "adjustments" allow for new discrepancies in sentencing. These adjustments for conduct include the defendant's acceptance of responsibility, role in the offense, and level of cooperation or obstruction. Prosecutors are given discretion to make adjustments based on these criteria to thereby increase or decrease a potential sentence.

The greatest area for federal prosecutorial discretion outside the charged offense lies in the concept of "relevant conduct," which means the offender's past antisocial behavior apart from the present charge. "Relevant conduct" includes conduct alleged in charges dismissed or conduct that resulted in acquittals or that was never charged at all. The relevant conduct format was adopted to offset plea bargaining by requiring consideration of prior behaviors uncharged or existing in dropped or acquitted charges. But the standard is capricious: the Sentencing Commission has failed to explain why it requires relevant conduct sentencing for some crimes, such as narcotics crimes or fraud, but not others, such as bank robberies.

As Tonry and others have observed, the relevant conduct standard poses difficult fairness issues because it mandates an increased sentence, on a finding less than beyond a reasonable doubt, that the defendant did something illegal before the convicted crime.[18] The prosecutor has to prove only that the offender committed the other antisocial behavior, and if so, the offender receives a more severe sentence than the conviction by itself would warrant. By contrast with state systems, federal judges *must* factor into sentencing a numerical value for these antisocial behaviors even if they have not resulted in a conviction or been otherwise established by any traditional criminal standard of proof.

Discretion and Bargaining

The federal guidelines also take discretionary power away from the sentencing judge and hand it largely to the less experienced prosecutor, who has the sole authority to decide whether and how severely to frame a charge and whether a defendant's cooperation warrants a sentence reduction. Even a defendant who cooperates still might not receive a shorter sentence if the assistance falls short of the prosecutor's expectations.

Victoria Toensing, the head of the Justice Department's Criminal Division in the Reagan administration and a key player in the development of the sentencing guidelines, says their purpose was truth in sentencing, not power for prosecutors. "Do I want to give [discretion] to a federal judge who has been confirmed by the Senate and supposedly has some experience in the law, or to a 28-year-old prosecutor right out of law school who has no practical experience?"[19] Nonetheless, despite her irony, the traditional checks-and-balances approach to sentencing succumbs in the guidelines precisely so as to enhance prosecutors and restrict judges' power.

The sentencing guidelines have become administrative handcuffs clamped on judges. A prosecutor who negotiates a disposition by setting charges and offering a plea effectively restricts the sentencing range. The judge as a result becomes a handcuffed accountant, subordinate to prosecutorial strategies, rather than a moral agent free to roam widely in the statutory range. The prosecutor has assumed much of the judge's sentencing authority by presenting "relevant" conduct solely for sentence enhancement and by shaping the sentence through the charging decision, plea bargaining, and the sentencing hearing.

The severity of the guidelines encourages their own circumvention; their rigidity subverts the goals of uniformity and proportionality. Circumvention of statutory mandates becomes routine via plea concessions, which occur with frequency, especially in drug cases. This very circumvention reflects a response to the inflexibility and severity of the federal sentencing machine.[20] One judge has responded to a survey about the guidelines by noting with disgust: "[T]he Guidelines . . . have made charlatans and dissemblers of us all. We spend our time plotting and scheming, bending and twisting, distorting and ignoring the law in an effort to achieve a just result. All under the banner of 'truth in sentencing'!"[21]

In sum, four problems arise with the federal guidelines: (1) inexperienced prosecutors can shape sentences more so than experienced judges do; (2) judges sentence not as moral reasoners but as computers without being able to consider important individual, differentiating circumstances; (3) the guidelines require judges to take into account past behavior before the conviction, including dismissed, acquitted, and never-filed criminal charges—a policy of seeming injustice because individual failings are considered whereas individual mitigating circumstances are not;[22] (4) the harshness of the guidelines encourages plea bargains.

MANDATORY SENTENCES

The second troublesome feature of our current sentencing scene at both federal and state levels is mandatory-minimum sentences, which provide that a specified circumstance requires (1) that the court *must* sentence the defendant to prison and (2) that its duration will be longer than without that circumstance. The underlying assumption is that all offenders committing the same crime resemble each other in culpability. State mandatory

laws, which share many of the problems of inflexibility in the federal guidelines, tell judges what sentence to impose rather than set boundaries for
sentencing.

Every state since 1980 has enacted laws mandating minimum prison sentences based on the legislative assumption that harsher penalties reduce
crime and that judges cannot be trusted to impose harsh sentences. Most
mandatories apply to murder or aggravated rape, drug offenses, possession
of firearms, or repeat felonies. Between 1985 and mid-1991, Congress enacted at least twenty new mandatory penalty provisions; by 1991, more
than sixty federal statutes and many state laws defined hundreds of crimes
subject to mandatories.[23]

During the 1980s and 1990s, political figures of both parties campaigned
on "tough on crime" platforms promoting these mandatory sentences.
Some of the broadest mandatory-minimum sentencing statutes of the past
twenty-five years are these: New York's 1973 Rockefeller drug law targeted
narcotics traffickers and users; Massachusetts' 1974 Bartley-Fox Amendment required that possessors of unregistered handguns receive a one-year
prison term; and the 1977 Michigan Felony Firearm Statute added two
years to any sentence involving firearm possession. The federal drug control
acts of 1986, 1988, 1990, and 1992 assigned long mandatory prison terms
to drug traffickers that are doubled for offenders with prior convictions.
Mandatory "three-strikes-and-you're-out-for-life" provisions targeted triple
felons, including nonviolent felons.[24] In its first two years on the books,
about 70 percent of the cases tried under it involved three strikes that were
nonviolent, with drug use the most common offense.[25]

Severe mandatory minimums for all offenders contradict incapacitation's
goal of reserving prison space for the most dangerous offenders. Tough
mandatory minimums without regard to age also reserve expensive prison
space for aged inmates well past the end of their criminal careers and
thereby transform increasing parts of prisons into tax-supported old folks'
homes. Mandatory-minimum statutes also induce prosecutors to reduce
charges and overturn guidelines. Moreover, in lengthening the sentences of
some offenders while reducing others, mandatory minimums actually increase sentence disparity. Political-inspired mandatory sentencing has
wrecked proportionality because of charge and plea manipulation caused
by their very inflexibility.

Mandatories have thus become courthouse bargaining chips. They apply
most frequently to low-level, first-time offenders with defenses and, thus,
an incentive to go to trial. Mandatories can be avoided only by striking a
plea deal with the government. Where prosecutors apply mandatories
against some defendants but not against others charged with the same conduct, the problem of disparity reappears. Prosecutors' covert plea bargaining vitiates the mandatories' objectives of deterrence, reduced disparity, and
even-handed punishment. The nation now has widespread de facto sentence

manipulation by prosecutors—persons who lack the experience and careful selection process given judges.

EVALUATION OF SENTENCING REFORM

Our nation's sentencing policy might have improved in the 1970s but for at least three political developments. First, a new rationale for sentencing to replace a morally based rehabilitation was preempted by the conservative mantra of "truth in sentencing," making prison sentencing more mechanical and generic rather than proportionate to the individual offense. Second, fixing sentence lengths has increasingly become the plaything of politics; legislatures have continually increased sentences to make legislators look tough, generating in the end both rigidity and demagoguery. Third, our sentencing policy has become extremely harsh—second in the world only to Russia.[26]

Severity

The most distinguishing feature of our combined federal and state sentencing policy now is the fixation on absolute severity of incarceration coupled with the assumption that only imprisonment behind bars counts as true punishment. Despite tiresome conservative complaints of leniency, the average lengths of prison sentences in the United States are six to ten times greater than in other Western countries. The current ten-, twenty-, and thirty-year minimum sentences for our drug crimes are impossible in other civilized countries. Despite tripling average prison sentences for violent crimes between 1976 and 1999, federal crime legislation passed in 1994 conditions future state prison construction grants on still more increases in sentence lengths for violent offenders, using 1993 as a base.[27] Our current sentencing laws suggest that the only limiting principle of punishment has become "if it deters, then it is good." Prison sentences have become so severe that a person can receive nineteen years for driving a car with crack cocaine in it or twenty-five years for stealing a slice of pizza.[28]

This severity is unwarranted. In recent years, 36 percent of drug offenders and 21 percent of the national prison population have been low-level, nonviolent first offenders whose offense did not involve sophisticated criminal activity.[29] The average sentence for these nonviolent prisoners—most sentenced under mandatory laws—was 81.5 months, that is, about seven years—hardly lenient by any measure.[30]

It makes neither fiscal nor penal sense to punish nonviolent offenders with longer sentences than violent ones. The once-perceptive U.S. House of Representatives explained in 1970 why such highly severe penalties do not work:

The severity of existing penalties, involving in many instances minimum mandatory sentences, has led in many instances to reluctance on the part of prosecutors to prosecute some violations, where the penalties seem to be out of line with the seriousness of the offenses. In addition, severe penalties, which do not take into account individual circumstances, and which treat casual violators as severely as they treat hardened criminals, tend to make conviction . . . more difficult to obtain.[31]

No Individuality

Even if our federal and state sentencing policy can survive its aberrant severity, which it cannot, its devotion to mandated sentences gives rise to a faceless rigidity that ignores individual differences in offenders. This policy contradicts our human experience of allocating blame based on differing culpability. For example, our everyday practice is to ascribe different culpability to a careless shooting compared to a purposeful one, and we view bulk drug sales by a major drug importer more blameworthy than street sales by a poor young ghetto dweller.[32]

In just deserts policy, however, two offenders who commit the same offense with similar criminal records receive the same penalty. If one is unemployed and homeless, and the other has a job and supports a family, a just sentence would treat them differently because the second offender seems more responsible and less likely to repeat. As in the *Olson* case at the start of this chapter, the offender's spouse and children—who have committed no crime—will lose a partner and a parent for so long as the offender is in prison and may also lose a home and a car and be forced onto welfare at public expense. The prisoner, besides losing his liberty, may find when he gets out that he has also lost his family—considerations seemingly appropriate for the sentencing judge.[33]

To make the label of the crime alone blindly determine the sentence invites injustice. A wife who kills a long-abusive, threatening husband receives the same sentence as a premeditating gang murderer. A defendant who plays a minor role in a drug transaction that involves large quantities, even after receiving a reduction for a minimum role, nonetheless can be facing a very lengthy sentence because of the quantity of drugs involved. That defendant may be an indigent mother with a young dependent or an uneducated off-loader of a boat carrying huge quantities of drugs without knowing the precise quantity.

Family responsibilities have also been all but eliminated as a consideration by the guidelines. Women prisoners are more likely to have dependents who lived with them prior to incarceration. Often, when mothers are incarcerated, children lose their primary caretaker and become subject to placements outside the home. Incarcerated women are more likely to lose their children to foster care than men. Thus, gender-neutral sentencing reforms actually can disproportionately harm incarcerated women and their children.

The guidelines also fail to consider the difference between male and female rates of recidivism. Many statistical studies show that women are less likely to be repeat offenders. Judges nonetheless must treat men and women equally when determining possible recidivism, even though there may be a demonstrable difference in recidivism rates. Prior to the recent sentencing reforms, judges could consider the anti-social differences between men and women to avoid imposing uniformly long sentences. Equal treatment policy has won over sentencing that takes into account crime's gender differences. A more nuanced sentencing system would not make uniform the punishments of women and men but would instead provide flexible sentences necessary to protect society from both crime and unproductive expense. Gender-neutral laws do achieve uniformity in *sentencing*, but not uniformity in *punishment*, because these laws disproportionately harm women more than men.[34]

Deterrent Effects

The strongest argument for mandatory penalties is that they deter would-be offenders and thereby reduce crime. However, the consensus of research bodies about deterrence is hardly encouraging.

After an exhaustive examination, the National Academy of Sciences Panel on Research on Deterrent and Incapacitative Effects concluded, "In summary . . . we cannot assert that the evidence warrants an affirmative conclusion regarding deterrence." Professor Daniel Nagin of Carnegie-Mellon University has been more explicit:

The evidence is woefully inadequate for providing a good estimate of the magnitude of whatever effect may exist. . . . Policymakers in the criminal justice system are done a disservice if they are left with the impression that the empirical evidence . . . strongly supports the deterrence hypothesis.[35]

The National Academy of Sciences Panel on Understanding and Control of Violent Behavior reached the same conclusion in 1993. After showing that the average prison sentence per violent crime *tripled* between 1975 and 1989, the panel asked if increasing the prison population had an effect on violent crime and answered, "very little," an answer, as Tonry points out, taking account of both deterrent and incapacitative effects.[36]

Ironically, most mandatory penalty provisions enacted during the 1980s and 1990s concerned drug crimes, which are especially insensitive to deterrent goals because vacancies created by drug arrests are filled immediately. As a result, according to criminologist Alfred Blumstein:

There is no evidence that harsh drug law enforcement policies have been at all successful. Of course, that result is not surprising. Anyone who is removed from the street is likely to be replaced by someone drawn from the inevitable queue of replacement dealers ready to join the industry. It may take some time for recruitment and training, but experience shows that replacement is easy and rapid.[37]

One of the most careful studies of mandatory sentences was the New York Bar's evaluation of New York's "Rockefeller drug laws," which required severe mandatory-minimum sentences for drug crimes and forbade plea bargaining. The study found no discernible effects on drug use or crime in New York. Mandatory penalties for drug crimes have not demonstrably reduced drug trafficking.[38] In fact, New York's severe drug laws have become counterproductive. Owing largely to the increase in drug offenders, the state's prison population shot up from 21,621 in 1980 to nearly 70,000 by 1999. Governor George Pataki has begun arranging for the early release of low-level offenders so as to free up space for truly dangerous felons. As long as New York City keeps rounding up street-level drug dealers and prosecuting them under the Rockefeller laws, the pressure on the state prison system will continue. The pressure will also continue on cost-conscious elected officials to undermine its own draconian laws.[39]

In 1997, the Rand Corporation published a study assessing the cost-effectiveness of mandatory-minimum sentences for drug offenses.[40] Using a variety of expert statistical techniques Rand estimated how much U.S. cocaine consumption would be reduced by investing an additional $1 million in longer sentences for drug dealers, as compared with investing that money in conventional law enforcement—arrest, prosecution, and incarceration—or drug treatment. Spending $1 million on longer prison sentences would reduce cocaine consumption by about 13 kilograms (about 28 pounds). Investing it in law enforcement would reduce it by 27 kilograms. Putting the same amount of money into treatment programs, by contrast, would reduce consumption by more than 100 kilograms.

As for reducing cocaine-related crime, Rand found that every dollar invested in drug treatment was ten times more effective than law enforcement and fifteen times more effective than mandatory minimums. The reason, Rand concluded, is that when a supplier is jailed, he or she is usually replaced by another supplier, whereas treatment directly reduces the market for drugs. Rand concluded that "mandatory minimums produce the smallest bang for the buck by far."[41]

It is true that the past few years have seen a broad decline in our violent crime rates, suggesting that mandatory penalties may be causing the decline. With the exception of crack cocaine, however, no such decline appears in other drug offenses, which continue to spiral upward despite pervasive mandatory sentences. Mandatory penalties seemingly do not play a role in the reported decline in other crime. The 1997 Rand study of mandatory drug sentences finds that they are not only ineffective in reducing crime but also wasteful and deserve repeal.[42] A more recent Harvard study by a prosecutor, William N. Brownsberger, a Massachusetts assistant attorney general, finds that mandatory drug sentencing laws waste prison resources on nonviolent, low-level offenders and reduce prison space needed for violent criminals.[43] Attorney General Brownsberger's conclusion about mandatory drug sentences applies equally well to all mandatory sentences:

When incarceration becomes routine, it cannot deter crime and may even be seen as a positive rite of passage. . . . Mandatory penalties for drug offenses lead to the inflexible over-application of harsh punishment, further diminishing its deterrence value, misallocating scarce resources and exacerbating high incarceration rates. Our main conclusion from this report [is] that we need to moderate our mandatory drug sentencing policies.[44]

As to the larger issue of causes for nondrug crime decline, a 1997 study by the Justice Department agrees with most criminologists, namely, that the causal explanation for the recent crime decline is not found in mandatory sentences but in a temporary decline in the juvenile population coupled with a shift from crack cocaine (closely tied to homicide and assault rates) to other drugs.[45]

The conclusion remains that mandatory penalties have no significant effects on rates of serious crime.[46] These data, or ignorance of them, generate a striking policy dissonance. Legislators who enact mandatory sentencing laws support them for symbolic and political reasons, while justice officials and criminologists in the trenches oppose them for institutional, research, cost, plea bargaining, and inefficiency reasons.[47] These researchers, including many judges, know well that mandatory penalties simply do not work because they ignore offender differences, shift power from judges to prosecutors, cause widespread plea bargaining, produce distortions in case records, and result in expensive penalties as indiscriminate as they are ineffective.[48]

CONCLUSION: THE INJUSTICE

Several principles—or their lack—appear in the preceding description of our nation's current sentencing policies. One of the first, which applies both to state commissions and to the federal guidelines, is that sentencing has become legislative more than judicial, defined in advance of, and apart from, an offender's courtroom appearance. A second is that both systems' sentencing machines reflect a patently incorrect assumption that all those who commit the same crime are possessed of equal moral culpability. Allied to this observation is the curious systemic paradox that the effort to avoid the evil of sentencing disparity has also avoided the justice of individualized consideration: we have replaced disparity with faceless offenders en masse.

We have done all this with a remarkable penal myopia that envisions the normative sentence as incarceration in a prison to the virtual exclusion, especially in the federal system, of less expensive, more nuanced, and more effective intermediate sanctions such as probation, work furlough, community service, fines, and house arrest. As we have become tough at the expense of being smart, we have also created a state and federal sentencing regime that works mostly by number rather than by moral culpability. The very language of "just deserts" connotes the individual's moral culpability—the very thing our mathematical classifications overlook. We are left with a sentencing regime with little or no rationale for any given sentence.

In our courtrooms and in our cases there is almost no articulated concern as to whether a particular defendant should be sentenced in the interests of deterrence, rehabilitation, retribution, or incapacitation and no mention of the defendant's experience, character, and work service or accomplishments and failures. Judges are not allowed to take them into account because under both regimes of state mandatories and federal guidelines, these matters count, if at all, less than pre-set mathematical formulas.

Where does this analysis leave us for the competing purposes of punishment defined at the start of this chapter?

Rehabilitation—the notion that punishment should "fix" the offender—has been tacitly disavowed in most jurisdictions. Today no sentencing philosophy adopts rehabilitation as its explicit systemic penal goal, although some judges invoke it for rare offenders.

Deterrence—the notion that severity of punishment prevents crime by its example—fares no better. Although "tough on crime" politicians still cite it as a goal, research on the effects of severity and on mandatory penalties, as well as on the death penalty, resolutely shows little to no deterrent effect from these severe and expensive penal policies. The reason is not new or hard to fathom: criminals simply do not calculate the risks of apprehension or punishment before they act.[49]

Incapacitation—the notion that criminality can be predicted and prevented in advance by lockup—prompts some to argue that crime would be reduced substantially by incarceration of all defendants convicted of certain crimes. The vast increase in lengthy prison terms needed to implement such policies cannot be justified in cost-benefit terms. The central moral problem remains one of accurate prediction. A strategy of selective incapacitation that targets repeat offenders more likely incarcerates low-risk offenders unlikely to commit volume crime if left in the community. Overprediction of dangerousness or future criminal activity is bound to occur.[50] Even the best prediction instruments overpredict by 3 or 4 to 1. For each future high-rate offender incapacitated, two or three noncriminogenic people would also have to be confined.[51]

This analysis leaves just deserts as the remaining contender justifying punishment policy, the idea that offenders who commit the same or similar crime with the same mental state should receive the same sentence on moral grounds. Just deserts theories rest on the idea that punishment should be *deserved* and on the notion that crimes and punishments can be abstractly ranked in order of severity. In principle, retribution would shape the sentence narrowly to the individual's unique moral status. In our nation's sentencing courts, however, offenders, in fact, are viewed as a faceless crime class rather than as individuals. In practice, just deserts politics makes punishment both far more severe and more impersonal than retribution would dictate and by encouraging plea bargains creates disparities as extreme as any that existed under indeterminate sentencing.[52]

Given these four recognized justifications for sentencing—rehabilitation, deterrence, incapacitation, and just deserts—if each for differing reasons fails, our collective sentencing policy today appears purposeless, lacking both rationality and coherence.

Some lawmakers naively assert that all four of these penal purposes can coexist. However, the first three sentencing purposes—rehabilitation, deterrence, and incapacitation—are utilitarian, concerned exclusively with avoiding future offenses. The last purpose—just deserts—is not utilitarian because it sees punishment as a necessary end in itself without regard to preventing future crime. The utilitarian goal of avoiding future crime and the retributive goal of imposing just punishment for past crime cannot be reconciled. Avoiding future crime conflicts with deserved punishment for past crime, distinctions erased in the guidelines' gross averages of past sentences.

If incapacitation were the sole determinant for sentencing, prison terms would reflect predictors of future crime: the higher the likelihood of crime, the longer the sentence. Two of the best predictors of criminality are low education and unemployment. Thus, chronic unemployment and low educational skill suggest recidivism and would increase a sentence. Indeed, if incapacitation were the only distributive principle, little reason exists to wait until an offense is committed to impose sanctions. It would be more efficient simply to screen the general population for dangerous traits and "convict" those found with those traits and incapacitate them in advance— a policy wholly inconsistent with punishment based on prior culpability.

If deterrence were the sole distributive principle for punishment, the probability of apprehension would help determine the sanction needed to deter effectively. Offenses with a low probability of arrest would be punished more severely to compensate for the perceived low probability of apprehension. Sentences would then reflect not the gravity of the offense or the dangerousness of the offender but only the difficulty of being caught—a policy also incompatible with degrees of culpability in a desert-sensitive system.

If rehabilitation governed sentencing, responsiveness to treatment would be central. A minor but resistant offender might call for a long term of incarceration, and a serious but compliant offender might call for no incarceration if long-term treatment would avoid recidivism in the one case, and no treatment at all were needed in the other. Indeed, under a pure rehabilitation principle, as with a pure incapacitation principle, no reason exists to wait for any crime to occur. The at-risk population could simply be screened, disabled, and rehabilitated for possessing known criminogenic traits. Sanctions could be imposed to compel treatment and thereby avoid anticipated crime—a policy of preventive detention in advance of crime wholly inconsistent, again, with principles of moral desert.

Just deserts and utilitarian sentencing principles are thus at loggerheads. Utilitarian principles not only look to different criteria but also fail to view culpability factors central to desert. The nature of the crime committed may be of little import under some utilitarian purposes if rehabilitation, deterrence, and/or incapacitation can be achieved, as they well might, independently of the offender's true culpability.

Factors that determine punishment under utilitarian principles differ from those under a desert principle. To advance either of these goals, a sentencing system must sacrifice the other. Nothing can reconcile these differences; they simply reflect different goals, time periods, and moralities. Utility addresses how to avoid future crimes. Desert concerns itself with the past—how to give morally deserved punishment for a past offense.

Our present-day federal and state sentencing policies trying to do both— or neither—necessarily collapse by default into unprincipled emotionalism of victims at sentencing—a venting of anguish, tears, and verbal assault as in daytime talk-show confrontations. Our collective sentencing policies show an abandonment of both judicial detachment and systemic rationale.[53] Both the federal guidelines and the proliferating federal and state mandatories, with minor exceptions, ignore relevant individual culpability and result in sentences that seek simultaneously to deter future crime and punish past crime in the name of "just deserts," all the while ignoring the offender's individual moral culpability. Overall, the system's need is not for blanket categories or blindfolded judges but what Aristotle called equity, "the correction of the law where it is defective owing to its universality."[54]

NOTES

1. *Olson v. Walker*, 162 Ariz. 174, 781 P.2d 1015 (App. 1989).

2. D. Lipton, R. Martinson, and J. Wilks, *The Effectiveness of Correctional Treatment: A Survey of Treatment Evaluation Studies* (New York: Praeger, 1975).

3. M. Frankel, *Criminal Sentences: Law without Order* (New York: Hill and Wang, 1972). See also M. Tonry, *Sentencing Matters* (New York: Oxford University Press, 1996).

4. K. Davis, *Discretionary Justice: A Preliminary Inquiry* (Baton Rouge: Louisiana State University Press, 1969).

5. R. Messinger and B. Johnson, "California's Determinate Sentencing Laws," in *Determinate Sentencing: Reform or Regression* (Washington, D.C.: U.S. Government Printing Office, 1978).

6. M. Tonry, *Sentencing Matters*, 10–11, to whom this analysis is indebted (hereafter, Tonry).

7. Id.

8. F. Zimring and G. Hawkins, *Incapacitation: Penal Confinement and the Restraint of Crime* (New York: Oxford University Press, 1995).

9. See R. Frase, "Sentencing Guidelines in the States: Still Going Strong," 78 *Judicature* 173 (1995); M. Wesson, "Sentencing Reform in Colorado: Many Changes, Little Progress," 4 *Overcrowded Times* 14–17, 20 (1993). See also Tonry, 10–11.

10. Tonry, 15.

11. Id., 14–15, 89.

12. The Sentencing Reform Act (SRA) of 1984, Pub. L. No. 98–473, 98 Stat. 1837 (1984) (codified at 18 U.S.C. §§ 3551–3586, 3621–3625, 3742 [1988] and 28 U.S.C. §§ 991–998 [1988]). The Sentencing Commission, "an independent agency in the judicial branch composed of seven voting and two nonvoting, ex officio members, has the principal purpose to establish sentencing policies and practices for the federal criminal justice system by promulgating detailed guidelines prescribing the appropriate sentences for offenders convicted of federal crimes" *U.S. Sentencing Comm'n, Guidelines Manual* § 1A1 (1994) (hereafter, Guidelines). In *Mistretta v. United States*, the Supreme Court held the SRA and the sentencing guidelines constitutional against a challenge of excessive delegation of legislative authority and violation of the separation of powers. 488 U.S. 361, 412 (1989).

13. P. Robinson, "Sentencing Reform," 8 *Crim. Law Forum* 12 (1997).

14. U.S. Sentencing Commission, *Sentencing Commission Guidelines Manual* (St. Paul, Minn.: West, 1994).

15. K. Stith and J. Cabranes, "Judging under the Federal Sentencing Guidelines," 91 *N W L.R.* 1247, 1265 (1997).

16. M. Flaherty and J. Diskupic, "Despite Overhaul, Federal Sentencing Still Misfires," *Washington Post*, A1 (Oct. 6, 1996).

17. Stith, 1264.

18. Tonry, 93.

19. S. Estrich, *Getting Away with Murder* (Cambridge, Mass.: Harvard University Press, 1998), p. 80.

20. See U.S. Sentencing Commission, *The Federal Sentencing Guidelines: A Report on the Operation of the Guidelines System and Short-Term Impacts on Disparity in Sentencing, Use of Incarceration, and Prosecutorial Discretion and Plea Bargaining* (Washington, D.C.: U.S. Sentencing Commission, 1991). Federal judge Lawrence Irving of San Diego chose to resign from the bench to protest these laws. U.S. district judges Jack Weinstein of Brooklyn and Whitman Knapp of Manhattan have refused to preside over drug cases because of the harsh sentencing guidelines. Judge Harold H. Greene of the U.S. District Court in Washington, D.C., refused to impose a guideline sentence of seventeen and a half to twenty-one and a half years for selling one tablet of Dilaudet, holding that such a sentence would violate the Eighth Amendment prohibiting cruel and unusual punishment.

Fifty of the 680 federal judges refuse to hear any drug cases because of sentencing guidelines. The 1990 and 1991 judicial councils of all twelve federal circuits asked Congress to reconsider federal mandatory sentencing laws and recommended more judicial discretion. See L. Forer, *A Rage to Punish* (New York: Norton, 1994), 5.

21. Stith and Cabranes, 1247, 1265.

22. I. Nagel and S. Schulhofer, "A Tale of Three Cities: An Empirical Study of Charging and Bargaining Practices under the Federal Sentencing Guidelines," 66 *So. Cal. L.R.* 501–566 (1992).

23. Tonry, 134 ff.

24. Id., 146–147. See also A. Reiss and J. Roth, *Understanding and Controlling Violence* (Washington, D.C.: National Academy Press, 1993).

25. M. Massing, "The Blue Revolution," *N.Y. Review of Books,* 35 (Nov. 19, 1998).

26. Tonry, 13.

27. Id., 100–101.

28. See E. Slater, "Pizza Thief Receives Sentence of 25 Years to Life in Prison," *L.A. Times,* A1 (Mar. 3, 1995); Note, 70 *So. Cal. L.R.* 171, 1740 (1995).

29. U.S. Dept. of Justice, "An Analysis of Non-Violent Drug Offenders," 2101–2103 (1994). In Arizona, as of June 30, 1997, of the 23,780 prison population, 4,026 were imprisoned for drugs only, and 57.8 percent of the entire prison population were nonviolent offenders.

30. Tonry, 151–152.

31. Id., 142, quoting the House of Representatives statement in the U.S. Sentencing Commission Report of 1991. Congress discovered that mandatory minimums actually yielded fewer convictions because of prosecutors' reluctance to prosecute crimes with such harsh penalties. Congress repealed almost all of the drug-related mandatory-minimum penalties in 1970. See Comprehensive Drug Abuse Prevention and Control Act of 1970, Pub. L. No. 91–513, 84 Stat. 1236 (codified as amended in scattered sections of 21 U.S.C.). See also 21 U.S.C. § 848 (1970).

32. N. Morris, *The Future of Imprisonment* (Chicago: University of Chicago Press, 1974), 37.

33. Tonry, 18–19, uses this example.

34. Note, 70 *So. Cal. L.R.* 1717, 1740 (1995).

35. D. Nagin, "General Deterrence: A Review of the Empirical Evidence," in *Deterrence and Incapacitation,* ed. A. Blumstein (Washington, D.C.: National Academy Press, 1978). See also Tonry, 137.

36. Tonry, 137. See also Reiss and Roth, *Understanding and Controlling Violence*. Recent crime rate reductions are explainable by the economic boom and temporary demographic reductions in the size of the teenage population, the most prone to crime.

37. A. Blumstein, "Prisons," in *Crime,* ed. J. Q. Wilson (San Francisco: ICS Press, 1994). See also Tonry, 141.

38. Joint Committee on New York Drug Law Evaluation, *The Nation's Toughest Drug Law: Evaluating the New York Experience* (New York: New York Bar Association and Drug Abuse Council, 1978). See also Tonry, 141.

39. Massing, "The Blue Revolution," 35, indicating growing support to rescind the Rockefeller laws as counterproductive.

40. J. Caulkins, C. Rydell, W. Schwabe, and J. Chiesa, *Mandatory Minimum*

Drug Sentences: Throwing Away the Key or the Taxpayers' Money? (Santa Monica: Rand Corporation, 1997).

41. Massing, "The Blue Revolution," 36.

42. Caulkins et al., *Mandatory*.

43. W. Brownsberger, *Profile of Anti-Drug Law Enforcement in Urban Poverty Areas of Massachusetts* (Cambridge: Robert W. Johnson Research Foundation, 1997). Brownsberger studied 1,175 inmates in the Massachusetts state prison system and found no deterrent effect but did find nearly half of those sentenced to that prison system had no record of any violent crime.

44. Id., vii, ix.

45. As reported in "Drop in Homicide Rate Linked to Crack's Decline" (summary of Justice Department Study), *New York Times*, A17 (Oct. 27, 1997).

46. Tonry, 141.

47. Id., 160.

48. Id. For explanation of recent crime reductions, see note 36.

49. "It has always befuddled me that we can seriously assume that the members of our society who behave the least rationally will engage in the rational process that underlies the deterrence theory. When coupled with the mathematical computations that the sentencing guidelines require, it is hard to believe that anyone is serious about deterrence." A. Mitva, "Justice Reform," 43 *Cleveland S.L.R.* 5, 7 [1997].

50. Zimring and Hawkins, *Incapacitation*.

51. Tonry, 138–139.

52. Id.

53. Robinson, "Sentencing Reform," is helpful for this theoretical analysis.

54. Aristotle, *Nicomachean Ethics*, in *The Complete Works of Aristotle,* ed. Jonathan Barnes (Princeton: Princeton University Press, 1983).

2

A JUDICIAL VIEW OF PLEA BARGAINING

The Court's authority—possessed of neither the purse nor the sword—
ultimately rests on substantial public confidence in its moral sanctions.
—Felix Frankfurter, *Baker v. Carr*, 369 US 186 (1962) (dissenting)

Plea bargaining is the process by which a criminal defendant and a prosecutor barter to resolve a criminal case.[1] Over 90 percent of federal and state criminal cases settle by plea agreement as opposed to trial.[2] The guilty plea, rather than the trial, has become the embarrassing centerpiece of our criminal courts, on which could be engraved, per a recent cartoon, "Liberty, Justice, and Plea Bargaining." Plea bargaining at best appears as a mixed blessing—if at all. The centrality of "copping a plea" invites this inquiry into its causes, forces, and expectations, as well as its impact on mandated and guideline sentences.

CAUSES OF THE PLEA BARGAINING CLIMATE

A major, but subtle, cause of plea bargaining is the complexity of today's criminal trial. Because of its detailed procedures, trial has ceased to be an efficient routine disposition of a criminal charge. Instead, the courtroom players engage in a form of condemnation without adjudication: they threaten the defendant, in effect, with a greater sanction for invoking the constitutional right to trial.

Over the two centuries since our courts have constitutionalized most

136125

parts of the jury trial, higher courts have transformed it into such time-consuming complexity that it can work well only exceptionally. By contrast, the common-law trial was a summary proceeding largely judge-directed and lawyer-free; the present complex law of evidence lay far in the future; extended *voir dire* was unknown, and appeal was, as a practical matter, unavailable. Two centuries ago, felony trials took place with such remarkable dispatch that English common-law judges discouraged defendants from pleading guilty. A guilty plea then was shorter than a trial, but not by much. This picture has now turned upside down.

Today's raison d'être of plea bargaining is expediency. Even its proponents would not contend that bargaining is a desirable route to justice. The practical claim for bargaining is that it approximates the outcome of true adjudication at greater speed and lower cost. Our Supreme Court frankly explains why it treats plea bargaining as an essential component of the administration of justice: "If every criminal charge were subjected to a full-scale trial, the States and the federal government would need to multiply by many times the number of judges and court facilities."[3]

The strongest defenses of our present bargaining practice are expediency and the reluctance of our officials to allocate enough resources for trial. No principled argument exists for plea bargaining. Reformist efforts often reduce to proposals to reject secret covenants secretly made in preference for open covenants secretly made—a reform undeserving of the name.

Plea bargaining has become not some adjunct to our justice system; it *is* the system. Allocating criminal punishment through this sort of dappled street bazaar is, of course, unappealing.[4] Our cosmetic solution lies in proclaiming the abstract right to our elaborate trial process. But this assertion is only window dressing, because we mouth it while imposing guilt on almost every defendant through a very uncosmetic bargaining process well short of trial. The unfairness lies in determining a defendant's guilt without investigation, evidence, testimony, or impartial fact-finding.[5] This unfairness may harm especially the poor and unsophisticated who accept bargains because of the threat of harsher penalties after trial and for that reason surrender the system's much advertised protections. Ironically, judges often give the bargained-for sentences because of what prosecutors and defense lawyers do *not* say at sentencing because the sentencing hearing intends, at bottom, to support the deal struck by the attorneys.

Attorney caseloads are a major cause of plea bargaining. From the standpoint of the lawyers, bargaining becomes a necessity not for any reason inherent in the defendant or in the facts of a case but for caseload management. Neither prosecutors nor defense attorneys want to try criminal cases. Prosecutors cannot move their cases without getting guilty pleas; defense attorneys cannot acquire new clients and get them to enter more guilty pleas if they have to try many cases. A defense attorney's financial motivation is to encourage a client to give up the right to trial for the benefit of moving the caseload. Most defense attorneys—the notable exceptions being those known as true trial lawyers—depend on plea agreements to make their fees and move cases. Trials are a wrench in this turnstile.

ADVANTAGES

Negotiated resolution of criminal cases seemingly serves the superficial interests of all concerned.[6] The prosecutor's objective in each case is to obtain the optimum level of punishment at the least cost in order to free resources for other prosecutions. By tailoring each plea offer to the expected costs of trial, the likelihood of success, the expected evidence, and sentence, the prosecutor can maximize the supposed deterrence from the office's finite resources. Similarly, the defendant who seeks to minimize punishment is better off accepting the plea offer if the negotiated punishment is lower than the anticipated posttrial sentence. From both perspectives, plea bargaining not only saves court time and litigation costs but also seems to serve both the public interest in maximizing deterrence expectations and the defense interest in minimizing the sentence.

Role economy is a further advantage of plea bargaining. Attorneys, judges, and court personnel often process several pleas per day.[7] Plea proceedings do not require the time to empanel a jury and present arguments and evidence. Nor does plea bargaining require the bailiffs, clerks, witnesses, and other personnel needed for a trial. Nor does it entail trial-related expenses such as laboratory testing and expert witness testimony.[8] Given their present procedural complexity, if trials rather than pleas were the norm, a great increase of prosecutors, defense attorneys, judges, and staff would be needed.

Plea bargaining thus appears to benefit both defendants and prosecutors much as settling a civil suit benefits each party. The defendant trades the uncertainty of conviction by verdict and a more severe sentence for the certainty of a less severe one.[9] The prosecutor achieves quick conviction on at least some of the charges, saves the time required for witnesses and trial, and remains free to process more cases.[10] Because it expedites caseloads with little expense in resources and mutually benefits both parties, plea bargaining appears to be a useful and economic tool.

SHORTCOMINGS

Despite these advantages, plea bargaining is hardly innocuous.[11] Several distinct shortcomings appear. The first relates to crime victims. As a group victims usually find bargaining offensive. They often believe that the sentence imposed on a pleading defendant is more lenient than it would be for the original charge. The present justice system grants victims several newly created rights, including the right to be notified and attend court proceedings; the right to confer with the prosecutor; and the right to information about the conviction and sentencing.[12] By using these rights to convey their emotional reaction to the crime, victims can affect the plea and the discretion of both the prosecutor and the judge in shaping the sentence. This informational contact sometimes permits victims to have direct input in the plea bargain, but they often resent bargains whether or not they are informed.

Another shortcoming of bargaining is prosecutorial integrity. Prosecutors often overcharge in order to gain negotiating leverage for a plea. Manslaughter on its face is thus chargeable as second-degree murder; a simple burglary is chargeable as both burglary and trespass and usually also as attempted theft. Overzealous prosecutors heavily weigh the scales of justice on their side not because the defendant has *really* done the precise crimes charged but rather because from the very start of the case they feel the need to generate leverage in order to coerce a plea.

For sophisticated defense attorneys and defendants, this practice of overcharging means that charges do not really mean what they say. Overcharging turns out in the end to be counterproductive because astute defense counsel and defendants perceive it exactly for what it is. The original charges are not taken as seriously as they would be if they strictly conformed to the facts, so a smart defense attorney advises a client to hold out because the charges are inflated. Thus, instead of encouraging a climate favorable to a plea, overcharging impedes that result: bluster on the part of the prosecutor encourages bluster on the part of the defendant.

A further problem is record fraud. If the plea is to a lesser or to a fictional offense, the crime pled to has a distorting effect on criminal justice records. The conviction becomes a suspect unit for counting crime, for making restitution awards, for parole, for sentencing guidelines, and for crime and criminal justice agency records. In the absence of a factually accurate plea, officials find themselves searching for the "real" offense concealed behind the fictional plea in order to restore the proper fit between the charge and the plea. As a result, the public over time comes to assume that recorded convictions for lesser offenses invariably mask greater charges. The guilty plea feeds a pervasive sense of fiction and inaccuracy both inside the justice system and in the public observing it.

Bargaining has other serious flaws. A primary one is sentencing uncertainty.[13] The prosecutor need not recommend a particular sentence until the defendant pleads. The plea usually does not bind the judge to the sentencing recommendation. The prosecutor cannot always guarantee the defendant the bargained-for outcome. The trial judge can upset hard-fought negotiations by not accepting the agreement.

Sophisticated defendants use this uncertainty to their advantage. They can come to view the court system as they view society at large, as a "con game" that they can manipulate at will.[14] Ideally, the justice system should disabuse them of this notion.[15] Instead, the system encourages this manipulative attitude via the bargaining process itself.[16]

Subtle coercion to surrender the right to trial is another shortcoming. Procedural rules permit a judge to reject a plea resulting from threats or coercion.[17] However, the bargaining process itself can be inherently coercive aside from any overt threats by the prosecution.[18] The promise of a lenient sentence in return for a plea wedges the defendant in the dilemma of having to forgo trial or face more severe sanctions after trial. Prosecutors commonly use the threat of trial as a tool to induce a plea.[19] Judges may also pose an implicit threat by imposing higher sentences on defendants who insist on their constitutional right to trial. This coercive process prompts defendants who are potentially innocent or whose conduct does not merit the original charge to plead guilty to escape a more severe result after trial.[20]

CONFLICTS OF INTEREST

These serious shortcomings reflect subtle conflicts of interest. The elected district attorney usually sees a personal goal as career enhancement. An effective crime control strategy contributes to that goal, but marginal deterrence effects are likely to be imperceptible to the general public. A high conviction rate, a good relationship with influential private attorneys, and an absence of high-profile trial losses contribute more effectively to political standing. Although the district attorney may want occasionally to try a case that could be resolved more efficiently by settlement, more often the officeholder wants to ensure conviction even if it requires a generous plea offer because, after all, the conviction rate or "batting average" makes the best electoral argument. The elected prosecutor's image thereby often differs from best serving the public interest.

Deputy prosecutors who actually negotiate plea agreements do not usually share the elected district attorney's political ambition. If the deputies can elude monitoring by their superior and appear to remain committed to a deterrent philosophy, they can seek optimal sentences even at the expense of their chief's reelection chances. The deputy's immediate goal, in fact, usually is not to find the optimal strategy for controlling crime or reelecting the superior but instead to maximize the deputy's own welfare, defined by some loose combination of trial experience, career advancement, job satisfaction, and leisure. Pursuing an optimal crime control strategy may advance the deputy's career, but other factors are likely to do so more directly.

By contrast, the elected chief prosecutor often has unique personal and professional reasons to avoid trying risky cases. The chief prosecutor's elected position means that some guilty pleas negotiated case by case may diverge from the public interest in optimal supposed deterrence. This divergence usually takes the form of unduly lenient sentence offers in order to ensure high conviction rates.

On the defense side, loyalty problems are more acute and financial but result in a similar dissonance. Like prosecutors, defense attorneys regularly have personal or professional reasons for trying a case when their clients would be better served by settlement. Defense attorneys sometimes have powerful incentives to avoid a trial, even one that serves the client's interest. While the incentives vary with the attorney–client relationship, the net effect is nearly always the same: a sharp divergence between the economic and efficiency interests of attorney and client, with powerful financial incentives for the attorney to settle promptly rather than try the case.

These agency problems become less serious when a defendant has retained paid counsel. Attorneys compensated on an hourly basis generally do not face financial pressure to minimize the time spent on a case. Nor do they feel a personal incentive to settle quickly. But defense attorneys are almost never paid in that fashion. Only a minority of defense attorneys are retained by paying clients; nearly all of them work for a flat fee in advance. Since court rules usually prohibit them from withdrawing after a court appearance, retained attorneys must go to trial if settlement negotiations fail, and in that event, the additional services must be rendered free of charge. Accordingly, the financial pressure on defense counsel to settle early is intense.

A defense counsel who has reasonable expectations of settling a case, or in order to induce client agreement to settlement, benefits by exaggerating to the client the risks of trial and by overstating the likely penalty. Indeed, it serves the bargaining interests of *both* counsel to exaggerate the expected severity of sentence following trial. Post-trial sentencing fires must be made to appear hotter than those following a plea.

Because the interests of both prosecutors and defense counsel diverge from those of their clients, *both* sides regularly lack zeal for trial. The two sets of agency problems may seem to cancel each other out, but they don't, because they operate on different levels. For plea negotiation no marketlike solutions protect either the public or the accused. The process is incapable of public monitoring of the penal prices negotiated in guilty pleas. On the defense side, reputation helps to encourage client loyalty by retained counsel. The resulting attorney–client relationship is not the voluntary contractual arrangement lauded in law schools but a partly involuntary union heavily infected by conflicts of scheduling, timing, financial interest, and the virtual absence of effective means to monitor client loyalty. These structural flaws damage both innocent defendants and the public interest in proportionate sanctions.

The only alternative to bargaining—going to trial—avoids these problems. Trials in open court with sentences imposed by a neutral fact-finder protect due process rights, minimize the risk of unjust conviction, and further the public interest in adequate punishment. Low-visibility plea negotiation undercuts all these interests. Bargaining lawyers possess inadequate incentives for proper performance; prospects for effective monitoring are limited or nonexistent; and the coercive dynamics of negotiation creates weighty pressure for defendants falsely to condemn themselves. Plea agreements defeat the public interest in effective law enforcement while they simultaneously deny defendants the advertised benefits of a trial. In the process, bargaining inflicts undeserved punishment on innocents who could win acquittal.

INNOCENTS' DILEMMA

Conviction of the innocent is a serious concern. The Supreme Court stated in *In re Winship*:

It is critical that the moral force of the criminal law not be diluted by a standard of proof [or a procedure for conviction] that leaves people in doubt whether innocent men are being condemned. It is also important in our free society that every individual going about his ordinary affairs have confidence that his government cannot adjudge him guilty of a criminal offense without convincing a proper fact finder of his guilt with utmost certainty.[21]

The nightmare that most plagues bargaining is the innocent defendant facing a life sentence if convicted who is offered a pretrial bargain of a few years in prison. The huge disparity between the posttrial sentence and the pretrial negotiated sentence tempts the innocent defendant to accept the offer. The sentencing differential may reflect low probability of conviction, or it may stem from limited prison space. In either case, the defendant may be better off with the offer than without it: a murder defendant who has a 50 percent chance of winning at trial wants a regime that allows the option of, say, a ten-year sentence via plea. The situation is a constraint, to be sure, but preventing the offer only makes it a greater dilemma. The wrenching part of the picture is the duress working against the right to vindicate oneself by trial.

The duress problem certainly harms innocent defendants. Coercive plea bargaining can deny any realistic right to trial. The most important, real-world fact about our justice system at our millennium is that the accused enjoy few truly realistic strategic choices no matter how many rights our constitutions exult. In the majority of cases, they have little true opportunity to exercise these rights because their exercise is too expensive, time-consuming, and risky. Because trial can impose a stiff tariff on those choosing it, sentencing pressures cause most to bargain away its lofty privileges.

Innocent defendants may plead because they lack sophistication in bargaining and are unable to verify their innocence.[22] The number of such innocent defendants may be minimal.[23] Nevertheless, innocent persons may become trapped in a process that leaves them no viable avenue for acquittal because they exercise their right to trial in the face of almost certain conviction. The plea process has no effective means for protecting these truly innocent defendants.

STATUTORY OVERBREADTH

The bargaining problem goes beyond definitions. A causal relationship exists between mandatory punishment, the coercion of guilty pleas, and the resulting erosion of the right to trial. The long-standing pattern of our criminal law has usually been overbroad definition of crimes coupled with broad prosecutorial and judicial discretion. Legislatures writing criminal codes show more concern with capturing the behavior they wish to punish than with excluding behavior they wish to ignore. This practice not only creates broad criminal liability, but also overlapping crimes as a single criminal act falls within the definition of several offenses ranging from trivial misdemeanors to serious felonies. Moreover, defendants can often be charged with more than one offense for what seems like a single act.

The system has historically compensated for this overbreadth in two ways: (1) prosecutors have been given absolute discretion *not* to charge any given crime, and (2) judges traditionally have exercised discretion to sentence within a very wide range. The second protection is critical. Without it, in a world of fixed sentences, a prosecutor filing the charge can determine not merely the charge but also the posttrial sentence and thereby inflict severe punishment on defendants who do not really deserve it when no disinterested court would apply such punishment in isolation.

Where mandatory sentences govern, prosecutors use the dangerous and repetitive offender bargaining chips by charging defendants with these sentence enhancement allegations, only to dismiss them later as part of a bargain. Lack of uniformity inevitably leads to sentence disparities regardless of who makes the decisions. Prosecutors no less than judges are susceptible to arbitrariness when exercising unguided discretion. When deputy prosecutors, sometimes fresh out of law school, determine on a case-by-case basis whether to enforce mandatory sentence enhancements, uneven sentencing results are inevitable.[24]

ROLE REVERSAL

The statutory overlap and inconsistency of most American criminal codes thus effect a pervasive and contradictory reversal of role and function in the bargaining process: the system locates vast, unstructured, and unreviewable discretion to charge, to enhance, to aggravate, to bargain, and to fix sentence in the least experienced, most hidden, least correctable, and least answerable sector of the justice system, and at the same time this system tacitly divests the public's more experienced, more carefully chosen, and more responsive judiciary from any comparably significant role in these decisions. Judges' circumscribed courtroom discretion is reviewable and correctable; the wide-ranging manipulation of charges and penalties by prosecutors hides from public view in prosecutors' offices, where it remains as uncorrectable as it is unreviewable. This role reversal probably does not meet the public's expectations, nor is this reversal consistent with the way these role players are chosen, nor is it compatible with the differing ways these officials are made responsive to the public.

Mandatory sentencing gives prosecutors enormous bargaining power. A causal relationship exists among mandatory punishment, the coercion of guilty pleas, and the resulting erosion of the right to trial. Sentences usually reflect simply whether defendants choose to exercise their right to trial. Those convicted after trial usually receive some sentence enhancement; those who plead guilty receive lesser sentences at the whim of prosecutors because of their cooperation. Prosecutors thus use sentence enhancements to coerce guilty pleas and to discourage the right to trial. The severity and arbitrariness of mandatory sentences combine to make the right to trial an unacceptable risk even for innocent persons, who, by definition, have no incentive to cooperate in securing a conviction for something they didn't do.

THE ILLUSORY RIGHT TO TRIAL

Arizona offers a compelling and probably typical example of the illusory nature of trial. In that state, severe mandatory sentencing has promoted rampant plea bargaining and, in tandem, decreased the realistic availability of the right to trial.

In 1976, the Arizona legislature passed a severe, charge-based mandatory sentence-enhancement law, which permitted prosecutors to induce guilty pleas by charging a firearm possession whenever a defendant was eligible and then dismissing the charge in return for a plea to the underlying crime.[25] Immediately after the statute went into effect, the guilty plea rate in the state's largest court system increased significantly. In 1976, the calendar year immediately preceding the effective date of the new law, 10.4 percent of criminal cases proceeded to trial.[26] In the following two years, while the new law was in effect, the trial rate fell to 8.74 percent. The average percentage of cases going to trial dropped to 5.73 percent during the first three full years of sentencing under the 1978 code.

A 1982 law further increased the sentencing of persons convicted of felonies while on probation or parole.[27] This statute, still in effect, requires a sentence for the new offense of life imprisonment without release for twenty-five years. After this law was enacted in 1982, the percentage of cases going to trial in Maricopa County, the state's largest, declined sharply. In the three years immediately preceding the implementation of the mandatory 1982 law, the trial rate had been about 5.73 percent.[28] This figure fell to 4.27 percent during the four years immediately after the 1982 law went into effect.[29] While the 1982 statute may not have been the sole cause of this decline in the trial rate, the bargaining leverage it granted prosecutors suggests that it was the primary cause.

Overall, in less than a decade the criminal trial rate fell from 10.40 percent to 3.77 percent.[30] During the same period, judicial, prosecutorial, and public defender resources increased at a greater rate than the trial court's caseload, suggesting that the decline in the trial rate cannot be attributed to caseload pressure but rather to prosecutors' use of the hammer of mandatory penal enhancements to coerce pleas and thereby deny access to trial. Prosecutors then drop the enhancements in return for the defendant's giving up the right to trial.[31] In sum, mandatory sentences effectively make the right to trial too risky to be exercised, even for an innocent defendant.

Plea bargaining offers the only realistic option for a defendant facing severe mandatories. Prosecutors accordingly use the dangerous and repetitive sentencing enhancements as plea bargaining chips by charging defendants with sentence enhancements, only to dismiss them later as part of the bargain. In a recent year in Arizona, prosecutors dismissed mandatory repetitive offender allegations in 76 percent of all cases in return for a guilty plea.[32] Plea bargaining may be a necessary evil, an essential lubricant without which the machinery of justice would break down, but it is utilized in arbitrary ways that counter mandatory sentence philosophy. Armed robbery is pled down to robbery, aggravated assault to assault, completed crimes to inchoate ones. Uniform statutory sentencing thus disappears. In Professor Tonry's words:

Mandatory penalties elicit more devious forms of adaptation. When Michigan judges in the 1950s and the 1970s acquit factually guilty defendants, or when Arizona prosecutors in the 1980s permit people who have committed serious crimes to avoid mandatories by pleading guilty to attempt or conspiracy, or when prosecutors and judges fashion new patterns of plea bargaining solely to sidestep mandatories, important values are being sacrificed.[33]

PROSECUTORIAL VERSUS JUDICIAL DISCRETION

Prosecutors, in effect, have more clout than judges regarding realistic availability of the right to trial. The prosecutor decides not only which offenses to charge but also whether to seek sentence enhancement and aggravation, whether to offer a plea, what that plea agreement will be, and whether there will be a stipulated sentence. These are the most significant decisions shaping a criminal case and the option of trial, and there is no judicial or legislative control over them. The decisions of prosecutors, typically recent law graduates, are discretionary, hidden from public scrutiny and judicially unreviewable. Ironically, the visible courtroom rulings of the more experienced judiciary are reviewable, but these rulings have less penal impact than the hidden, discretionary decisions of prosecutors.

In short, where a legislature drafts broad criminal statutes and then attaches mandatory sentences to them, prosecutors have an unchecked opportunity to generate easy pleas because of statutory overbreadth and inflexible sentences. This difficulty can be avoided in several ways. Reducing legislative overbreadth in criminal statutes is the most obvious and the most unlikely. If the behavior that falls within a given statute merits the mandatory sentence, the strategic problem disappears. But reducing statutory overbreadth has its costs because it occupies prosecutors and courts with minuscule elements of detailed crimes, thereby increasing the expense and difficulty of trial. As one alternative, one might do away with mandatory sentencing.

EXEMPLARY MODELING?

A further problem with plea bargaining reflects the exemplary nature of public trial and condemnation. Like medieval morality plays, our criminal justice system assumes, in part, that the public spectacle of wrongdoing, capture, and punishment deters crime. Guilty pleas drive a gaping hole through these assumptions. If too few contested trials occur, the public will not learn the moral lessons on which an exemplary criminal law depends. By agreeing to such pleas, the parties abandon not only their own rights but also their moral roles as pedagogical surrogates for a larger public interest. Public support for the justice system depends on public confidence in resolving high-profile cases where the community has a greater than ordinary interest in knowing the full facts. The same is true when a crime involves a sensational public figure.

In such cases, rumors and suspicions abound that there is more than meets the media's eye. The sparse information contained in the charge and the monosyllabic guilty plea offer too little information to allay those suspicions. Indeed, in cases like the killings involving Martin Luther King or the Kennedys or the O. J. Simpson cases, "more is at stake than one-to-one justice between State and accused or accused and victim. . . . Anything short of complete disclosure in such cases inflames public cynicism about our system of justice to a dangerous point."[34] At one time, in some places, such concerns led to prohibitions of guilty pleas in capital cases, a rule still followed in the military justice system.

Most seriously among its negative features, contemporary plea bargaining aggravates, rather than erodes, the criminal mentality of most pleading defendants. In their day-to-day dealings most criminals view the world at large as a con game where people and institutions are to be regularly manipulated for the criminal's benefit. This mentality, of course, is what gets them hauled into court in the first place. The court, we assume and want them to know, is the institution that will forthrightly disabuse them of this manipulative attitude once and for all.

Rather than disabusing them of this attitude, however, the court's plea bargaining dialectics actually encourage it. Each side takes repeated bargaining positions and engages in delay, bravado, and bluster. Defendants who are the least bit sophisticated conclude that the justice system operates by bluster and dickering just like what they attribute to the outside world. Plea bargaining is but another kind of street bazaar con game where deceit, bravado, and putting on a stolid face can generate a "good deal." In the process, the defendant learns, if it was not known already, that instead of standing for principle, the justice system echoes the manipulative talents of the outside world. To this extent, rehabilitation is seriously undermined because the system reinforces a devious mentality analogous to the mindset that got the criminal into trouble in the first place.

ALTERNATIVES

Because of these serious drawbacks to plea bargaining, alternative methods of easing the court caseload abound. These reforms range from complete abolition of bargaining to various forms of mandated sentencing and enforcement of prosecutorial bargains or eliminating lawyers. While each reform has its advantages, most of these proposals correct one problem by merely creating another.

Many commentators favor a complete abolition of plea bargaining.[35] They argue that abolishing bargaining does not unduly burden courts or prosecutors.[36] However, bargaining still occurs subversively even in those systems that discourage or forbid it. Even in European countries such as Germany, whose criminal justice system does not include plea negotiations, tacit concessions for defendants who plead guilty often occur.[37] In England, a pleading defendant receives an explicit sentence reduction for cooperation in eliminating a trial.

In American jurisdictions plea bargaining takes place covertly even when it is banned outright. Jurisdictions that have eliminated plea bargaining have not collapsed from overloaded dockets. In Alaska, New Orleans, and Ventura County, California, where plea bargaining has been eliminated, and in Oakland County, Michigan, where it has been partially eliminated, dockets have not overflowed. But these policies overlook continuing sub-rosa bargaining. Many prosecutors in these areas continue to offer explicit or implicit concessions. Defense attorneys continue to seek pleas from fear that judges might penalize defendants who insist on trial.[38] The pressure to compromise in order to secure cooperation and avoid wasting resources tempts courts, prosecutors, and defense attorneys to seek covert concessions.[39]

Proponents of plea bargaining contend that eliminating bargaining would clog already overworked trial courts. Some discount the idea that eliminating plea bargaining necessarily increases caseload.[40] They argue that the jury system itself increases the length of trials and urge reform of it rather than bargaining.[41] They contend that a bench trial performs the same adversarial fact-finding function as a jury trial with less cost.[42] The Philadelphia bench trial system seems to support this theory.[43]

Other commentators advocate reform of the bargaining process itself. Mandated sentencing reduces the uncertainty of the process by requiring judges to impose statutorily determined sentences on defendants guilty either by plea or by trial.[44] A prosecutor can promise with some certainty that if the defendant pleads guilty to such a crime, it is the statutory sentence that the judge will impose. However, such a system has its own flaws. Mandated sentencing removes discretion from judges who merely rubber-stamp sentencing decisions made by nonjudicial officers, prosecutors, and defense counsel. Stipulated sentences effectively cause judges to lose their sentencing discretion. Above all, mandatories themselves prompt plea bargaining as a means to escape their severity. The Federal Sentencing Guidelines have merited deserved criticism for this reason.[45]

Substantial evidence emerges from research sponsored by federal sentencing commissions that lawyers, often with judicial approval, do regularly bargain around severe sentencing guidelines and mandatories. Sometimes this deviation occurs by having the defendant plead guilty to an offense where the maximum sentence is less than the applicable range. Sometimes it is done in even more byzantine ways. The judge may disregard the guidelines altogether if the prosecutor files a motion requesting a mitigated sentence because of the defendant's "substantial assistance to the government." If the prosecutor's real motive is to avoid an unduly harsh sentence, courtroom observers and record-keepers cannot know whether the claimed substantial assistance was useful or even provided at all. Such bargaining distorts mandatory federal guidelines at sentencing in at least a third of all sentencings.

Generally, any proposal that limits judicial discretion creates problems elsewhere. Judicial discretion imposes vital control on the sentencing process by ensuring proportionality and individual tailoring of punishment. A judge can offset a prosecutor who recommends sentences too high or low for the charge.[46] Such discretion offsets overt duress, such as overcharging or overrecommending, by ensuring that the plea escapes prosecutorial threats or promises.

A counterpoint variation on the proposal to limit judicial discretion would give the prosecutor absolute discretion to fix sentencing.[47] Under the present system, the prosecutor brokers plea agreements which the judge has discretion to reject. Giving the prosecutor ultimate authority to fix sentences eliminates the uncertainty that surrounds the plea process.[48] The sentencing guidelines take this approach by mandating numerically calibrated sentences within various ranges. Under these guidelines a prosecutor can predict with great certainty the sentence of a pleading defendant. But in this system prosecutors, rather than judges, decide the sentence—a basic role reversal.

The federal guidelines also address eliminating case-by-case bargaining.[49] Replacing the current system with statutorily fixed, nonnegotiable concessions would not necessarily decrease the numbers of guilty pleas.[50] Such a scheme might equally increase the likelihood that guilty defendants would plead guilty to get the fixed sentence, while innocent ones would take their chances on acquittal.[51] Defense attorneys may be tempted to overstate to their clients the benefits of taking the fixed-plea discount rather than risking trial.[52]

The prosecutor could set a maximum sentence that the judge can tailor downward but not upward.[53] The judge could then reduce unduly severe sentences and protect defendants who have consented to ill-advised bargains or who have been the victim of overcharging or prosecutorial vindictiveness. However, this variant on judicial discretion poses the concern discussed earlier that judges thereby acquiesce in prosecutor-imposed sentences disproportionate to the crime charged.[54] Sophisticated defendants can capitalize on such a system by refusing to negotiate to reduce the maximum penalties. Prosecutors, for their part, may drive sentencing recommendations upward to offset a judge's tendency to impose less severe sentences.[55]

Another proposal aims to eliminate lawyers from the initial stages of the process and limit the ban on self-incrimination.[56] Such a system would permit innocent defendants to identify themselves more readily and facilitate detection of the guilty, supposedly because defense attorneys would not be available to "coach" defendants into "stories" based on what the defense attorney believes the prosecutor needs to hear. Such a system would also curtail bargaining because inexperienced defendants supposedly would be less likely to hold out for favorable deals as they would under the guidance of a defense attorney.

Abolition of bargaining could help protect innocent defendants. Any system that pushes innocent defendants to trial minimizes the number of innocents convicted. But it does so only at the cost of maximizing the punishment each receives. This result stands every known theory of distributional justice on its head. Losses, especially unjust losses, are better spread than concentrated.

In any scenario, prosecutorial pressure on the defendant to take a plea ought to be lessened, although achieving this aim is difficult. Bargaining is inconceivable without the prosecutor's offer to modify the charge or to recommend a sentence. A wily prosecutor frames charges usually at the highest possible level in order to increase leverage in bargaining, thereby discharging his role in a manner approaching that of a huckster. These practices demean the office and cast doubt on the voluntariness of pleas. Devotion to the role of minister of justice and narrow attention only to circumstances relevant to the crime are indispensable qualities in the prosecutor. Manipulation of charging for clearing calendars or creating a tough reputation signals the public that the prosecutor will extend unconscionable rewards in return for a plea.

In *Bordenkircher v. Hayes*,[57] the prosecutor offered to recommend a five-year sentence if the defendant would plead guilty and at the same time ools. Pstated that, if the offer were declined, he would seek to re-indict the defendant under the state's habitual offender act, which would subject the defendant to mandatory life imprisonment. When the defendant went to trial, and the prosecutor carried out his threat, the Supreme Court found the prosecutor's actions legitimate leverage. This finding exonerated the prosecutor from the suspicion of vindictiveness that would violate due process.

This opinion rests on the curious assumption that only spontaneous afterthoughts are vindictive whereas planned and threatened retaliation is not. The announcement of the fateful choice to the accused during negotiations no more dispels a suspicion of vindictiveness than arming oneself with a gun dispels a suspicion of intent to kill. Aggressive involvement of the prosecutor in bargaining by voicing threats of steeply enhanced charges should render any plea involuntary.

CONCLUSION: THE INJUSTICE

Plea bargaining remains a central but incongruous part of our complex justice system. It is unlikely ever to be abolished. The debate over its merits addresses values of proportionate justice and economy. Current bargaining practices compromise the notion that the severity of punishment should match the severity of the charge. Bargaining does permit defendants and attorneys to individualize sentencing. But in bargaining the value of just deserts becomes threatened by the competing values of economics, bluster, and barter. The plea bargaining process turns a court into a street bazaar where justice is hawked, bought, and sold at a crass level far below the lofty constitutional principles taught in law schools. Plea bargaining attorneys crowding courtroom halls have become the new money changers in the temple. Bargaining reinforces, rather than reduces, the criminal's view of the world as yet another scam.

From an ironic standpoint, the prevalence of plea bargaining reflects the rigidity and severity of sentencing guidelines and mandatory-minimum sentences. The harsher these policies appear, the greater the institutional incentive to avoid them by fashioning a tempered, individual disposition through plea bargaining. The system in this respect resembles a balloon: severity and impersonality impinging on one end cause increased pressure at the other end for circumvention by bargaining. The very severity and uniformity intended to correct sentence disparity produce the very evil sought to be avoided: disparate plea bargains.

A subtle bait-and-switch process works in the justice system: in the abstract the system offers lofty proclamations about the constitutional protections of trial by jury, but in practicality it loads exercise of those rights with so many draconian consequences that, for almost all defendants, it is safer to "buy justice" in the stalls of court bazaars than in the courtroom itself. Our criminal law has become a process for extracting guilty pleas. We have made the consequences of refusing a plea bargain so onerous that few can risk a trial. Our complex due process has erected a residence too expensive to occupy. Plea bargaining gives the cold shoulder both to constitutional rights and also to the goals of sentencing guidelines and mandatory sentences, and in the process reinforces the criminal world-view of manipulation.

NOTES

1. *Black's Law Dictionary 1152*, 6th ed. (St. Paul: West Pub., 1990).
2. R. Scott and W. Stuntz, "Plea Bargaining as Contract," 101 *Yale L.J.* 1909–1968 (1992), 1989, n.1 (hereafter, "Contract").
3. *Santobello v. New York*, 404 U.S. 257, 260 (1971).
4. "Contract," 1911–1912.
5. Id.
6. The most powerful and influential development of this thesis appears in Frank H. Easterbrook, "Criminal Procedure as a Market System," 12 *J. Legal Stud.* 289 (1983).
7. Stephen J. Schulhofer, "A Wake-Up Call from the Plea Bargaining Trenches," 19 *Law and Soc. Inquiry* 135, 143 (1994) (hereafter, "Wake-Up Call").
8. "Contract," 1911.
9. Frank H. Easterbrook, "Plea Bargaining as Compromise," 101 *Yale L.J.* 1969, 1975 (1992).
10. Id.
11. "Wake-Up Call," 143.
12. 42 U.S.C. § 10606 (b) (3)-(5), (7) (Supp. 1996).
13. "Contract," 1953–1954.

14. R. Gerber, "A Judicial Perspective on Plea Bargaining," *Ariz. Atty.* 38, 39 (Sept. 1, 1988).

15. Id.

16. Id.

17. Fed. R. Crim. P. 11(d).

18. C. Brunk, "The Problem of Voluntariness and Coercion in the Negotiated Plea," 13 *Law and Soc.* 527, 528–529 (1979).

19. Id.

20. "Contract," 1946–1948.

21. *In re Winship*, 397 U.S. 358, 364 (1970).

22. Id.

23. "Wake-Up Call," 143.

24. A. Alschuler, "An Exchange of Concessions," 142 *New L.J.* 937, 938 (1992) (hereafter, "Concessions").

25. Act of June 23, 1976, Ch. 111, 1976 Session Laws 438, 438–445.

26. G. Lowenthal, "Mandatory Sentencing Laws," 81 *Cal. L.R.* 61–124 (1993), to which this analysis is indebted. Cf. Act of June 23, 1976, ch. 111, 1976 Ariz. Sess. Laws 438, 438–445.

27. Laws 1982, ch. 322, § 10, as reflected in the present version of A.R.S. § 13–604.02(A) (1989).

28. G. Lowenthal, "Mandatory," 83.

29. Id., 85.

30. Id.

31. Id., 95.

32. Id.

33. M. Tonry, *Sentencing Matters* (New York: Oxford University Press, 1996), 161.

34. A. Goldstein, "Criminal Justice Systems: Guilty Pleas and the Public Interest," 49 *SMU L.R.* 567, 575 (1996).

35. See generally S. Schulhofer, "Plea Bargaining as Disaster," 101 *Yale L.J.* 1979 (1992) (hereafter, "Disaster").

36. "Wake-Up Call," 143.

37. "Concessions," 937.

38. Id.

39. "Wake-Up Call," 104.

40. Id.

41. Id.

42. Id., 142.

43. Id.

44. "Contract," 1083–1087.

45. "Concessions," 938–939.

46. "Disaster," 1994–1998.

47. "Contract," 1953–1957.

48. Id.

49. "Wake-Up Call," 141.

50. Id., 142.

51. Id.

52. Id.

53. "Contract," 1957–1960.
54. "Disaster," 1094.
55. Id., 1093–1094.
56. "Contract," 1951–1953.
57. 434 U.S. 357 (1978).

3

DEATH AND ITS REBIRTH

We are told by my friend, "Oh, the killer does it, Why shouldn't the State?" I would hate to live in a State that was no better than a murderer.
　　　　　　　—Clarence Darrow, *Attorney for the Damned* 96 (1989)

In February 1999 Oklahoma executed Sean Sellers, the tenth juvenile offender put to death in our country in that decade, more than any other country executing offenders who committed their crime as a juvenile. Sellers suffered from serious multiple personality disorder plus severe brain damage from a childhood injury. After his conviction he ministered to thousands of troubled teenagers to help them find a right path in life. His death raises again the propriety of our American enthusiasm for capital punishment.

According to a recent Gallup Poll, most Americans believe that the death penalty deters murder,[1] a belief trusting that severe punishment can alter behavior. In reality, however, our burgeoning national stampede to the execution chamber is a counterproductive technique for reducing crime.

History puts our current death penalty policy in perspective. Blood revenge, the earliest form of capital punishment, dominated primitive societies. Its initial spirit was retaliatory. People killed to avenge their kin. Any blood relative, no matter how removed, could be the victim of the avenger's retribution.[2]

Primitive criminal codes endorsed personal revenge. Hammurabi's *Floruit* ("If a man destroy the eye of another man, they shall destroy his eye") and *Exodus* ("Eye for eye, tooth for tooth, hand for hand, foot for foot") reinforced individual retribution. The command "life for life, eye for eye, tooth for tooth," in its day an ethical advance, sent the message that excessive penalties harmed the community and punishment should be proportionate to the offense. The Talmud required that vengeance fit the crime. If by only taking "measure for measure" God exercised self-restraint, "*a fortiori* must the victim of the offense, the blood avenger, exercise it and never take vengeance beyond the measure of the damage or mischief caused to him."[3]

As crimes progressed from personal to governmental status, increasing numbers of offenses joined Europe's list of capital crimes. Deterrence certainly motivated medieval England: torture and death followed by degradation became its norm for crime control. The number of British crimes punishable by the "bloody code" rose from 8 at the end of the fifteenth century to 223 by 1800.[4] During the reign of England's Henry VIII, more than 65,000 hangings took place, all of them public spectacles.

REFORM MOVEMENTS

A more liberal democratic political philosophy in the eighteenth century slowly countered the death penalty's assumed efficacy. Voltaire wrote in 1748:

Is it possible that nations who boast of their reformation, of trampling superstition under foot, who, indeed, supposed that they had attained the perfection of reason, could believe in witchcraft, and, upon the strength of such belief, proceed to burn poor women accused of that crime, and this, more than a hundred years after the pretended reformation of their reason?[5]

Cesare Beccaria[6] and Jeremy Bentham[7] nurtured the trend to end lethal brutality. Even severe Blackstone joined the opposition to excessive punishments:

For though the end of punishment is to deter men from offending, it never can follow from thence that it is lawful to deter them at any rate and by any means; since there may be unlawful methods of enforcing obedience even to the justest laws. . . . But, indeed, were capital punishments proved by experience to be a sure and effective remedy, that would not prove the necessity . . . of inflicting them upon all occasions when other expedients fail. I fear this reasoning would extend a great deal too far.[8]

The exemplary value of capital punishment lay at the core of the debate then as it does now. Consider James Stephen's celebrated dictum "The fact that men are hanged for murder is one great reason why murder is considered so dreadful a crime."[9] From the same example Beccaria drew the opposite lesson:

The punishment of death is pernicious to society, from the example of barbarity it affords. . . . Is it not absurd, that the laws, which detest and punish homicide, should, in order to prevent murder, publicly commit it themselves?[10]

Beccaria's position greatly influenced abolitionist thought: the death penalty was too quickly administered, too momentous to deter; it instilled compassion rather than fear in the observer. Crime would decline not from the "terrible but momentary spectacle" of the death of a wretch but by "the continued example of a man deprived of his liberty, condemned as a beast of burden, to repair, by his labor, the injury he has done to society."[11]

Leading Americans urged abolition. In 1774, lecturing at the house of Benjamin Franklin, Dr. Benjamin Rush urged building a "House of Reform" so criminals could be detained "until purged of their antisocial habits."[12] Hanging, he argued, did not deter, but rather increased, crime: when a government puts its citizens to death, "it exceeds the powers entrusted to it."[13] In 1792, Rush developed this theme in a famous tract, *Considerations on the Injustice and Impolicy of Punishing Murder with Death*, arguing that capital punishment lessened the horror of taking life and influenced the suicidal to end their lives. Loath to see a capital sentence imposed, jurors let murderers go free. Prison avoided such problems:

If the punishment of murder consisted in long confinement and hard labour, it would be proportioned to . . . our feelings of justice, and every member of society would be a watchman or a magistrate to apprehend a destroyer of human life, and to bring him to punishment.[14]

During the 1830s and 1840s, opponents of the death penalty began to shape state penal law in ways we have now forgotten. In the 1840s, Horace Greeley, founder of the *New York Tribune* and one of the leading critics of the death penalty, influenced Michigan, Rhode Island, and Wisconsin to abolish the penalty.[15] Other states gradually made public executions illegal.

This minihistory reveals an important change in public versus private executions that has a modern resonance. Public executions reflected, in part, religious rituals, at least at their inception: a condemned prisoner repenting on the gallows would supposedly remind spectators of the possibility of salvation, while the execution proved the wages of sin. In the years of our public executions, criminals were encouraged to recant publicly their sins and plead for the mercy of God. The refusal of attendant crowds to be sobered by them helped end public executions.

Michel Foucault views the public aspect of execution as a failed lesson of terror because it fostered solidarity among offenders and turned the condemned into antiheroes. Public executions evolved into festive theaters of the absurd. After witnessing a beheading in Rome in 1845, Dickens wrote, "Nobody cared or was at all affected. There were no manifestations of disgust, or pity, or indignation, or sorrow. My empty pockets were tried several times in the crowd immediately below the scaffold, as the corpse was being put in its coffin." The crowd saw the scene as a sport, placing bets on the flow of blood from the head. Turgenev described the mob at the execution of a notorious criminal as a mindless, primal force, generating "an enormous, rumbling noise." The crowd was exuberant and "over-joyed" at the appearance of the condemned before the scaffold. Public executions such as these were eventually abolished because spectators' normal inhibitions changed into riot and disrespect for law. The crowd identified with the victim, not the executioner, and the spectacle became revolting. Meting out capital punishment away from the public gaze became preferable.

The irony of this piece of history is that mass indulgence in the passion of revenge was precisely what public executions were supposed to prevent. Yet this boisterous tradition of public vengeance continues today in our own nation's execution carnivals. On January 10, 1986, a crowd of more than 200 gathered at the South Carolina Department of Corrections for the electrocution of James Terry Roach, who had pleaded guilty five years earlier, at the age of seventeen, to the murder of two teenagers. The crowd carried signs and banners with messages like "Save Energy, Use a Rope," "Fry Him," "Let the Juice Flow," and "Bon Voyage." In 1989, some 300 people gathered outside the state prison in Starke, Florida, to celebrate the execution of Ted Bundy, who had murdered at least thirty women. "The sheer light-hearted boisterousness" of the event was "extraordinary," like a "football rally," replete with beer, T-shirts, and signs that read "Roast in Peace" and "This Buzz Is for You," with the crowd "a sham of the criminal justice process."[16]

Generated, in part, by this very degradation associated with executions, the modern abolitionist movement resulted from England's 1949 Royal Commission on Capital Punishment, the United Nations reports of the 1950s, and the 1956 *Canadian Report on Capital Punishment*, all abolitionist on principle. This movement prompted six more states—Oregon in 1964; West Virginia, Vermont, Iowa, and New York in 1965; and New Mexico in 1969—to abolish the death penalty.

DEATH PENALTY'S RESURRECTION

Airline bombings in 1958 and 1959, air piracy in 1960 and 1961, and the assassination of President Kennedy in 1963 prompted Congress to re-enact the death penalty. But in 1972, in *Furman v. Georgia*,[17] the U.S. Supreme Court held the death penalty unconstitutional because of its arbitrary procedures. As a consequence, existing state statutes disappeared from the books because of their unpredictability. *Furman* did not address whether death in principle was cruel and unusual punishment. The Court merely stated that the caprice in existing capital sentencing statutes violated due process standards. The door remained open for more precise statutes promising more uniform standards for death.

In 1976, a more conservative Supreme Court held that capital punishment in principle does not violate the Constitution and added, pointedly, that even without any evidence states could assume it had a deterrent effect, ruling in *Gregg v. Georgia*,[18] that death could be imposed via defined procedural standards ensuring sentencing uniformity. Following statutory changes, executions resumed in 1977, and by the mid-1980s had become routine events with little public attention and little media publicity. Between 1977 and 1999, 566 prisoners were executed in the United States.[19] By 1990, an average of two executions occurred per month; by 1998, that figure had tripled.[20]

At our millennium, death penalties have become more commonplace, especially in southern states. The death row population as of 1999 is over 3,500, about five times greater than it was in 1977.[21] With its sixty new death penalties, the 1994 Violent Crime Control Act will undoubtedly increase the numbers even more, all with the expectation that capital punishment deters crime.[22]

WHO COMMITS HOMICIDE?

Capital punishment's primary attraction lies in its assumed deterrent potential. Hence, data about homicidal conduct relate to this supposed deterrent effect.

Criminal homicide, rarely a planned act, reveals predictable behavior patterns involving inner-city culture, rage, alcohol, and weapon availability. Black males are more likely to commit criminal homicide than females, who are more prone to homicide than white males and white females.[23] Criminal homicides are heavily male, minority, and, apart from the South, inner-city-related. Homicide generally results from a domestic quarrel, jealousy, an argument over money, romance, or a robbery. Most of the known victim–offender relationships are close, intimate, and frequent, and the usual homicide site is a familiar home. Homicide more readily occurs if violence is an accepted part of subcultural values.

There are sharp regional differences in homicide, with the South having by far the highest murder rate, almost double that of the Northeast, a divergence that has persisted since the nineteenth century. The former slave-holding states of the old Confederacy all rank in the top twenty states for murder, led by Louisiana, with a rate of 17.5 murders per 100,000 people in 1996. The ten states with the lowest homicide rates are in New England

and the northern Midwest, with South Dakota's the lowest at 1.2 murders per 100,000 people.

The high southern murder rate is a key factor behind our disproportionately high homicide rate compared with other democratic, industrialized nations. In 1996, the last year for which data are available, our murder rate was 7.4 per 100,000 people. The closest country was Finland, at 3.2 per 100,000 people, followed by France at 1.1, Japan at 0.6, and Britain at 0.5.

Alcohol plays a major role in homicides. Weekend homicides typically involve alcohol prior to the killing. Many murders occur on the evening of receiving a paycheck squandered on alcohol. In a careful study at the Florida State Penitentiary at Faiford, Shaw Grigsby found that 75 percent of all murderers had been drinking alcohol just prior to their crime.[24] International data support the same conclusion.[25] These data are important because alcohol addresses capital punishment's supposed deterrent effect: the more a killer has been drinking, the more suspect is the expectation that the killer contemplates the available punishment.

Deterrence appears in another guise in light of the blurred nature of murder and assault. From the standpoint of motive and intent, assault and murder are inseparable. Most murders are complete assaults; their motives, means, and origins do not usually differ. Whether the assault ends in murder usually turns on the presence of a weapon and whether it has fatal potential such as a knife or large-caliber gun. Murders and assaults are matters of weapon and alcohol convenience: if our government were really serious about controlling killings, the progression from assault to homicide could be reduced by restricting weapons and alcohol.

DETERRENCE RESEARCH

Does capital punishment really deter crime, as politicians and the public profess? Eight research approaches appear: (1) analysis of homicide rates in contiguous states with and without capital punishment, (2) examination of any change in the homicide rate after the penalty has been abolished or reinstated, (3) the impact of an execution on the subsequent homicide rate, (4) comparison of the rates of police murder in states with and without capital punishment, (5) whether prisoners are more likely to kill in abolitionist states, (6) the same question regarding paroled murderers, (7) the impact of the penalty on noncapital felonies, and (8) whether the penalty more effectively deters murder than does life imprisonment.[26] Each of these research topics addresses whether the death penalty lives up to the expectation that it deters crime.

Contiguous States

Early research on deterrence involved comparing homicide rates in contiguous states where one jurisdiction had abolished capital punishment and the other(s) retained it. If the states share economic, demographic, and other social characteristics, any difference in murder rates should relate to the presence or absence of the death penalty.

Thorsten Sellin conducted the classic studies utilizing this approach.[27] For five sets of similar contiguous states, he found no statistically significant homicide differences between those that punish by death and life imprisonment or even within the same state before and after the repeal or adoption of capital punishment.[28] Sellin's conclusion: capital punishment cannot statistically be shown to deter criminals from committing murder.

More recent research shows that the murder rate on average is almost twice as high in death penalty states as in neighboring states without it. Our national homicide rate has stayed generally constant even as executions increase in number.[29] The murder rate has lately dropped in some areas, but the decline has occurred more slowly in our thirty-eight execution-prone states than in the twelve states that do not execute.

Abolition/Retention of the Death Penalty

A second approach used by Sellin[30] examines jurisdictions that have either abolished or reinstated the death penalty, thus giving a "before"-and-"after" comparison. In the past century, several states repealed their capital statutes. Sellin's early studies looked at their "before" and "after" homicide rates; later studies examined the rates in contiguous states that had not made a change.[31] Both kinds of studies found no increased deterrence in jurisdictions that retained or reinstated the death penalty, with the homicide rate closely following the same trend in contiguous noncapital punishment states.

Recent studies reinforce this conclusion strongly. In 1995 the average murder rate per 100,000 people was 4.1 among the 12 states without the death penalty but 7.5 among the 32 states with it.[32] Conservative criminologist John DiJulio noted in 1998 that although the state of New York executes "rarely," murders are "way down" in the city, and that while Texas "leads the execution pack," murders "are up in Dallas." From such data he concludes that he doubts whether even the cleverest social science statistician "could explain any significant fraction of recent inter-jurisdictional variance in murder rates by reference to the death penalty."[33]

Impact of an Execution

Research also examines the effect of an execution on the murder rate in the same jurisdiction. Robert Dann examined the impact of five executions in Philadelphia for sixty days after executions, assuming that if capital punishment deterred murder, homicides would decline afterward. Dann found that the murder rate actually increased slightly in this sixty-day period.[34] When William Graves studied homicide rates in Los Angeles, San Francisco, and Alameda Counties to discover whether fewer murders occurred after a publicized execution than before, he found that murders actually increased on the days prior to, and on the day of, the execution, declined slightly in the two-day period following the execution, and then returned to the norm, suggesting that persons contemplating homicide are taught by the state's taking of life to act sooner.[35] Others using his data found that homicides were higher in the weeks after, than in the weeks before, executions.[36]

Steven Stack found a small deterrent impact for executions receiving much national publicity[37]; cases without publicity created no deterrent effect. The result should not be surprising: as executions become more common, press coverage declines, so the penalty soon loses any deterrence resulting from publicity.

Killings of Police Officers

If the death penalty deters better than life incarceration, criminals should be less likely to kill police officers in states that retain the penalty. Several studies address this question.[38] Despite different researchers, methodologies, and time periods, the results are remarkably similar: killing law enforcement officers occurs no more frequently in states without capital punishment; policing does not become more hazardous with the abolition of the death penalty or safer by its adoption.[39] The penalty simply does not impact the police workplace. The police themselves know this. A 1995 Hart Research Associates poll showed that 67 percent of nearly 400 U.S. police chiefs don't see capital punishment as any deterrent. The chiefs ranked the death penalty *last* among effective ways to reduce violent crime.

Homicides Committed by Prisoners

In comparing the homicidal behavior of prisoners in retentionist and abolitionist states, Sellin found over 90 percent of these killings occurred in states with capital punishment.[40] Wendy Wolfson found that the percentage of imprisoned murderers who recidivate approximates the same number in retentionist and abolitionist jurisdictions,[41] finding "seriously flawed" the argument that these individuals can be deterred by the same death threat that did not deter them from killing in the first place.[42]

Homicides Committed by Parolees

Researchers have also asked whether paroled murder inmates are less likely to kill again in states that retain the death penalty. If so, the presence of the death penalty could account for the lesser risk.

The result is negative: homicide parolees generally commit less crime than other paroled groups. Correctional administrators regularly describe murderers as the most adaptable of prisoners and the offense group less likely to murder again or commit any other crime than the typical burglar, robber, forger, or thief.[43] The small repeat rate applies to murder parolees who absconded from parole or committed technical violations, reinforcing the Royal Commission's observation that the release of life-sentenced murderers involves little criminal risk by comparison with other released criminals.[44]

Bedau found that over a seventy-six-year period in twelve states, only 12 of 2,646 murderers were convicted of murder again after being released.[45] Similarly, Sellin studied 56,265 inmates released on parole over a three-year period, of whom 6,835 had been convicted of willful homicide. Of these parolees, 310 committed a new offense; only 21 committed murder. Similarly, those who committed armed robbery, aggravated assault, and rape were more likely to commit murder when released than were paroled murderers.[46] The presence of a death penalty is immaterial to these data.

Researchers have also tracked the behavior of murderers with sentences commuted as a result of the *Furman* decision. James Marquart and Jonathan Sorenson compared forty-seven persons in Texas taken off death row by *Furman* to a control group of 156 inmates sentenced to life imprisonment for murder or rape, the same offenses for which the *Furman* inmates received death. Despite the fact that both groups spent an average of approximately one decade in prison, only 14 percent of the *Furman*-commuted inmates committed a new felony upon release.[47] Little criminal difference appeared upon release between those convicts originally sentenced to death and those sentenced to life imprisonment. Gerraro Vito, Pat Koester, and Deborah Wilson[48] also studied *Furman*-commuted inmates, including those removed from death row in twenty-six states by that decision. The repeat homicide rate for this group was 1.6 percent, well below that of nonmurderer parolees,[49] prompting the conclusion that "societal protection from convicted capital murders is not greatly enhanced by the death penalty."[50]

These independent researchers conclude that an operative death penalty offers no additional protection from murder over life imprisonment.

Deterrence of Noncapital Felonies

William Bailey examined whether executions deterred persons from committing noncapital felonies.[51] Johannes Andenaes,[52] Marlene Lehtinen,[53] Ernest van den Haag,[54] and Walter Berns[55] had suggested that the death sentence could educate people to obey the law; could deter those crimes where an unintended killing results, as in armed robbery; and that it could conserve scarce criminal justice resources.

Bailey's analysis finds no support for deterrence in any scenario and no relationship between capital punishment and the index felony rate. He concludes:

[T]his pattern holds for the traditional targeted offense of murder, the person crimes [*sic*] of negligent manslaughter, rape, assault, and robbery, as well as the property crimes of burglary, grand larceny, and vehicle theft. In other words, there is no evidence . . . that residents of death penalty jurisdictions are afforded an added measure of protection against serious crimes by executions.[56]

Multiple Regression Analysis

In a seeming departure from these findings, Isaac Ehrlich[57] in 1975 reported that each execution saved seven to eight lives based on a regression analysis of multiple contributors to homicide (such as unemployment rate, age distribution of the population, proportion of citizens who own handguns, etc.).[58] Ehrlich argued that geographical proximity by itself presented an incomplete comparison of homicide statistics. The ideal approach to his mind would examine annual murder figures on a nationwide basis. Comparing the number of homicide convictions with executions, he concluded that an additional execution per year over the period in question (1933–1969) may have resulted, on average, in seven or eight fewer murders.[59]

Ehrlich's contention that capital punishment may deter murder provoked many studies challenging his conclusion[60] and inquiring into whether deterrence appeared in the early 1970s, when many states revised their capital statutes. A nationwide study in 1988,[61] comparing murder rates in abolitionist and retentionist states from 1973 to 1984, concluded that death penalty states actually suffer higher rates of homicide than states whose maximum punishment is life imprisonment, with rates even higher than the national average.[62] In contiguous states that had the death penalty but refused to impose it, the homicide rate for 1973–1984 was either comparable in capital and noncapital states or, in some instances, higher in states with the death penalty.[63] Other studies, such as those mentioned earlier, found no lower incidence of murder of police in capital as opposed to noncapital states.[64] Publicity accompanying an execution does not result in a lower homicide rate.[65] The rate of homicide does not change in a state without the death penalty compared with the period when capital punishment was reintroduced.[66]

Researchers using Ehrlich's methodology and data have reached conclusions[67] directly contrary to his. The overwhelming evidence on deterrence continues to point in the opposite direction.[68] With Ehrlich's findings called into question,[69] the deterrent advantage of capital punishment over life imprisonment remains discredited in social science research. No credible social science evidence suggests that general deterrence results from capital punishment as opposed to life imprisonment. Although certainty of punishment does offer some deterrence, capital punishment itself does not,[70] at least not one greater than life imprisonment. In sum, the popular belief that capital punishment more effectively deters murder than does life imprisonment is a myth.[71]

Why is the death penalty not an effective deterrent? As any courthouse observer can note, most homicides occur between angry or drunk acquaintances without rational calculation or attention to consequences. Punishment cannot deter if killers do not consider it in advance. In the very rare cases when they do, life imprisonment and death appear alike. Douglas Heckathorn found no difference in deterrence of two sanctions if both appear severe, even if one is, in fact, harsher than the other.[72] Apparently, those very rare killers who do contemplate punishment find little difference between being put to death and spending life in prison.

A JUDICIAL VIEW

I enter this debate personally, as one who has wrestled with it in court, not to add forests of paper to the tonnage already extant but to comment on four differing aspects of the death penalty beyond the raw statistics of supposed deterrence.

The first relates to premeditation. Capital statutes throughout this country uniformly take premeditation as the touchstone of depravity. Like Aristotle, our capital statutes view those acts most culpable that are most carefully deliberated. The heinous nature of homicide stems primarily not only from causing death but, more pointedly, from the lucidity of that choice.[73]

Under this standard, our official administration of capital punishment must do some serious soul-searching. An American execution involves repeated levels of carefully considered appeals[74] where multiple layers and years—averaging eleven—of judicial and executive thought precede execution. From the first trial judge to the state's governor and all the way to the Supreme Court, each of these reflective reviews involves carefully premeditated willingness for the death of the offender. These lengthy judicial and executive reviews constitute premeditated choice of official death well beyond the length or lucidity of any murderer's thoughts. If we take the Aristotelian concept of premeditation as the hallmark of culpability, must not our layers of thoughtful death endorsement embarrass us by the very standard we use to measure a murderer's depravity? "If they kill me, that's deliberate murder; I can't make my peace with this," said Joseph Payne before his 1996 execution.[75]

The second observation stems from Camus[76] and others: the death penalty sends a counterproductive message. Politicians regularly defend the death penalty on the grounds that human life is so sacred that to snuff it out demands the highest penalty possible.[77] Only by using the highest penalty, they argue, can we deter the taking of life and spread the message that life, above all other values, is never to be taken.

The death penalty directly contradicts this message. If human life is so sacred that it is never to be taken, the same logic impugns governmental killing of a criminal. Our death penalty instead exemplifies that killing is permissible, even desirable, by any powerful avenging entity. The illogic increases dramatically when juvenile offenders like Sean Sellers are executed. My state of Arizona has sentenced both sixteen- and eighteen-year-old killers to death. Only six countries in the world have done this in the 1990s—Pakistan, Saudi Arabia, Iran, Nigeria, Yemen, and the United States, an embarrassing group of allies.[78]

Data now support this brutalization effect. Besides the Dann and Graves studies mentioned earlier, a 1995 California study analyzes homicide rates in 1992 and 1993 on a monthly basis, for a four-month period preceding and following the execution of Robert Harris. The average number of monthly California homicides was 306; in the four months following Harris' execution, the average number rose to 333, a 9 percent increase. When the California murder rates during its abolitionist and retentionist years are compared, average annual homicides were twice as high during years in which executions occurred as in years when no one was executed. The researchers conclude that the example of officially caused death actually prompts homicidal behavior.[79] A recent ten-year study of international homicide similarly finds that the death penalty tends to incite more violence rather than deterring.[80] In the 1993 debates in Parliament regarding restoring the death penalty in England and Northern Ireland, the legislative consensus in Parliament was that restoring capital punishment would incite more violence on the part of fanatics and would-be martyrs.[81]

A third reflection, drawn from experience on the trial court, is that the unmanageable capital sentencing discretion condemned by *Furman* has not disappeared but has simply moved from overt sentencing statutes to covert prosecutorial decisions. The charging discretion between first- and second-degree murder, the choice to seek or not seek the death penalty, the caprice with which plea bargains are crafted and offered, and the political advantages for prosecutors invoking the death penalty illustrate the very same caprice condemned by *Furman*—though now it hides in private prosecutorial choices unreviewable in court. These arbitrary decisions directly impact exposure to death; none of these areas is judicially reviewable. As the O. J. Simpson case illustrates, the death option lies wholly within the unruled and unreviewable political whims of individual prosecutors.[82] A recent *New York Times* study of major urban prosecutors' offices (Philadelphia, New York, Pittsburgh, Syracuse, Chicago, Houston, Dallas, Los Angeles, and New Orleans) finds that seeking the death sentence varies capriciously with elected prosecutors' individual preferences.[83]

Judicial election campaigns also illustrate that unconscionable judicial candidates use their devotion to the death penalty to bolster their election chances.[84] As these examples of politically minded prosecutors and judges show, the caprice condemned by *Furman* has simply moved from public sentencing statutes to private political whims. The *National Law Journal* has rightly concluded that justice in capital murder trials still is "more like a random flip of the coin than a delicate balancing of the scales."[85]

The fourth consideration has to do with error. Since 1973, according to the Death Penalty Information Center in Washington, at least eighty-two people have been released from death row because DNA or other evidence established that they were not guilty of the crimes for which they had been sentenced to die. Those were the lucky ones. No one knows how many innocent people have actually been executed. The eighty-two released of the 566 executed since 1977 show a ratio of one freed for every seven put to death, a hideous error rate for so final a punishment.[86]

In their 1992 book *In Spite of Innocence*, Michael Radelet, Hugo Bedau, and Constance Putnam tell of 23 additional innocent people executed since 1900. They claim that 400 people were wrongly convicted and sentenced to die during that period. One of the best-known cases is that of Randall Dale Adams, who sat twelve years on Texas' death row for the murder of a police officer. It took a documentary film, *The Thin Blue Line*, to reveal that the perjured testimony of witnesses, including the actual murderer (who accepted a plea bargain), had put him there. The prosecutor there is quoted, apparently accurately, as saying, "It takes a good prosecutor to convict and execute a guilty man; it takes a great prosecutor to convict and execute an innocent man"—a comment reflecting the hysterical compulsion to convict anyone for a sensational killing.

Official Washington is seemingly troubled by capital punishment. *Convicted by Juries, Exonerated by Science*[87] details twenty-eight cases of men who served a total of 197 years, including three who spent more than twenty-five years on death row, before DNA tests established their innocence. These data are not the bias of some ultraliberal zealot but official Justice Department research with a Foreword by Attorney General Janet Reno and testimonies by eight deputy district attorneys, police chiefs, forensic scientists, and law professors.[88]

Raising additional concern is the bizarre death row experience in Illinois, which has released twelve innocent death row prisoners while executing twelve since reinstating the penalty in 1977. DNA tests helped free four of the twelve; eight also had the investigative help of pro bono lawyers and journalists. A grand jury there brought charges against three former prosecutors, one now a judge, and four investigators, alleging they conspired to frame two of the innocent men eventually released.[89]

We are executing people more, but we are examining the cumbersome process that leads there less. Pro-death penalty politicians have drastically curtailed the legal representation available to condemned inmates as well as the length of time between sentencing and execution. Politicians race to dispatch the condemned before any exculpation or legal error can be brought to light. The goal has not been justice but to kill quickly. Even despite restricted appeals, federal courts have found constitutional error in nearly half of all the capital cases that reach them. Anthony Amsterdam has explained the piercing indictment this figure conveys:

In every one of these cases [in which federal habeas relief was granted], the inmate's claim had been rejected by a state trial court and by the state's highest court, at least once and often a second time in state post-conviction proceedings; the Supreme Court had usually denied *certiorari* at least once and sometimes twice; and a federal district court [in those cases reaching a court of appeals] had then rejected the inmate's claims of federal constitutional error infecting his conviction and/or death sentence.[90]

AN INTERNATIONAL EMBARRASSMENT

The international arena now shows the embarrassing result of our country's death penalty enthusiasm. Every Western industrial nation has stopped executing criminals except the United States. Canada, Great Britain, Australia, New Zealand, and all of Western Europe have halted the practice. The last execution for a crime took place in 1860 in the Netherlands, 1863 in Belgium, and 1892 in Denmark. Norway has not imposed death for a civil offense since 1875. Great Britain had its last execution in 1964. Canada abolished death for civilian offenses in 1976. Spain and France, among the last Western European societies to abolish capital punishment, did so in 1978 and 1981, respectively.[91]

The United States remains one of the few governments to permit execution of juvenile murderers. More than three-quarters of the few executing nations of the world set eighteen as the minimum age for execution.[92] Both the United Nations and the Geneva Convention prohibit the execution of juveniles under the age of eighteen. Although juveniles are rarely executed in our country, this sentence is possible in approximately half our states.[93] As of May 1998, sixty-nine juvenile offenders were awaiting execution in our country.[94]

The Supreme Court in 1989 ruled that executing people as young as sixteen is constitutional. More than ninety juvenile offenders have received death sentences since the 1970s, and ten have been executed. As of 1996, according to Amnesty International, more juveniles faced execution in the United States than in any other country. Even China and Russia ban the execution of juveniles.

Amnesty International reviewed the cases and personal histories of twenty-three juveniles sentenced to death. The overwhelming numbers came from acutely deprived backgrounds, often victims of severe physical and sexual abuse. More than half had mental illness or brain damage, serious substance abuse problems, and below average intelligence and had been abandoned by parents and raised by abusive, alcoholic relatives.[95]

The Supreme Court has ruled that the Constitution permits the execution of retarded people, although states may prohibit it if they choose.[96] Amnesty International has estimated that at least six people diagnosed as mentally handicapped or borderline cases were executed during the late 1980s.[97] Probably the best known mentally disabled person executed in recent years was Rickey Ray Rector, who suffered from extensive brain damage from a self-inflicted gunshot in the head and a subsequent partial lobotomy. He was executed by the state of Arkansas and by then-governor Bill Clinton during his 1992 presidential campaign. Clinton personally attended his execution to show his support for the death penalty. Rector had virtually no understanding of his impending death; in the apparent belief that he would return to his cell after being executed, he saved the dessert from his last meal.

Our cult of death has now put our country in an embarrassing international position. In the *Soering* case,[98] the European Court of Human Rights found that our American capital punishment practices violate the European Convention for the Protection of Human Rights and Fundamental Freedoms, which prohibits fortuitous, inhuman, or degrading punishment.[99] In 1985, after a couple was killed in Virginia, the investigation focused on their twenty-year-old daughter, a student at the University of Virginia, and her boyfriend, Jens Soering. When the two fled to Great Britain, the United States sought their extradition. An international rights lawyer urged Great Britain to refuse on the grounds that Soering would be subject to cruel, inhuman, and degrading treatment in facing death.[100]

The European Court of Human Rights refused to extradite Soering, indicating that convicted capital defendants in the United States generally spend many years after conviction confined on death row, waiting for indeterminate and usually incompetent appeals to run out, and that, fifteen days before their scheduled execution, move to an unlighted cell near the electric chair, where they are watched constantly before being executed, often eleven or more years after their crime.[101] The court also noted that international human rights law, unlike American law, prohibits imposition of the death penalty on one under eighteen years at the time of the crime[102] and that Soering would be especially susceptible to inhuman treatment in the United States.

Soering shows the irony of our capital punishment culture. The European legal community now finds that we violate its human rights standards as well as our own. Even the United Nations (UN) has taken us to task. Our death penalty is tainted by racism, economic discrimination, politics, and an excessive deference to victims' rights, a UN human rights investigator reported in 1998 as he and a UN panel called for a moratorium on capital punishment. Bacre Waly Ndiaye, a lawyer and death penalty expert from Senegal, concluded in his fifty-four-page report that capital punishment in the United States operates outside international standards and violates international law. The United States is one of only five countries to permit the execution of defendants who committed their crimes before they were eighteen, a violation of the International Covenant on Civil and Political Rights, which the United States has signed.

Capital punishment is also racist in application. Although white people make up nearly three-fourths of our population, they occupy barely half of death row. Our death sentences are most often reserved for murderers of white people. As the UN summarizes, "Many factors, other than the crime itself, appear to influence the imposition of a death sentence. Class, race and economic status, both of the victim and the defendant, are said to be key elements." The American Bar Association has put it more bluntly: "[E]xecutions should cease until effective mechanisms are developed for eliminating the corrosive effects of racial prejudice to capital cases."

The rest of the world is similarly outraged by our willingness to execute killer children and the mentally retarded. As the UN report points out, numerous global treaties prohibit executions for crimes committed by persons under the age of eighteen and international law clearly prohibits imposing a death sentence on juvenile offenders.

More ironic still, this country's long human rights tradition has looked to international norms to define what is "cruel and unusual." When our Supreme Court struck down the penalty of denationalization in 1958, it noted, citing a United Nations survey, that "civilized nations of the world are in virtual unanimity that statelessness is not to be imposed as a punishment for crime."[103] In finding the death penalty a cruel and unusual punishment for rape, the Court in 1977 found that it was "not irrelevant" that only three of sixty nations retained the death penalty for that crime.[104] The Court also noted the trend "worldwide" against application of the felony-murder doctrine to a nontriggerman when it held capital punishment disproportionately severe for one who did not kill, attempt to kill, or intend to kill.[105]

However, when confronted with similar international standards showing the worldwide trend away from capital punishment, particularly as applied to juveniles,[106] our highest court scoffs at the notion that our Eighth Amendment should adopt any international norms. The bottom line: we pick and choose those international norms that support our status quo.

The international perception of our justice system has worsened over the last decade. Renowned cases like those of Rodney King, Mumia Abu Jamal, and Abner Louima—and the fact that blacks are on death row 3½ times their proportion of the population—symbolize the growing belief that our death penalty is racist. Abolitionist countries often have a policy of not extraditing suspected offenders to a country where they might be executed.

No country in the European Community will extradite persons to face our capital punishment. This is tantamount to the U.S. government's refusing to allow a U.S. citizen to face an almost universally condemned practice in another country (say, cutting off the hand of an accused robber).

The majority of the world's nations no longer use the death penalty, which they regard as archaic and barbaric. Nonetheless the United States ranks fifth in the world in the number of executions despite the steady, worldwide drumbeat toward abolition, which continues at a pace of at least two countries a year. We increasingly find ourselves at odds with governments that view the death penalty as archaic, inhumane, and arbitrary.

CONCLUSION: THE INJUSTICE

Crime rhetoric in this country focuses more on popular symbols than on workable crime solutions. The impotence and embarrassment of our death addiction escape us. Sizable segments of our gullible public believe that the death penalty deters murder and that executions protect us from crime.[107] Politicians nurture these unfounded fears by proclaiming that any vigorous attack on crime must include capital punishment, which, of course, they loudly support.

These beliefs rest on myth and defiance of social research and the international community. Death penalty proponents assume an efficacy for capital punishment that does not exist in fact. No empirical data in the voluminous research literature support this expectation. The contrary is far more likely: the death penalty fosters killing attitudes and a culture of brutality.

Capital punishment is a mirage that diverts attention from fruitful solutions to crime like controlling education, alcohol, idleness, drugs, and weapons. Our politicians find it easier to flaunt a purely symbolic, but impotent, death penalty than to pursue workable and less expensive ways to reduce crime. Capital punishment offers a counterproductive and costly placebo for a seducible public.[108] Like the emperor's new clothes, the death penalty serves nothing beyond political puffery except to exemplify the very behavior it professes to condemn. In the international community, which our government regularly lectures on human rights, our devotion to the death penalty has won us the dishonor of being placed on Amnesty International's 1999 list of the world's six most prominent human rights violators.

NOTES

1. K. Jamieson and T. Flanagan, *Sourcebook of Criminal Justice Statistics* (Albany: Hindelang Cr. Justice Research Center, 1989), 229.

2. G. Scott, *History of Capital Punishment* (New York: AMS Press, 1950).

3. D. Cohn, "The Penology of the Talmud," 5 *Israel L. Rev.*, 53, 66 (1970).

4. H. Bedau, *The Death Penalty in America* (New York: Oxford University Press, 1982), 3.

5. Voltaire, *A Commentary*, appended to C. Beccaria, *An Essay on Crimes and Punishments*, Ingraham, trans. (London: Verso, 1819) (hereafter, Beccaria), 190.

6. Beccaria.

7. J. Bentham, *The Rationale of Punishment* (London: Verso, 1830).

8. W. Blackstone, *Commentaries on the Laws of England* vol. 4 (Chicago: University of Chicago Press, 1979), 10.

9. Quoted in H.L.A. Hart, *Law, Liberty, and Morality* (Stanford: Stanford University Press, 1963), 58.

10. Beccaria, 104–105.

11. Id., 99.

12. Bedau, *Death Penalty*, 8. Rush, according to Bedau, is the father of the abolition movement in the United States.

13. Id.

14. Id.

15. Michigan abolished the death penalty in 1847, Rhode Island in 1852, and Wisconsin in 1853.

16. W. Kaminer, *It's All the Rage* (New York: Addison-Wesley, 1995), 36, 172. See also "Foreword" by William Brennan in 8 *Notre Dame J. Law, Ethics and Public Policy* (1994).

17. 408 U.S. 238 (1972).

18. 428 U.S. 158 and 169 (1976).

19. K. Maguire and T. Flanagan, *Sourcebook of Criminal Justice Statistics* (1991), 684. See also *New York Times Magazine*, 23 (October 25, 1998).

20. Bureau of Justice Statistics (Washington, D.C.: Department of Justice, 1992), 2.

21. V. Kappeler, M. Blumberg, and G. Potter, *The Mythology of Crime and Criminal Justice*, 2d ed. (Prospect Heights, IL: Waveland Press, 1996), 307ff. (hereafter, Kappeler).

22. Violent Crime Control and Law Enforcement Act of 1994, Pub. L. No. 103–322, codified at 18 USC § 924. The 1994 crime bill created many new death penalty offenses, including espionage, killing foreign officials, wrecking trains, bank robbery, hostage taking, murder for hire, racketeering, genocide, and car-jacking.

23. These are representative urban figures. See "Law and Order," *Time*, 48–56 (Jan. 15, 1996).

24. Bedau, 186. The foregoing analysis is from Wolfgang's study in Bedau, 464.

25. See L. Schwartz, "Conflict without Violence and Violence without Conflict in a Mexican Mestizo Village," in *Collective Violence*, ed. J. Short and M. Wolfgang (New York: American Academy of Politics and Social Science, 1970), 151, where the author finds "an overwhelming correlation between alcohol and violence."

26. Id., 215. See also Kappeler, 309, whose useful categories are followed here.

27. Thorsten Sellin, *The Death Penalty* (Philadelphia: American Law Institute, 1959, 1982); Thorsten Sellin, *The Penalty of Death* (Ann Arbor: Sage Publications, 1980).

28. Sellin (1980). The same result applies to major cities: "The State of New York executes rarely but murders are way down in New York City. Texas leads the execution pack but murders are up in Dallas." John DiJullio, *Wall Street Journal*, A 15 (Jan. 16, 1998). See also Kappeler, 310.

29. *Arizona Republic*, A28 (Oct. 5, 1997).

30. Sellin (1980).

31. H. Zeisel, "The Deterrent Effect of the Death Penalty," in *The Supreme Court Review, 1976*, ed. Philip Kurland (Chicago: University of Chicago Press, 1977).

32. *Arizona Republic*, B5 (Feb. 18, 1997).

33. Letter to Editor, *Wall Street Journal*, A15 (Jan. 16, 1998).

34. R. H. Dann, "The Deterrent Effect of Capital Punishment," Friends Social Service series, 25 (1935). See also Kappeler, 311.

35. W. Graves, "A Doctor Looks at Capital Punishment," 10(4) *Journal of the Loma Linda University School of Medicine*, 137–141 (1956). See also Kappeler, 311.

36. Graves (1956). See also W. Bowers et al. *Legal Homicide: Death as Punishment in America, 1864–1982* (Boston: Northeastern University Press, 1984), 284.

37. S. Stack, "Publicized Executions and Homicide," 52 *Am. Soc. Rev.*, 532–540 (1987).

38. T. Sellin (1980); A. Cardarelli, "An Analysis of Police Killed in Criminal Action," 59 *J. Crim. L. Crim. Pol. Sc.*, 447–453 (1968); W. Bailey and R. Peterson, "Police Killings and Capital Punishment: The Post Furman Period," 25 *Criminology*, 1–25 (1987). See also Kappeler, 312.

39. V. Kappeler, 312, whose analysis is followed here.

40. T. Sellin (1980), 113.

41. W. Wolfson, "The Deterrent Effect of the Death Penalty upon Prison Murder," in Bedau, *The Death Penalty in America*, 167.

42. Id. See also Kappeler, 313, for an excellent summary.

43. H. Bedau, *The Death Penalty in America*, 180.

44. These and the following stated data are collected in R. Gerber, "A Death Penalty We Can Live With," 50 *Am. J. Juris.*, 251 (1974).

45. See H. Bedau, *The Death Penalty in America*; Sellin (1982).

46. See generally Sellin (1980).

47. J. Marquart and J. Sorensen, "Institutional and Post-Release Behavior of *Furman*—Commuted Inmates in Texas," 26 *Criminology*, 685–687 (1988). See also Kappeler, 321–322, whose analysis is summarized here.

48. R. Bohm "Return of the Dead: An Update on the Status of *Furman*—Commuted Death Row Inmates," *The Death Penalty in America: Current Research*, (Cincinnati: Anderson, 1991).

49. Id., 95. See also Kappeler, 322.

50. Kappeler (1996), 322. Sellin found a similar result: paroled murderers are less likely to kill again than convicts paroled after being convicted of other violent offenses. Sellin (1980).

51. W. Bailey, "The General Prevention Effect of Capital Punishment," in Bohm, *Death Penalty*.

52. J. Andenaes, *Punishment and Deterrence* (Ann Arbor: University of Michigan Press, 1974).

53. M. Lehtinen, "The Voice of Life: An Argument for the Death Penalty," 23 *Crime and Delinquency*, 237–252 (1977).

54. E. van den Haag, "In Defense of the Death Penalty," 14 *Cr. L. Bul.*, 51–68 (1978).

55. W. Berns, *For Capital Punishment* (New York: Basic Books, 1981).

56. W. Bailey, in Bohm, *Death Penalty*, 35. See also Kappeler, 313–314, where the Bailey research is summarized.

57. I. Ehrlich, "Capital Punishment and Deterrence," 85 *J. Pol. Econ.*, 741 (1977).

58. Ehrlich's study received widespread notice. It was the only study cited by solicitor general Robert Bork in a brief before the U.S. Supreme Court that purported to show that executions deter homicide. *Challenging Capital Punishment: Legal and Social Science Approaches*, ed. R. Hass and J. A. Inciardi (Newbury Park, CA: Sage Publications, 1988). See also Kappeler, 314–315, for a careful analysis followed here.

59. I. Ehrlich, "The Deterrent Effect of Capital Punishment: A Question of Life and Death," 65 *Am. Ec. R.*, 397–417 (1977). For a criticism of the position that the death penalty is a deterrent to the commission of murder, see J. Fox and M. Radelet, "Persistent Flaws in Econometric Studies of the Deterrent Effect of the Death Penalty," 23 *Loy. L.A. L. Rev.*, 29 (1989).

60. For an extensive critique of Ehrlich's findings, see F. Zimring and G. Hawkins, *Capital Punishment and the American Agenda* (Cambridge: Cambridge University Press, 1986); D. Baldus and J. Cole, "A Comparison of the Work of Thorsten Sellin and Isaac Ehrlich on the Deterrent Effect of Capital Punishment," 85 *Yale L.J.*, 170 (1975).

61. R. Peterson and W. Bailey, "Murder and Capital Punishment: The Post-Furman Era," 66 *Soc. Forces*, 774 (1988).

62. Id., 785.

63. Id., 786–788.

64. W. Bailey and R. Peterson, "Police Killings and Capital Punishment," 25 *Criminology*, 1 (1987).

65. W. Bowers, "The Effect of Executions Is Brutalization, Not Deterrence," in Hass and Inciardi, *Challenging*.

66. See R. Lempert, "The Effect of Executions on Homicides: A New Look in an Old Light," 29 *Crime and Delinq.*, 88 (1983); Peterson and Bailey, "Murder."

67. P. Passell and J. Taylor, "The Deterrent Controversy: A Reconsideration of the Time Series Evidence," in *Capital Punishment in the U.S.*, ed. H. Bedau and G. Pierce (New York: Oxford University Press, 1976).

68. Bowers, et al. (1984).

69. There was so much debate surrounding Ehrlich's work that the National Academy of Sciences Panel on Deterrence and Incapacitation conducted a thorough study of Ehrlich's findings. The panel concluded that "we see too many plausible explanations for his finding a deterrent effect other than the theory that capital punishment deters murder. . . . [His] results cannot be used at this time to pass judgment on the use of the death penalty." Klein et al., "The Deterrent Effect of Capital Punishment: An Assessment of the Estimates, in A. Blumstein et al., *Deter-*

rence and Incapacitation: Estimating the Effects of Criminal Sanctions on Crime Rates (Washington, DC: Nat'l Academy of Sciences, 1978), 358.

70. Id.

71. Bowers et al. (1984); Kappeler (1996), 316.

72. D. Heckathorn, "Why Punishment Does Not Deter," in *The Ambivalent Force: Perspectives on the Police*, ed. A. Blumberg and E. Niederhoffer (New York: Holt, 1985). See also Kappeler, 316, whose careful analysis is followed here.

73. Typically, A.R.S. § 13–1101, Arizona's first-degree homicide law, defines the most culpable degree of the four degrees of homicide in terms of the ability for "reflection."

74. R. Pascucci, "Special Project, Capital Punishment in 1984: Abandoning the Pursuit of Fairness and Consistency," 69 *Cornell L. Rev.*, 1129, 1241 (1984); J. Browning, "The New Death Penalty Statutes: Perpetuating a Costly Myth," 9 *Gonz. L. Rev.*, 651, 660 (1974).

75. *Time*, 69 (Nov. 11, 1996).

76. A. Camus, "Reflections on the Guillotine," in *Resistance, Rebellion, and Death*, J. O'Brien, trans. (New York: Vintage Books, 1961), 175.

77. J. Browning, "New Death Penalty," 673–74.

78. *Time* 52 (Jan. 19, 1998).

79. M. Godfrey & V. Schiraldi, "How Have Homicide Rates Been Affected by California's Death Penalty?" *In Brief* (San Francisco: Center for Juvenile and Criminal Justice), 2–3 (Apr. 1995). See also "At What Cost?" *San Francisco Banner Daily Journal*, 4 (Feb. 4, 1988) (in New Orleans, from July to September 1987, the homicide rate increased 16.9 percent despite eight executions during the same period of time). Recent research strongly supports the brutalization argument: see E. Thomson, "Deterrence vs. Brutalization," 1 *Homicide Studies*, 110–128 (1997).

80. J. Wilkes, "Murder in Mind," *Psychology Today*, 27, 28 (June 1987).

81. *National Law Journal*, A17 (July 7, 1997).

82. C. Black, *The Inevitability of Caprice and Mistake* (New York: W. W. Norton, 1981), 33.

83. T. Rosenberg, "The Deadliest D.A.," *New York Times Magazine*, 21–52 (July 16, 1995). Prosecutors' death discretion undermines *Furman*, which "rested on specific empirical claims about the possibility of reliable and even-handed administration of the death penalty," J. Steiker, "The Long Road from Barbarism," 71 *Tx. L.R.*, 1131 (1993).

84. S. Bright and P. Keenan, "Judges and the Politics of Death," 75 *B.U.L.R.*, 759 (1995). It is not unusual for elected judges to campaign on promises to impose the death penalty.

85. *National Law Journal*, 2 (June 11, 1990).

86. B. Herbert, "Mistakes Were Made," *New York Times*, Sec. 4, K-19 (Jan. 11, 1998).

87. E. Connors, *Convicted by Juries, Exonerated by Science* (Upland: Diane Publishers, 1997).

88. E. Smith, "Innocents Convicted," *Arizona Republic*, B7 (Aug. 9, 1997) summarizes these data.

89. "How a Vision Failed," *ABA Journal*, 26 (Feb. 1997).

90. For Amsterdam's data, see W. Brennan, "Foreword," 8 *Notre Dame J. Law, Ethics and Public Policy*, 4 (1994), an issue devoted to the death penalty.

91. Kappeler, 310.

92. V. Streib, *Death Penalty for Juveniles* (Bloomington: Indiana University Press, 1987), 30.

93. The United States stands nearly alone among civilized democracies in retaining capital punishment, an irony for a country that prides itself on leading the world in human rights. As early as 1966, the United Nations General Assembly unanimously adopted the International Covenant on Civil and Political Rights (International Covenant), which reserves death for the most serious crimes and prohibits its imposition on those under eighteen.

See International Covenant on Civil and Political Rights, Dec. 16, 1966, art. 6, 999 U.N.T.S. 171. The UN General Assembly has repeatedly affirmed the desirability of abolishing capital punishment. See G.A. Res. 28/57, U.M. GAOR, 26th Sess., Supp. no 29, ¶ 3, U.M. Doc. A/8429 (1972); G.A. Res. 32/61, U.M. GAOR, 32d Sess., Supp. No. 45, ¶ 1, U.M. Doc. A/3245 (1978). In addition, in 1983, the Council of Europe provided that, except in wartime: "The Death Penalty shall be abolished. No one shall be condemned to such penalty or executed." Nov. 4, 1950, Protocol No. 6, art. 1, 213 U.N.T.S. 222 (hereafter European Convention).

Discussions for abolition took place under the Carter administration; President Reagan let them lapse, but President Bush, after the collapse of the Soviet Union, put the discussions back on Congress' agenda. The Senate gave its advice and consent to a modified ratification of the covenant on April 2, 1991. The United States has now finally ratified the U.N. Covenant with important reservations, such as executing persons under the age of eighteen when they committed their crimes. We refuse to comply with the prohibition against cruel, inhuman, or degrading treatment or punishment except to the extent that such treatment violates the Fifth, Eighth, or Fourteenth Amendments.

94. *Harpers Index*, 13 (June 1998). Anomalies abound. According to the same index, the state of California spent $3,400,000 between 1993 and 1998 to prevent birds from being executed on its electronic prison fences.

95. W. Kaminer, *Rage*, 96.

96. *Penny v. Lynaugh*, 492 U.S. 302 (1989).

97. Amnesty International, *When the State Kills: The Death Penalty: A Human Rights Issue* (New York: Amnesty International, 1989), 229.

98. "Case of Soering," 161 Eur. Ct. H.R. (ser.A) (1989), reprinted in 28 *I.L.M.*, 1063 (1989).

99. European Convention for the Protection of Human Rights (signed Nov. 4, 1959), art. 3 ("No one shall be subjected to torture or to inhuman or degrading treatment or punishment").

100. "Case of Soering," 28 *I.L.M.*, 1088.

101. Id., 1086.

102. Id., 1099.

103. *Trop v. Dulles*, 356 U.S. 86, 102 (1958) (plurality opinion).

104. *Coker v. Georgia*, 433 U.S. 584, 596 n.10 (1977). According to a 1965 United Nations survey, aside from the United States, only China (Taiwan), Malawi, and the Republic of South Africa still use capital punishment for rape. U.M. Dept. of Economic & Social Affairs, Capital Punishment, 1968, at 40, U.N. Doc. ST/SOA/SD/9–10, U.M. Sales No. 62.IV.2 (1968), cited in Brief for Petitioner at 50, *Coker*, 433 U.S. 584.

105. *Enmund v. Florida*, 458 U.S. 782, 796–97 n.22 (1982). The Court limited this principle to some extent in *Tison v. Arizona*, 481 U.S. 137, 157–158 (1987), when it announced that a death sentence could be imposed on a major participant in an underlying felony who displayed reckless indifference toward human life.

106. In *Stanford v. Kentucky*, 492 U.S. 361, 369 n.1 (1989), the Court pointedly noted that only "American conceptions of decency . . . are dispositive" rejecting the dissenters' reliance on the overwhelming world trend against executing juveniles.

107. K. Jamieson and T. Flanagan, *Sourcebook of Criminal Justice Statistics* (Albany: Hindelang Criminal Justice Research Center, 1988), 230.

108. Cost of keeping and eventually executing a prisoner from arrest to death ranges from three to six times the cost of maintaining that person in life imprisonment. Kappeler, 319–320. In California, it has been estimated that taxpayers could save $90 million per year by abolishing the death penalty. See, for details, R. Tabak and J. Lane, "The Execution of Injustice: A Cost and Lack of Benefit Analysis of the Death Penalty," 23 *Loy. of L.A. L.R.* 136 (1989). Cf. also (Judge) L. Forer, *A Rage to Punish* (New York: W. W. Norton, 1994), 115, where she estimates that the cost of prosecuting a death case alone would pay for more than fifty years' incarceration.

4

PRINCIPLE AND THE FELONY-MURDER RULE

Perhaps in time the so-called Dark Ages will be thought of as including our own.

—Georg Christoph Lichtenberg

A staple of the criminal law of almost all American states, the felony-murder doctrine finds the felon guilty of murder if anyone for any reason dies during the felony. The rule holds the felon liable for murder even if the death occurs during preparation before, or flight after, the felony. It does not matter that the death occurs accidentally; homicidal mental state is irrelevant. The only intent required is the intent to do the felony. The rule imposes strict homicidal liability on felons even for deaths caused by third parties such as a victim, the police, or a bystander.

The rule is unfair, unprincipled, and inconsistent with other criminal and civil standards. Two cases illustrate the problem. In a civil case, *Hall v. Booth*,[1] one member of a hunting party accidentally shot and killed a thirteen-year-old boy. The victim's father sued the entire group on a theory of vicarious liability, arguing that each member of the group should be equally liable for the shooting. The court refused to extend liability beyond the person who fired the shot. It labeled the shooting an unforeseeable event that broke any chain of liability for the nonshooting hunters.[2]

In contrast, *People v. Hickman*,[3] a criminal case with a supposedly higher standard of proof, imposed felony-murder liability on all burglary participants for the fatal act of a police officer pursuing the group. Three boys in

Joliet, Illinois, set out to burglarize a warehouse. Seeing the police, they fled into an adjacent parking lot, where a pursuing officer mistakenly shot and killed another officer. Each of the boys, including Hickman, who was unarmed and, like the others, did not cause the death, was convicted of felony murder solely for their group participation in burglary—a principle contrary to that which exonerated the hunters in the civil case.[4]

These two cases expose a serious incongruity: our legal system shows more care in assessing civil liability than in assessing felony murder in our criminal courts. The defendants in both these cases were victims of bad luck. None of the actors, criminal or civil, showed intent to kill, both deaths were unintended, and the actors all expressed remorse. None of the defendants anticipated a death. The only factual difference between the cases lies in the identity of the defendants, a group of socially acceptable recreational hunters in one case, youthful burglars in the other. The ultimate difference in their legal fates—acquittal versus guilt—lies in the unprincipled felony-murder rule. Its persistence reflects legal fiction, political timidity, and wrong lessons.

HISTORY

The English origins of our felony-murder rule are obscure. Its earliest sources are not judicial decisions but scholarly commentaries.[5] Coke may have originated the doctrine in stating in 1644 "that a death caused by an unlawful act is murder."[6] In 1762 a formal statement of felony murder appears in Sir Michael Foster's reconstruction of the law of homicide in his *Discourse of Homicide*.[7] Lord Holt later gave the rule a new lease on life through fuller explication. Hawkins and Foster built on Holt to shape the modern rule. In his *Commentaries on the Laws of England* Blackstone declared, "If one intends to do another felony, and undesignedly kills a man, this is also murder."[8]

One of the likely sources of the rule is the medieval theory of "tainting," where culpability for death results regardless of the actor's mental state. Taint requires "expungement." Medieval England assumed that if one person caused the death of another, the killing upset the natural order. Some legal response was necessary to expiate the killing and to expunge the taint. Expunging the taint of a killing differs subtly from justly punishing for causing death with fault because taint arises regardless of fault or blame. Expunging taint reflects a grossly metaphysical concept of punishment. Nonetheless, tainting remains one of the shadowy props for the rule.[9]

Under early English law, felonies as well as murders were generally punished by death. Thus, it made little difference whether the felon was put to death for the unintended murder or for the underlying felony. In its earliest incarnation, the felony-murder rule was even broader, better characterized as an "unlawful act-murder" rule, because any death arising from any un-lawful act became a murder.

In its origins, the English doctrine prevented an actor who killed acci-dentally during the course of a felony from escaping the death penalty. That world saw all killings as murder, so it made sense, under this standard, to preclude felons from avoiding punishment for murder by claiming ac-cident. Thereafter the concept spread, without good reason, into the much broader rule that turned any death in the course of even nondangerous felonies into a murder.[10]

By the nineteenth century the doctrine was in full force in English courts. At its apogee, it then spread to the American colonies,[11] where the few offenses then classified as felonies were all capital crimes. Thus, it made no difference whether a felon was executed for one felony or another. Later, however, the harsh nature of the rule was curtailed by making only the most egregious crimes—those inherently involving a risk of death—carry the death penalty.

ENGLISH VERSUS AMERICAN LIMITATIONS

Over the years, English courts put limitations on the rule's harsh effects. They began resolutely to limit the rule early in this century, which coincided with the effort to proportion punishment for common-law murder. The limits generally were twofold. They required either that (1) the defendant's conduct in committing the felony involve an act of violence while carrying out a felony of violence, or (2) the death be the natural and probable consequence of the defendant's criminal conduct.[12] These limits could not correct the rule's illogic. England eventually abolished the rule in its entirety in 1957.[13]

By contrast, American legislatures and courts remain markedly unmoved in their loyalty to felony murder. Some states retain the extreme common-law rule. Most states limit it to the enumerated felonies in the murder statute.[14] Jurisdictions that do not follow the enumerated felonies approach usually limit it to inherently dangerous felonies.[15] To determine if a felony is inherently dangerous, some of these jurisdictions consider only the ele-ments of the felony in the abstract, while others consider the circumstances surrounding the crime.[16] The factual approach includes all felonies as po-tentially inherently dangerous but also recognizes that inherently dangerous felonies can be perpetrated in a nondangerous manner.[17]

The drafters of the Model Penal Code originally proposed elimination of the felony-murder rule, but the realization that it would be politically dif-ficult to do so led them to keep it, albeit in a more restricted form. Only New Hampshire and Hawaii followed the code's ideal of felony-murder exclusion.[18]

CRITICISM

The felony-murder rule has an extensive history of thoughtful condemnation. At least since 1834, when His Majesty's Commissioners on Criminal Law found the rule "totally incongruous with the general principles of our jurisprudence," the rule has won condemnation by both English and American writers and scholars.[19] Notwithstanding trenchant criticism, the rule still operates in nearly all the states because lawmakers lack the courage to amend or repeal it. In most of its modern statutory forms, it suffers not only from serious moral weakness but also from the congenital deficiencies of its obscure birth. It has no respectable common-law ancestry; its doctrinal frailty ought never to have survived the seventeenth century. Though England has now abolished it without regret, its continuing prominence in our courts teaches unprincipled and inconsistent messages to those who need to learn the contrary.

THE ARIZONA EXAMPLE

Because Arizona's felony-murder rule is extreme by any standard, modern or medieval, and seems to be the broadest in this country, it serves as an example of the illogical results flowing from the core of any version of the rule.

The Arizona legislature ignored the recommendation of the Model Penal Code to abolish or narrow the rule and instead broadly expanded it.[20] Arizona now expansively defines felony murder as first-degree murder, subject to the death penalty, when anyone, including a nonparticipant, dies, even accidentally, during the commission or attempt to do any of the felonies listed in the statute.[21] The list of these underlying felonies has ballooned well beyond the common law's limitation to inherently dangerous felonies. Nonlethal offenses subject to the Arizona felony-murder rule include, among others, the sale or importation of drugs, including marijuana; sexual conduct with a minor (which includes consensual conduct); arson of any structure; escape; any degree of burglary; and inducing a minor to violate drug laws.[22]

Inclusion of these nonviolent felonies in the rule marks a vast departure from even the extreme English rule, which, at its most punitive, justified its severity by restricting the underlying felonies to those necessarily threatening to life. The felonies included in the Arizona code go well beyond this category of inherent lethality. The Arizona statute also significantly dilutes causality, another common-law protection, by covering the death of any person, by whatever cause, or none at all, during the commission, attempted commission, or flight from the underlying felony.[23] Temporality ("during"), in effect, replaces causality. Case law reflects this overbreadth. In *State v. Lopez*, defendant Lopez suffered a felony-murder conviction despite having been arrested and handcuffed before police shot and killed his accomplice.[24]

Nonlethal felonies and broad causation in the Arizona rule lead to first-degree felony-murder liability in the following hypothetical (only for the time being) scenarios, among others:

1. the death by heart attack of an uninvolved spectator present at a sale of a small amount of marijuana;

2. the death of an angry parent who trips on a step and falls after finding his daughter and her boyfriend engaged in consensual fondling on the front porch;

3. the death of a cyclist hit by a police car, accidentally, while the police car is pursuing a misdemeanant-juvenile escapee from a juvenile detention center;

4. the vehicular death of a motorist evading an ambulance carrying a person suffering smoke inhalation from an arson fire;

5. the death of a minor child by falling from a playground swing while being induced by an older brother to carry a marijuana roach to a nearby friend.

Though such a rule may have made minimal sense at common law, where the few felonies that existed were all punished with death, modern legislatures have created a wide variety of felonies that are not inherently dangerous. Application of the rule's rigor to such felonies yields dramatic results. In addition to those just listed, a seller of liquor in violation of a felony statute becomes a murderer if his purchaser falls asleep and dies of exposure.[25] A person who traffics in marijuana even could be guilty of murder.[26] Similar results could apply in both the drug and sexual areas where an underlying, nonlethal felony is far removed geographically and temporally from the fatality.[27]

FELONY-MURDER PROBLEMS

In any version the generic American felony murder rule reveals at least four distinct problems, each of which alone is fatal to principled justice. The first is its departure from otherwise universal *mens rea* principles.

Mens Rea Problem

According to the otherwise uniform principles of criminal law, offensive conduct combined with criminal intent produces culpability. Lesser mental states, of course, yield lesser liability. Mental state, or *mens rea*, is the decisive factor in determining culpability. Felony murder, however, requires no specific *mens rea* as to the death; it encompasses deaths that could be prosecuted under other murder statutes such as negligent homicide. It also comprises a narrow category of cases that can be prosecuted as murder only because the death happened during the commission of a felony.

The universal criminal rule, apart from the felony-murder instance, is that "[e]ach crime . . . has its distinctive *mens rea*."[28] Thus, liability for a conventional, first-degree homicide requires murder and intent to murder. Felony murder, however, requires no such homicidal *mens rea*. The rule transfers mental state from the intent to commit the felony to the act of death itself. Here, where the stakes are as high as the death penalty, the rule ignores the felon's true state of mind and, in its place, concocts an ersatz homicidal mental state from evidence of a felonious mental state less culpable than homicide.

The felony-murder rule transfers the intent to commit a felony to the death even if the death is accidental or unanticipated. The rule presumes this fictive homicidal mental state merely from evidence of the underlying felony. Even accomplices to the felony become liable for another's killing. Homicide liability befalls anyone who intended, committed, or fled from a felony where someone died, thus resulting in strict accomplice liability. Felons have been convicted of murder when the victim kills a cofelon or a third party, when a third party kills another during the felony, and even when a cofelon kills himself.

The doctrine contradicts our most basic conception of proportionality because someone is severely punished for unintended results.[29] The U.S. Supreme Court has stated that "[i]t is fundamental that 'causing harm intentionally must be punished more severely than causing the same harm unintentionally."[30] The rule violates this principle by treating felony murder as first-degree murder because culpability for an unintended or accidental death is made, artificially, to match that of premeditated homicide.[31]

The felony-murder rule is thus a striking exception to the usual principles of *mens rea*.[32] The criminal law does not otherwise predicate liability simply on conduct causing death. Principled arguments in favor of the doctrine's view of the mental state requirement are impossible to find.[33] Grading crime according to the culpable mental state of the actor is the modern approach to culpability. Making true mental state so grossly irrelevant as to replace it with less-than-homicidal mental state otherwise denies due process.[34] Criminal punishment is normally imposed only after the actor becomes blameworthy under accepted principles of moral responsibility. *Mens rea* has long been the Anglo-American cornerstone of any just system of criminal responsibility; without it the system loses its moral ballast.

Defenders of the rule, faced with this analysis, have suggested that a strict liability offense like felony murder is no stranger to the criminal law and that, in fact, many administrative and regulatory offenses reflect strict liability and that felony murder merely fits their pattern. Supporters also claim that the rule induces felons to exercise care during felonies, prompts them to refrain from committing felonies in the first place, and warns them that they cannot hide behind claims of accident or mere negligence.

These claims are as spurious as they are creative. In the first place, felony murder does not fit the mold of strict liability regulatory crimes. It is not an administrative or public welfare regulation carrying a token penalty but a serious common-law crime of a moral rather than regulatory nature. The conduct in question is not routine or morally neutral. In addition, there is no avalanche of felony killings to which the masses are prone, and strict liability is not needed to combat any widespread behavioral threat of free riders. The administrative conditions unique to true regulatory offenses simply do not fit felony murder.

The rule also stands apart from public welfare crimes, which do not ordinarily parallel a serious crime. The omission of *mens rea* from strict liability public welfare offenses reflects low-level culpability and mass vulnerability. Felony murder, on the other hand, is a variety of the rare crime of murder whose essence is malice and whose penalty can be death, a crime showing serious moral culpability rather than administrative oversight. In these senses, the rule is far removed from the strict liability model in regulatory and public welfare offenses.

Tort Wrongful Death Problem

In addition to these problems of transferred mental state, the felony-murder rule generates evidentiary inconsistency compared to civil law. The way courts handle civil defendants charged with causing death starkly contrasts to the way the rule operates in criminal cases. In a typical civil wrongful death suit, such as the hunting accident mentioned earlier, the defendant's state of mind is not presumed but must be proven. Evidence of this state of mind, from either the plaintiff or the defendant, is always relevant because the defendant's actual mental state is a necessary predicate for both liability and damages. Explanation, excuses, and defenses show intent or negligence as well as degrees of foreseeability, awareness of risk, and deviation from the standard of care. Mental state bears heavily on liability to the point where a jury could legitimately exonerate a wrongful death civil defendant who acted by accident.

By contrast, our criminal law, whose standards of proof and procedural protections boast of more care than the civil law, tells an opposite story. Felony-murder defendants cannot testify about proximate or intervening cause[35] or about their true mental state at the time of the death.[36] The only relevant mental state is the intent to do the underlying felony.[37] Felony murder makes explanations, excuses, and accident irrelevant. Intent to do the felony alone suffices for homicidal motive not because such a homicidal motive really exists in fact but simply because of the misfortuity of a death.

By contrast, in a wrongful death tort suit with lower standards of proof, excluding the defendant's mental state evidence would certainly violate due process. Furthermore, a negligent act resulting in death never presumes an intent to kill or even to injure, nor is mental state transferred from one tort to another. Oddly, it does precisely that in a felony-murder trial where the ultimate stakes are not dollars but death.

History helps explain how such an aberration could develop in England. In that country, during the early development of the common law, murder was considered an offense against the Crown. A potential civil action for death merged into the crime and was prosecuted solely by the Crown. A third party injured as a result of a death had no recourse. However, by the mid-nineteenth century the private wrongful death action became available in England. But that development was limited to England, not to its former colony. In the United States all deaths arising from felonies continued to be crimes rather than wrongful deaths. As private civil actions for wrongful death began to develop in this country, the rationale for felony murder— that only the government can avenge a death during a felony—vanished.[38]

But the irony does not stop there. There continues to be a disconnect between the ways courts treat felony-murder criminal trials by comparison with civil wrongful death actions. In our civil law, when a tort involves more than one defendant, the other defendants become liable only via evidence showing substantial assistance or encouragement to the principal actor. Civil liability focuses on the existence and extent of the coparticipants' cooperative acts.

Not so with our criminal law. In a felony-murder prosecution such as the *Hickman* case, all participants in the felony are liable for all consequences, including an unintended death, even if these participants lack control over the result or strongly oppose it or even fail to cause it. Vicarious liability not only expands by comparison with a civil wrongful death; it consumes excuses as well. The excusing doctrine of intervening cause, which exists both criminally and civilly, becomes irrelevant in a felony-murder trial because minimal participation in the felony alone suffices for liability for the death despite another's intervention. Mere association with the felon becomes more dispositive than the causal acts of the participants. In the civil law, this doctrine of intervening cause exonerates the other participants of tort liability for an unintended death; not so in felony-murder cases like *Hickman*, where the officer's intervening fatal shot makes no difference to the nonshooting felons' liability.

As vicarious liability expands in the criminal law, the arena of excuses diminishes. The felony-murder rule requires only a mental state of intent to do the felony; no other mental state is required. Hence, the requirement of specific knowledge disappears. As a result, excuses—an assertion of lack of knowledge and intent—become irrelevant. The irrelevance of excuses contrasts sharply with tort law, where evidence of excuse and accident is universally permitted and may at times alone warrant an acquittal, as in the hunters' case earlier.

In addition to the problems of accomplice liability and evanescent excuses, the felony-murder rule adopts a peculiar broad notion of causality. The tort of wrongful death is helpful in showing the inconsistency. Central to proof in a civil wrongful death action is proximate causation, which entails at least four inquiries: (1) whether the actor had a legal duty to the plaintiff; (2) whether the duty was breached; (3) whether the risk created was the actual or "but for" cause of the harm, and (4) whether the risk was foreseeable. These inquiries determine whether it is just to extend liability to peripheral actors. Simply proving the actor is negligent is not enough; the negligence must also be the proximate cause of the injury. The causation requirement precludes liability for unforeseeable, unexpected, intervening, and nonparticipatory results.[39]

The opposite is the case for felony murder, which shows indifference to any causation at all. In some states the prosecution need not prove that the felon caused anything; it suffices for liability that the death simply occurred during the commission of the felony. In most states where causation either does not appear as a requirement or has been defined loosely as "but for," felons on trial are not allowed to raise the issue of proximate causation, that is, are denied the chance to say they neither intended nor caused the death. Most courts assume the death was reasonably foreseeable from the commission of the felony simply because it occurred in its time parameters, including flight afterward, as in *Hickman*. Courts disregard causation from a belief that felonies are themselves inherently dangerous and, given enough time, likely will lead to someone's death.[40]

We are left, then, with the irony that wrongful death civil defendants and their accomplices enjoy higher protections and greater latitude in testimony than do criminal defendants on trial for felony murder. Civil dollar penalties are more carefully scrutinized than a possible death sentence. Civil defendants may explain, seek to excuse, and suggest lack of intent, accident, and unforeseeability. Felony-murder defendants may not do any of this because their mental state and their noncausal conduct are made irrelevant by the rule. The civil law does not conclusively presume mental state for a wrongful death; the criminal law does exactly that for the more serious charge of felony-murder homicide. Something is grossly wrong when the civil system affords tort defendants more protections than the criminal system provides defendants threatened with loss of liberty and life itself. The real inquiry then becomes why we depart from the standard legal rules to impose homicidal liability on felons but adhere to these rules when evaluating wrongful death tortfeasors.

Like other fictions, such an unprincipled rule breeds disrespect. Our courts would never deny due process in this way to civil tort defendants in a wrongful death suit. Nor indeed would a court similarly restrict a defendant's evidence of mental state or causation in any other routine criminal case, such as a theft trial, where any defendant could readily offer evidence of mistake, error, and lack of intent. In a felony-murder case, however, where the penal stakes are life imprisonment or the death penalty, our criminal law does exactly that. In this respect the felony-murder rule surrenders to expediency rather than to principle and belies the criminal law's vaunted claim of respecting due process rights.

The Death Problem

The felony-murder rule presents a further problem for the death penalty. The Supreme Court's 1972 decision in *Furman v. Georgia* held then-existing schemes of capital punishment constitutionally deficient because of caprice.[41] *Furman* focused on the unprincipled selection process for the death penalty and required future death penalty statutes to have a nuanced narrowing process to select those truly qualifying for death.[42]

Narrowing the class of eligible death penalty candidates requires that the least culpable homicide defendants escape death penalty eligibility. If *Furman* requires narrowing the death eligible class, a properly applied narrowing device would "differentiate this [death penalty] case in an objective, evenhanded, and substantively rational way from the many . . . murder cases in which the death penalty may not be imposed."[43] Such a narrowing device supplies, supposedly, a rational basis for executing one defendant and not another and confirms that the death penalty matches the culpability of the murderer's mental state.

A first-degree felony-murder rule such as the Arizona paradigm mentioned earlier disrupts this pattern of individual scrutiny. Instead of identifying the least culpable offenders by malice and premeditation standards, the rule thrusts *all* undifferentiated, first-degree murderers into the pool eligible for death. Typically, the felony-murder defendant is factually among the less culpable. The rule makes no distinctions; it does not narrow eligibility but broadens it precisely because it ignores differences in mental state. The rule thus provides death penalty exposure equally to the deliberate rapist/killer[44] and to the robber whose victim dies of a heart attack, as well as to the robber's accomplice driver who is absent from the scene of the crime.[45] In its traditional form the rule even makes the defendant, like Hickman, guilty of first-degree murder when an officer or victim mistakenly kills a third person.[46] Such a nonpremeditating defendant falls into the death-eligible class just as much as a premeditating killer.

Similarly, a felon who extracts promises from his cofelon that no one will be hurt is subject to the rule when the cofelon breaks the promise.[47] Because the rule broadly equates any participant in the felony with a cold-blooded, deliberate killer, no matter how unforeseeable the death or how attenuated the participation, all felony participants fall into the class eligible for death regardless of their very differing mental states.

On the rule's blurring of vital *mens rea* distinctions, the language of the California Supreme Court shows the impossibility, under the rule, of narrowing the death-eligible class when homicidal *mens rea* is abrogated:

[Felony murder] includes not only [premeditated murder], but also a variety of unintended homicides resulting from reckless behavior, or ordinary negligence, or pure accident; it embraces both calculated conduct and acts committed in panic or rage, or under the dominion of mental illness, drugs or alcohol; and it condemns alike consequences that are highly probable, conceivably possible, or wholly unforeseeable.[48]

The impact of the rule in capital cases has not diminished under post-*Furman* procedures. In many states, a felon involved in any minor degree in the death can be worse off with respect to the death penalty than a first-degree premeditated murderer, because the rule, stripped of any *mens rea* index, provides no meaningful moral narrowing to discriminate real from accidental culpability. Just as before *Furman*, this large class of defendants includes all the various accomplices and accidental killers caught up in the rule's wide net regardless of mental state.

Because the usual class of first-degree murderers comprises two groups of defendants, felony murderers and premeditated murderers, the only ones eliminated by any narrowing device are those who kill with premeditation, that is, in cold blood, not those who cause an unforeseen death during a felony. In fact, however, the class of felony murderers includes not only cold-blooded killers but also accidental killers and accomplices. The rule thus operates contrary to narrowing; it greatly broadens the death-eligible class. A simple felony murder unaccompanied by any other aggravating factor ought not by itself match the culpability of premeditated murder. If anything, on its face a killing in cold blood shows more culpability because of real homicidal intent.

The felony-murder rule thus creates arbitrary and capricious capital sentencing by imputing homicidal responsibility for the unforeseeable manner of death to a defendant whose fatal involvement is attenuated. For example, a nontriggerman convicted of felony murder is several times removed from the locus of blame: the killing is murder only by reason of the felony-murder rule, he is responsible for the killing under accomplice liability principles, and he faces the executioner because of the manner in which the more culpable codefendant killed. Despite the nontriggerman's lesser culpability, he still faces a death sentence exactly as does the far more culpable intentional killer.

A proportioned measurement of culpability would consider the actual mental state of the defendant along with the felony. Premeditated murder becomes heinous precisely because a person purposely kills another after reflection. But felony-murder statutes embrace as first-degree murder any broad conduct that negligently causes death. Proportionality requires that a *mens rea* of premeditation be punished more severely than a *mens rea* of negligence. Equating negligent felony murder with premeditated murder ignores proportionality because the defendant is punished without regard to moral lucidity. Retribution for taking a life can be justified only if tempered by an evaluation of the defendant's homicidal *mens rea*. In the case of felony murder, the felon is exposed to the death penalty without regard to mental state; he is treated as though he premeditated and directly caused death.

Violated are not only *Furman* but also the ideals eloquently espoused in *Woodson v. North Carolina*[49] to treat each offender proportionate to individual moral culpability:

A process that accords no significance to relevant facets of the character and record of the individual offender or the circumstances of the particular offense excludes from consideration in fixing the ultimate punishment of death the possibility of compassion or mitigating factors stemming from the diverse frailties of human kind. It treats all persons convicted of a designated offense not as uniquely individual human beings, but as members of a faceless, undifferentiated mass to be subjected to the blind infliction of the penalty of death.[50]

Deterrence Impossible

To some supporters, one purpose of the modern felony-murder rule is to prevent killings. Holmes once expressed the idea that "the law ought to throw on the actor the peril that if a death results, even an unforeseeable one, he shall be punished as a murderer."[51]

The history of the original rule, however, does not reveal the deterrent focus underlying the modern rule. Coke, Foster, and Blackstone did not justify the doctrine on deterrence grounds. Nonetheless, deterrent reasoning tracks most of the modern rationale underlying its strict liability. As noted earlier, supporters claim that felony murder induces felons to exercise care during felonies, prompts potential felons to refrain from committing felonies in the first place, and warns prospective felons that they will not be able to hide behind claims of accident or negligence. These are unproven and highly questionable assumptions.

The deterrence argument has two underlying assumptions. The first is that the rule deters felons from causing death during the felony.[52] The second is that the rule deters the underlying felony itself by informing the felon of responsibility for any death during it.[53]

The deterrence argument is curious at best[54] regarding the vicarious liability of codefendants for the actions of the principal.[55] Simply stated, how does one felon deter another's unintended act? Supposedly, the threat of a murder conviction induces felons to commit felonies with greater care,[56] thereby reducing the number of accidental homicides. Realistically, unintended consequences and accidents are simply not deterrable. The same problem arises when the rule holds the defendant for murder when a third party, such as the victim or a police officer, as in *Hickman*, causes the death. The felon, having no control over these acts, cannot be deterred from this result. Moreover, any potential deterrence against unintentional killings evaporates because few felons know that the rule imposes strict liability for resulting deaths or believe that fatal harm will result from their felony.[57] Deterrence for felony murder is unlikely where there was no effective deterrence for doing the felony in the first place.

A good part of the deterrence assertion is illogical. It is unrealistic, if not impossible, to encourage an actor committing assault, aggravated assault, or similar felonies to take care in beating up the victim or to beat the victim up but stop just short of death. Ascribing such prudence to such an assailant is an *Alice in Wonderland* fiction because there is no way to cause great bodily harm safely.

Assertions that the doctrine exists to prevent killings that occur in the course of felonies and that it actually achieves this goal rest on blind faith. If the rule is to rest upon deterrent premises, its advocates need to comply with our normal insistence on proof of efficacy. Without a credible foundation in facts, deterrence is not a real justification but a poor excuse for infidelity to principle.

Lawmakers may actually believe the delusion or, more likely, know the spurious nature of the deterrent claim but remain content to let it stand. On such an important matter, why have we been willing to rest on assumptions and not demand proof that the rule actually produces deterrence? A working hypothesis is simply that there is, in fact, no evidence of any deterrence, but the public doesn't know this, and lawmakers don't care.

The rule necessarily lacks any plausible deterrent function. The felon, after all, has already disregarded the penalties available for the underlying felony. If the rule reinforces the disregarded deterrent effect of the felony's penalties, it would be more effective and hardly more fortuitous to select a certain ratio of convicted felons for the death penalty by lot.[58]

Lawmakers' Mind-Set

Why do our lawmakers retain this illogical rule when principled jurisdictions like England, its originator, narrow or abolish it? The answer is not difficult in the abstract. Nurtured in a climate of toughness rather than principle, our lawmakers either cannot see the rule's inconsistency or, if they do, cannot muster the courage to abolish it. In the real examples at the start of this chapter, scholars see no difference: the deaths were unintended, and the defendants in both cases regretted the results and were victims of bad luck.[59] None of the actors showed intent to kill, and neither group expected the fatal result. The difference in legal result reflects not only a difference in principle but also of identity, that is, who the actors are. In the *Hickman* case, it is a group of felons; in the other case it is a group of acceptable, recreational hunters.[60]

Legal theorists would say, with good reason, that an actor who kills someone accidentally should escape criminal and civil liability and that this principle should apply as much to "bad" actors as to good ones. On the other hand, a politician kneading the criminal law sees the result differently. For a "tough on crime" mind-set, a negligent killing during a felony differs as a polar opposite from a negligent killing apart from a felony. If "accidental" means innocent, no felon can possibly be innocent by definition, certainly not innocent enough to be excused. Because the felon started the entire factual process, the felon loses the protection of the accident defense otherwise available to all other civil and, indeed, to all other criminal defendants.[61] Felony murder is thus an exception not only to civil law but also to all other kinds of criminal prosecutions.

The identity of the actors becomes the touchstone. Felony-murder cases present easy opportunities for halo-polishers to impose moral condemnation because here the law is dealing with a bad person, a felon. By objectifying the person—seeing the actor as nothing more than an undeserving criminal—lawmakers also find it easier to aggravate punishment even to death, no matter the caprice. Civil cases of wrongful or accidental death do not present the same opportunity because there is no bad person on whom we can impose blame and, furthermore, because we have the habit to call such cases accidents.[62]

While lawmakers may well accept the general premise behind culpable mental state—moral fault as a prerequisite for criminal liability—they can just as easily disavow its implications. After all, for rare regulatory offenses such as littering, lawmakers do dispense with mental state.[63] For felony murder, a legislature may similarly assume it may dispense with the culpable mental state otherwise universally required for nonregulatory crimes. But unlike littering, felony murder can bring a death sentence.

The typical lawmaker probably does not perceive the disproportionality lurking in the rule. The culpability of the felon matches the politician's disdain for the death. The inconsistency in legal tests and courtroom verdicts is unimportant to a "tough on crime" mentality that disregards mental state for the felons convicted criminally but retains it for the tortfeasors exonerated civilly.[64]

CONCLUSION: THE INJUSTICE

Justice Frankfurter noted long ago that "[n]ot the least significant test of the quality of a civilization is its treatment of those charged with crime, particularly with offenses which arouse the passions of a community."[65] The lingering presence of the felony-murder rule that treats felon defendants with blatant inconsistency significantly blemishes our justice system's claim to teaching fairness. The rule teaches that the law and the courts are willing to avoid principle in dealing with bad actors—the very ones who need to learn something about principle. In *People v. Aaron*,[66] in striking down its felony-murder rule as fundamentally unfair, the Michigan Supreme Court perceptively noted that the underlying rationale for felony murder is that the necessities of justice will be denied those who do bad acts.[67]

The felony-murder rule contradicts a number of fundamental criminal law principles. In the first place, it relieves the prosecutor of the burden to prove at all, much less beyond a reasonable doubt, the otherwise universal requirement of criminal *mens rea*, namely, the intent to kill. The felon's true mental state, unlike that of any other *mens rea* defendant, criminal or civil, becomes irrelevant. There is thus no correlation between criminal liability and moral culpability.

Second, the rule works against the *Furman* requirement to narrow the class of death-eligible defendants to those whose moral turpitude truly merits death. By ignoring degrees of mental state, the rule thrusts into the death-eligible class felons whose true mental state may range from premeditation to negligence or from malicious intent to pure accident.

Further, the rule offers less protection to felony-murder defendants than does the civil law to wrongful death defendants. The latter group regularly offers evidence of causation, intent, knowledge, foreseeability, and mistake. By contrast, all this evidence is made irrelevant to felony-murder defendants, some of whom are facing capital punishment.

Finally, apropos the sentencing issues in chapter one, the rule does violence to the principle of "just deserts" central to federal and many states' sentencing schemes. Just deserts, however defined, is a retributive concept, resting on the notion that punishment reflects the individual's unique moral culpability apart from any utilitarian calculus. Insofar as felony murder is a strict liability offense obviating homicidal mental state for a homicide conviction, the rule belies the goal of sentencing according to individual moral culpability and instead reflects a univocal, cookie-cutter view of all felons within the ambit of death.

The rule is an unnecessary and unprincipled construct. It teaches the existence of two constitutions, one for general defendants, another—much more capricious—for felony-murder defendants. That this latter class often faces a death penalty is no barrier to bending principle. The rule serves no interests other than to advertise that our justice system will deviate from teaching principle when it deals with unprincipled actors.

NOTES

1. 423 So. 2d 184 (Ala. 1982).
2. Id., 185–186.
3. 59 Ill. 89, 319 NE 2d 511 (1974).
4. Id.
5. George P. Fletcher, "Reflections on Felony-Murder," 12 *Sw.U.L. Rev.*, 413, 421 (1980).
6. 2 Wharton's Criminal Law §§ 147 at 295–296 (Charles E. Torcia, ed., 15th ed. 1994 and Supp. 1998).
7. George Fletcher, *Rethinking Criminal Law* 281–282 (Boston: Little, Brown, 1978) (citing Michael Foster, *Discourse II of Homicide*, in *Crown Law* 255, 258 [Oxford: Clarendon Press, 1762]).
8. William Blackstone's *Commentaries on the Laws of England* (George Chase, ed., 4th ed. 1877; reprint, Chicago: University of Chicago Press, 1938), 947.
9. Fletcher (1978), 426.
10. Model Penal Code, Part II, § 210.2, 30–32 (Philadelphia: American Law Institute, 1980).
11. Fletcher (1980), 283.
12. Fletcher (1980), 426.
13. Homicide Act of 1957, 5 and 6 Eliz. 2, ch. 11 § 1.
14. See, for example, Arizona Rev. Stat. Ann. § 13–1105(a)(2).
15. See, for example, Montana 45–5–102 (forcible felonies).
16. 2 Wharton's Criminal Law, § 148 at 303–305.
17. Id.
18. Model Penal Code, Part II, § 210.2, comment 6 at 30–31 (1980).
19. "A living fossil" was the oxymoronic phrase Justice Brennan used to describe this "curious doctrine." *Tison v. Arizona*, 481 U.S. 137, 159, reh'g denied, 482 U.S. 921 (1987) (Brennan, J., dissenting). The nineteenth-century Victorian judge Sir James Fitzjames Stephen called the doctrine "astonishing" and "monstrous," with "little or no authority," with a credence "gained only from repetition." 3 J. Stephen, *A History of the Criminal Law of England* (1883), 57, 65, 75, 38. A California court stated that the rule "anachronistically resurrects from a bygone age a 'barbaric concept,' " *People v. Phillips*, 64 Cal. 2d 574, 583 N.6, 414 P.2d 353, 360 N.6, 51 Cal. Rptr. 225, 232 n.6 (1966). Another California court concludes that it "erodes the relation between criminal liability and moral culpability," *People v. Washington*, 62 Cal. 2d 779, 783, 402 P.2d 130, 134, 44 Cal. Rptr. 442, 446 (1965). Scholarly commentary on the rule and the related doctrine of "vicarious" or "accessorial liability" has approached ridicule. See G. Fletcher, *Rethinking Criminal Law* (1978); J. Dressler, "The Jurisprudence of Death by Another: Accessories and Capital Punishment," 51 *U. Colo. L. Rev.*, 17 (1979).
20. Model Penal Code, Part II, § 210.2 at 30–31 (1980).
21. Arizona Revised Statutes § 13–1105.
First degree murder; classification

A. A person commits first degree murder if . . .

2. Acting either alone or with one or more other persons such person commits or attempts to commit sexual conduct with a minor under § 13–1405, sexual assault under § 13–1406, molestation of a child under § 13–1410, marijuana offenses under § 13–1405, subsection A, paragraph 4, dangerous drug offenses under § 13–3407, subsection A, paragraph 7, narcotics offenses under § 13–1408, subsection A, paragraph 7 that equal or exceed the statutory threshold amount for each offense or combination of offenses, involving or using minors in drug offenses under § 13–3409, kidnapping under § 13–1304, burglary under § 13–1506, § 13–1507 or § 13–1508, arson under § 13–1703 or 13–1704, robbery under § 13–1902, § 13–1903 or § 13–1904, escape under § 13–2503 or § 13–2504, child abuse under § 13–3623, subsection B, paragraph 1, or unlawful flight from a pursuing law enforcement vehicle under § 28–622.01 and in the course of and in furtherance of such offense or immediate flight from such offense, such person or another person causes the death of any person. . . .

B. Homicide, as defined in subsection A, paragraph 2 of this section, requires no specific mental state other than what is required for the commission of any of the enumerated felonies.

22. Id.

23. Id.

24. *State v. Lopez*, 173 Ariz. 552, 845 P.2d 478 (App. 1992).

25. *People v. Pavlic*, 227 Mich. 562, 199 N.W. 373 (1924). If liquor is considered a drug, felony murder would be the result.

26. See *State v. Medina*, 172 Ariz. 287, 836 P.2d 997 (Ct. App. 1992).

27. *State v. Dixon*, 109 Ariz. 441, 511 P.2d 623 (1973), where the court's finding that a drug overdose death was too remote was reversed by the enactment of A.R.S. § 13–1105(B).

28. J. Hall, *General Principles of Criminal Law*, 2d ed. (Albany: Lexis Law, 1981), 142.

29. W. LaFave and A. Scott, *Substantive Criminal Law*, vol. 2 (St. Paul: West Publishing, 1986), 232: "Yet it is a general principle of criminal law that one is not ordinarily criminally liable for bad results which differ greatly from intended results." Fletcher states: "Punishment must be proportional to wrongdoing. When the felony murder rule converts an accidental death into first degree murder, then punishment is rendered disproportionate to the wrong for which the offender is personally responsible." Fletcher, "Reflections," 428.

30. *Edmund v. Florida*, 458 U.S. 782, 798 (1982) (quoting H. Hart, *Punishment and Responsibility* [1968], 162).

31. *People v. Aaron*, 299 N.W.2d at 317 (1980).

32. LaFave and Scott, *Substantive Criminal Law*, 159, § 6.8 (b).

33. Model Penal Code, Part II, § 210.2, comment 6 (1980).

34. *Morrissette v. United States*, 342 U.S. 246, 72 S.Ct. 240, 96 L. Ed. 288 (1952).

35. Donald Baier, "Arizona Felony Murder Rule: Let the Punishment Fit the Crime," 36 *Ariz. L. Rev.*, 701, 707 (1994).

36. Note, "Felony Murder: A Tort Law Reconceptualization," 99 *Harv. L.R.*, 1918, 1928 (1986), which parallels this analysis.

37. Id.

38. Id., 1921.

39. Id., 1928.

40. Id.

41. 408 U.S. 238 (1972).

42. Id., 239.

43. *Zant v. Stephens*, 462 U.S. 862, 877 (1983). The *Zant* decision made clear that this narrowing function was the only constitutionally required role to be played by aggravating circumstances in state sentencing systems that employ aggravating circumstances. See also *Gregg v. Georgia*, 428 U.S. 153, 197–198 (1976) (aggravating circumstances guide the sentencers in their deliberations). For a thorough discussion of *Zant* and the function of aggravating circumstances, see generally B. Ledewitz, "The New Rule of Statutory Aggravating Circumstances in American Death Penalty Law," 22 *Duq. L. Rev.*, 317 (1984).

44. See, for example, *State v. Lambright*, 138 Ariz. 63, 66–67, 673 P.2d, 1, 4–5 (1983) (en banc) (abduction, rape, torture, and murder of hitchhikers), *cert. denied*, 469 U.S. 892 (1984).

45. *People v. Stamp*, 2 Cal. App. 3d 203, 209–211, 82 Cal. Rptr. 598, 602–603 (1969), *cert. denied*, 400 U.S. 819 (1970). Two of the defendants robbed a business, while the third defendant remained in the car outside. During the robbery, the defendants forced the robbery victims to lie down on the floor and instructed them to remain there for five minutes after they departed. About fifteen or twenty minutes after the robbery, one of the victims, the owner, collapsed and later died of a heart attack induced by shock. All three defendants were found guilty of first-degree robbery and murder and sentenced to life imprisonment. The court of appeals affirmed, stating that the felony-murder doctrine is "not limited to those deaths which are foreseeable," but rather "a felon is held responsible for all killings committed by him or his accomplices in the course of the felony." Id. at 210, 82 Cal. Rptr. at 603. See also *State v. Edwards*, 122 Ariz. 206, 216, 594 P.2d 72, 82 (1979) (death of victim from heart attack, which occurred during robbery, formed basis for felony-murder conviction despite fact that death was unintended and accidental); *Durden v. State*, 250 Ga. 325, 330, 297 S.E.2d 237, 242 (1982) (robbery victim died of heart attack minutes after robbery; life sentence based on felony-murder conviction affirmed).

46. See, for example, *Griffith v. State*, 171 So.2d 597, 597–98 (Fla. Dist. Ct. App. 1965) (court lacked jurisdiction but said it would have held that defendant was liable when the robbery victim accidentally killed an innocent bystander).

47. *White v. Digger*, 483 U.S. 1044, 1045 (1987) (Brennan, J., dissenting) (defendant, who was not aware that confederates intended to kill robbery victims from beginning, voiced opposition to killing of victims, and did not participate in killings, convicted of felony murder and sentenced to death).

48. *People v. Dillon*, 34 Cal. 3d at 477, 668 P.2d at 719, 194 Cal. Rptr. at 412.

49. 428 U.S. 280 (1976).

50. Id.

51. Joshua Dressler, *Understanding Criminal Law* (New York: McGraw Hill, 1987), 464.

52. N. Roth and S. Sundby, "The Felony Murder Rule: A Doctrine at Constitutional Crossroads," 70 *Cornell L.R.*, 446, 450 (1985).

53. Id., 451. While this justification does have some adherents, it is, by and large, a minority view. Id., 451 n. 28 (citing Note, "The Merger Doctrine as a Limitation on the Felony-Murder Rule: A Balance of Criminal Law Principles," 13 *Wake Forest L. Rev.* 369, 374 ([1977])).

54. Oliver Wendell Holmes, Jr., provided an early formulation of this criticism:

"If the object of the [felony-murder] rule is to prevent [accidental killings], it should make accidental killing with firearms murder, not accidental killing in the effort to steal; while, if its object is to prevent stealing, it would do better to hang one thief in every thousand by lot." This statement by Holmes is often quoted, for example, by LaFave and Scott, *Substantive*, 232–233.

55. *Edmund v. Florida*, 458 U.S. 782, 798–799 (1982). The Supreme Court in *Edmund* held that it was inconsistent with the U.S. Constitution's Eighth and Fourteenth Amendment guarantees against cruel and unusual punishment to impose the death penalty on a defendant convicted of felony murder when he did not "kill, attempt to kill, or intend that a killing take place or that lethal force will be employed." Id., 797. The Court stated:

We are quite convinced, however, that the threat that the death penalty will be imposed for murder will measurably deter one who does not kill and has no intention or purpose that life will be taken. Instead, it seems likely that "capital punishment can serve as a deterrent only when murder is the result of premeditation and deliberation," for if a person does not intend that life be taken or contemplate that lethal force will be employed by others, the possibility that the death penalty will be imposed for vicarious felony murder will not "enter into the cold calculus that precedes the decision to act."

Id., 798–799 (quoting *Fisher v. United States*, 328 U.S. 463, 484 (1946) (Frankfurter, J., dissenting), and *Gregg v. Georgia*, 428 U.S. 153, 186 (1976).

56. J. Tomkovicz, "The Endurance of the Felony-Murder Rule: A Study of the Forces That Shape Our Criminal Law," 51 *Wash. and Lee L. Rev.*, 1429, 1449 (1994), which parallels this analysis.

57. Modern commentators uniformly denounce the rule and its illusory deterrence value. The American Law Institute's *Model Penal Code and Commentary*, Pt. II, 37–39, comment to § 210.2 (1980), recommends abolition of the rule. Fletcher's *Rethinking the Criminal Law* denounces it as "fictitious" and "violative of equal protection." The rule has been abolished not only in England, its birthplace, but also in India and severely restricted in Canada and most other Commonwealth countries. It does not exist at all in Europe. In the United States, where the rule does exist, it regularly is the subject of scholarly contempt, Note, "Felony Murder: A Tort Law Reconceptualization" (less protection than accorded wrongful death tort defendants); Note, "Should Courts Use Principles of Justification and Excuse to Impose Felony-Murder Liability?" 19 *Rutgers L.J.*, 451, 477 (1985) ("Russian roulette . . . cannot engender widespread public confidence").

58. Model Penal Code, Part II, § 210.1, comment 6, at 30 and 37 (1980).

59. Tomkovicz, "Endurance," 1472.

60. Id.

61. Id.

62. "Tort Law Reconceptualization," 1930.

63. Arizona Revised Statute § 13–1603 (littering) and historical note thereto.

64. Id. and Model Penal Code, Part II, § 210.1 at 30–31 (1980).

65. *Irwin v. Dowd*, 366 U.S. 717, 729 (1961).

66. 299 N.W. 2d 304 (1980).

67. Id.

II
IGNORING DATA

5

MARIJUANA MYOPIA

Marijuana gives rise to insanity—not in its users, but in the policies directed against it.

—Eric Schlosser

In 1989 Douglas Gray, a prior petty offender, bought a pound of marijuana in Alabama from Jimmy Wilcox, a just-released felon employed as an informer by the Morgan County Drug Task Force, which supplied the marijuana. After paying Wilcox $900 for the pot, Gray was charged with "trafficking in cannabis," tried, convicted, fined $25,000, and sentenced to life in a maximum security prison without parole. Wilcox, the informer, was paid $100 by the sheriff for his good services.[1]

Gray's plight is not isolated. As I write this, on my desk sits the file of Kenneth McKellar, in the Arizona State Prison since 1973 for possessing marijuana and selling one gram of heroin for $75.00 to a police officer. He pleaded guilty to one felony, his first, and at age nineteen was sentenced to life imprisonment, a sentence he is still serving twenty-five years later, his now-ruined life emptying the state's coffers at $25,000 a year.

WHAT IS IT?

Green, leafy *cannabis sativa* grows in almost any climate, spreads like milkweed, and sprouts stalks with fibers usable for rope, canvas, and paper. Its flowering buds secrete yellow resin rich with delta-9-

tetrahydrocannabinol, or "THC,"[2] its potent ingredient. The first American law on marijuana, passed by Virginia in 1619, actually required farmers to grow it. "Hemp" made sails and riggings, and its by-products made oakum for caulking. Some colonies even exchanged hemp as money. Some Founding Fathers, including George Washington, Ben Franklin, and Thomas Jefferson, grew hemp. Before the turn of the century, pharmacies legally sold marijuana in small packages as a cure for migraines, rheumatism, and insomnia.[3] At the same time lanky stems of cannabis grown for dope-making were so common in Lancaster County, Pennsylvania, that the townships of East and West Hempfield were named in their honor. As of 1999 hemp plants and seeds legally imported from China and Canada are already sold in pretzels, sneakers, and nutritional supplements in our nation.

HISTORY OF PROHIBITION

It has not always been so bucolic. Prohibition of pot in our country originated in racism and hysteria, echoes of which continue to this day. When the Mexican Revolution of 1910 prompted immigration to the Southwest, prejudices against immigrants soon included their marijuana habits. Police in Texas claimed marijuana incited violence, aroused a lust for blood, and generated superhuman strength. Mexican immigrants supposedly distributed this "killer weed" to unsuspecting schoolchildren.

Similar reactions occurred when sailors and West Indian immigrants introduced marijuana to the Gulf of Mexico. New Orleans newspapers associated it with African Americans, jazz musicians, prostitutes, and the underworld. The campaign against the marijuana menace connoted foreigners, inferior races, and social deviants taking strange drugs and making unprecedented music.[4] With the demise of Prohibition, government agents shifted enforcement from alcohol to cannabis, which they portrayed as leading to "reefer madness" and, later, the diametrically opposite "amotivational syndrome."

Harry J. Anslinger, who headed the Federal Bureau of Narcotics through five presidential administrations to 1962, almost single-handedly created out marijuana mania prior to President Reagan. He did not believe in a public health approach to any kind of addiction and dismissed treatment clinics as morphine barrooms. When the New York Academy of Medicine issued a report in 1944 concluding, as have many later such reports, that marijuana did not cause violent behavior, provoke insanity, lead to addiction, or promote opiate use, Anslinger dismissed its authors as "dangerous" and "strange" because their medical research contradicted his own biases.[5]

THE FEAR

On not-so-subtle racial grounds Anslinger campaigned to make marijuana illegal. His press releases and speeches argued that its users became homicidal, suicidal, and insane. He linked marijuana to poor Mexicans and blacks whose promiscuity and violence he saw threatening the nation's stability. The "killer weed" was a foreign influence transforming healthy Americans into sex-crazed maniacs like minority races. Anslinger hoped to make pot so terrifying that young people would be afraid to try it.

Allied government propaganda films soon appeared. *Reefer Madness, Devil's Harvest,* and *Marijuana: Weed with Roots in Hell* displayed imagined horrors of the drug as well as its contrarian culture. The great disparity between its alleged and actual effects gave young people additional reasons for trying it. A youth culture accordingly began to canonize the cannabis leaf as a symbol of anti-Establishment protest.[6] Anslinger's propaganda films gradually generated a counterculture opposite to their intention.

Anslinger started a movement rich with layers of unintended symbolism. Amid the anti-immigrant sentiment fueled by the Great Depression, southwestern politicians, aided by torpid and racist propaganda campaigns, petitioned the Treasury Department to outlaw marijuana. "Murder Weed Found Up and Down Coast," headlines warned; "Deadly Marijuana Dope Plant Ready for Harvest That Means Enslavement of California Children." Wanting to expand its domain by adding marijuana to its list of controlled substances, the Bureau of Narcotics generated, with Anslinger's help, a series of outrageous fables about atrocities committed by marijuana users, including the murder of a Florida family by an enraged son using pot. Newspapers that printed this and similar stories gave birth to the "dope fiend" icon of the pothead. Anslinger and the bureau found enthusiastic support for their campaign in the Hearst newspaper chain, which gave headline attention to any marijuana-related incident, such as "Marijuana makes fiends of boys in 30 days; hashish goads users to blood lust."

Anslinger traveled about the country with missionary zeal speaking to parents, teachers, judges, and politicians about marijuana's evils. He described marijuana as the "most violence-causing drug in the history of mankind," adding that it reduced "thousands of boys to criminal insanity."[7] In 1951 he told Congress that over 50 percent of hard drug users started on marijuana. "They took the needle when the thrill of marijuana was gone." Drug control officials, following Anslinger, initially denied that smoking marijuana would lead to heroin or cocaine use. They turned to the "gateway" theory in search of an alternative basis for drug prohibition only after scientific evidence and popular ridicule shredded the "reefer madness" argument that marijuana caused violence and insanity.

As Anslinger's unfounded argument related marijuana to underclasses and minorities, his ethnic references were at times impolitic. On official stationery he referred to "ginger-colored niggers" using pot. He told Congress that about half of all crime in the country was committed by "Mexicans, Latin Americans, Filipinos, Negroes and Greeks" and asserted that all these crimes could be traced directly to marijuana. Despite these unfounded assertions, he had been supplying morphine illegally for years to his friend Senator Joseph McCarthy, so that "communists would not be able to blackmail this great American senator for his drug-dependency weakness."[8]

During the Anslinger era our government grossly exaggerated marijuana's effects. Pseudoscientific publications fearfully described its dangers. Unwelcome immigrants dissimilar to the white culture were linked with violence and pot. Conservative Western states pressured the government to control its use. In 1937 the Supreme Court upheld the National Firearms Act, which prohibited the transfer of machine guns without a transfer tax stamp, which the government, of course, would not issue. Within a month of the Supreme Court's decision, the Treasury Department, sensing a strategy, sought legislation to establish a marijuana transfer tax, which became the Marijuana Tax Act, criminalizing possession of any marijuana. Until the Comprehensive Drug Abuse Act of 1970, marijuana was legally controlled through a transfer tax for which no stamps or licenses were made available.

DECLARATION OF THE DRUG WAR

The political climate regarding pot temporarily softened during the 1960s. In 1962 President Kennedy forced Anslinger to resign. Commissions appointed by Presidents Kennedy and Johnson, repudiating the strictness of prior policy, denied any direct link between pot and violent crime. Widespread marijuana use in the 1970s among white, middle-class college students caused a shift from an exclusively criminal approach to modest prevention sometimes coupled with punishment. In 1970 the Comprehensive Drug Abuse Prevention and Control Act differentiated marijuana from narcotics and reduced federal penalties for possession of small amounts.

But the pendulum of partisan politics swings both ways. In 1970 President Richard Nixon appointed the Schafer commission to study pot's health effects, legal status, and social impact. His National Commission on Marijuana and Drug Abuse, under the leadership of the former Republican governor of Pennsylvania, concluded in 1972 that marijuana should be decriminalized, demythologized, and desymbolized. "Considering the range of social concerns in contemporary America," the Schafer report said, "marijuana does not, in our considered judgment, rank very high." The commission rejected outright legalization and instead recommended that pot be decriminalized for possession only, with no arrest or criminal penalty beyond a fine similar to a speeding violation.

Feeling betrayed by his commission and by fellow Republican Schafer, Nixon rejected its nonpartisan findings as devious. His ire included health professionals sympathetic to marijuana's health claims, whom he called "soft-headed psychiatrists who are all on the stuff themselves." He had a similar reaction to the almost simultaneous nonpartisan conclusion of the

Canadian Commission on Non-Medical use of drugs, whose 1972 recommendation also called for blanket decriminalization of marijuana. A decade later the National Academy of Sciences Substance Abuse Commission again studied the health effects of marijuana and concluded again that it should be decriminalized. President Reagan, like Nixon, also rejected that impartial report.[9]

In 1977 President Jimmy Carter addressed Congress on the harm done by marijuana prohibition. Penalties against possession of a drug, he stated, should not be more damaging to an individual than the drug itself. He recommended that Congress eliminate all federal penalties for up to one ounce of marijuana. His message about counterproductivity was unheard. The drug war vastly expanded in President Reagan's administration, with Anslinger's earlier view of pot reborn in an abrupt cultural clash. To conservative parent groups supporting the Reagan revolution against deviance, marijuana symbolized the weakness and permissiveness of a liberal society and caused slovenly, lethargic teenagers and generational and racial tensions. Antidrug parent groups expanded the war nationwide, motivated, in good part, by parent–teenager conflict and racial and ethnic suspicion. Even Ross Perot helped launch the Texas War on Drugs.

Conservative groups allied with Reagan invested marijuana with power far beyond its ability. Robert Dupont, who at the National Institute on Drug Abuse (NIDA) had once supported decriminalization, decried the "tumultuous change in values" among the young—their pursuit of pleasure, their lack of responsibility—and asserted that "the leading edge of this culture change was marijuana use."[10] To this mind-set pot symbolized a culture schism causing widespread social disarray. In 1982 Reagan created the White House Drug Abuse Policy Office and appointed as its head a chemist, Carlton Turner, who had directed the Marijuana Research Project at the University of Mississippi. Like Anslinger, Turner saw marijuana as powerful enough to induce even homosexuality. The Drug Enforcement Administration (DEA), which had previously contemplated decriminalization, now under conservative political pressure called marijuana the "most urgent" drug problem facing the country. Goals of "zero tolerance" and "user accountability" revived the notion that drug offenders deserved severe punishment. The ensuing Comprehensive Crime Control Act of 1984, the Anti-Drug Abuse Act of 1986, and the Anti-Drug Abuse Amendment of 1988 raised federal penalties for marijuana possession, cultivation, and trafficking, all under an assumption that pot is medically harmful.

HEALTH EFFECTS

Is marijuana harmful? Some think so. The conservative *Arizona Republic*, echoing a common theme, editorialized in 1997 that pot needs strict criminalization because of its craving effects:

One study on rats suggests that people who regularly smoke large amounts of pot are changing the chemistry in their brains in exactly the same way as those who regularly abuse cocaine, heroin, amphetamines, nicotine and alcohol.

By measuring the effect of the sudden withdrawal of marijuana on rats, scientists were able to measure a neurochemical reaction identical to what occurs when a heroin addict goes cold turkey.

The difference is that the active ingredient in marijuana, THC, lingers in the bloodstream long after the high is over. That lingering effect masks some of the more extreme sensations associated with withdrawal. Addicts don't realize they are addicted. This research suggests that regular smokers of pot continue smoking not so much to get high as to ease the anxiety of withdrawal caused by the drug itself.[11]

At bottom, this representative argument leads to criminalizing all food and drink because deprivation of food and drink causes pangs of hunger and thirst, which, of course, we try to avoid.

Dispassionate medical data are the most helpful starting point. Viewed only as a health issue, marijuana creates a physical dependence in some, but not all, users. THC does diffuse widely throughout the body and remain there for some time just like legal drugs such as Valium, Thorazine, and quinine. But lifelong heavy marijuana users studied in Jamaica, Greece, and Costa Rica reveal little psychological or physiological damage apart from short-term memory deficiencies in heavy smokers. Laboratory animals injected with marijuana do suffer mild immunosuppression, but no study has conclusively linked THC to immune-system changes. Horror stories from the 1970s—that marijuana kills brain cells, damages chromosomes, and prompts men to grow breasts—are wild exaggerations.

Smoking marijuana can indeed damage the pulmonary system in a way similar to inhaling tobacco smoke. University of California–Los Angeles (UCLA) physician Donald P. Tashkin has found that marijuana smoke can cause chronic bronchitis, changes in cells of the central airway, and cellular impairment because a joint of pot delivers somewhat more carcinogenic tar than a tobacco cigarette of the same size. Some heavy marijuana users may eventually suffer cancers of the mouth, throat, and lung just like excess tobacco and alcohol users experience.[12] They sometimes also develop respiratory irritation akin to smoker's cough and lung illness. Doctors have found precancerous changes in the lungs of potheads. Massive use does suppress sperm counts, but users have the same infertility rate as nonusers. No lasting damage to the brain results even with decades of daily use. If marijuana ever caused a single death, it didn't leave any fingerprints. The most comprehensive study—of 65,000 users in the San Francisco Bay Area over ten years—found "no association between marijuana and overall mortality."[13]

Admittedly, Dr. Tashkin's pulmonary findings ought to be troubling for chronic marijuana smokers. For more than a decade, he has been comparing the lungs of pot smokers, cigarette smokers, and nonsmokers, examining changes in the airways and cellular damage that may lead to lung cancer. Pot smokers who inhale three or four joints a day suffer from chronic bronchitis as often as cigarette smokers who light up a pack or more a day. Both pot and cigarette smokers show similar unhealthy changes in the trachea and bronchial tubes as the cilia-covered cells that move soot out of the lungs begin to die, replaced by multiplying mucus-producing cells. The greatest damage appears in those who smoke both marijuana and tobacco because their pulmonary effects intensify each other.

A major breakthrough in understanding marijuana's medical effects came in 1988, when Allyn Howlett of St. Louis University discovered the chemical receptors that react to THC, the compound in marijuana that produces a high. The receptors set pot apart from any other kind of substance, including heavily addictive drugs such as heroin and morphine. "It's completely different from all the other drugs," according to Miles Herkenham, a brain researcher at the National Institutes of Mental Health in Bethesda, Maryland, who mapped the receptors in the early 1990s. Pot's influence on the immune system seems relatively subtle. "The paucity of receptors in the brain stem is crucial for explaining why it's a 'safe' drug," according to Herkenham. "It's impossible to take a lethal overdose."[14]

Medical research in the early 1990s showed that pot, unlike tobacco, might be beneficial. For glaucoma, marijuana reduces the fluid pressure in the eyes that causes irreversible damage to vision. For AIDS patients marijuana use addresses their immunosuppressed state and the danger posed by lung irritants and fungal illnesses such as aspergilliosis. Many AIDS patients with treatment-induced nausea, appetite loss, and wasting syndrome claim that marijuana has reduced pain and motivated them to eat.[15] Multiple sclerosis patients report that marijuana improves their motor functions and sustains them against the encroaching disease by relieving muscle spasticity and chronic or intermittent pain. It also counters nausea from chemotherapy. Almost half the oncologists in a 1990 survey had recommended it to their patients. Indeed, pot's core ingredient is already legal: Dronabinol, marketed as Marinol, a synthetic THC compound using the active ingredient in pot, is a legal drug prescribed for nausea, depression, and spasticity. The federal taboo on pot thus has an Orwellian ring to it—the official prohibition of a substance already approved under a different name.

In its capsule form, Marinol is more cumbersome than smoking marijuana in delivering pain relief. Here are some major differences:

• The onset of relief from the capsule takes an hour or more; smoking takes effect within minutes.

• The one-hour lag time means that oral dosage is difficult to adjust and monitor; a patient can cease or continue smoking in response to minute-to-minute results.

- Oral THC is metabolized through the liver, which neutralizes more than 90 percent of the chemical; smoking pot delivers the THC directly to the bloodstream.
- An oral dose lasts six unpredictable hours, and liver metabolism also means that its effects are variable; in the same patient, smoking pot lasts a predictable hour or two.
- Some patients whose livers metabolize the synthetic delta-9-THC partially into a more psychoactive, 11-hydroxy-THC get that much more stoned on the metabolite.
- A Marinol regime can cost upward of $600 a month; the cost of smoking crude marijuana could be negligible if cultivation for medical use were legalized.

As for non-THC alternatives, many have serious side effects. The antiemetics Compazine and Decadron, for example, pose a risk of liver damage. Marijuana is safer than many over-the-counter drugs. Asked to evaluate the medical benefits of marijuana, the DEA's own administrative judge Francis L. Young declared in 1988—inconveniently, from the DEA's point of view—that marijuana is "one of the safest therapeutically active substances known to man."[16]

We thus have the anomaly that the more costly, more cumbersome, less effective drug Marinol is legal while the more efficient, less costly same drug under a different name is criminal. Our law is out of step with our medicine.

Ironically, this excoriated drug also has painkilling powers. Animal studies by research groups at the University of California–San Francisco, the University of Michigan, and Brown University show that a group of potent cannabinoids, including the active ingredient in marijuana, relieves several kinds of pain, including the inflammation associated with arthritis, as well as severe forms of chronic pain.[17] A panel of experts convened by the National Institutes of Health acknowledged in 1997 that smoking pot is a useful treatment for many painful illnesses.[18] The Society for Neuroscience reported in 1997 at its annual meeting that its members' sophisticated animal research on pot reveals that the active chemicals in marijuana have a direct beneficial effect on pain signals in the central nervous system. Unlike opiate-based painkillers, pot's painkillers are not addictive, and continued use does not develop tolerance.

On the issue of danger by misuse to society at large, pot—which remains criminal—has a vastly superior record by comparison with legal drugs. Although the misuse of legal, over-the-counter medications such as Advil, aspirin, acetaminophen, and antihistamines each year kills thousands of Americans (estimates range from 100,000 to 200,000), pot is one of the few therapeutically active substances for which there is no well-defined fatal dose. Lester Grinspoon, a professor of psychiatry at Harvard Medical School, provides evidence that marijuana can relieve the nausea associated with chemotherapy, prevent blindness induced by glaucoma, serve as an appetite stimulant for AIDS patients, act as an antiepileptic, ward off asthma attacks and migraine headaches, alleviate chronic pain, and reduce the muscle spasticity that accompanies multiple sclerosis, cerebral palsy, and paraplegia.[19] The federal government remains deaf and blind to this unwelcome research: it has been more interested in trying to find marijuana's professed, but elusive, ill effects. Government opposition also discourages drug companies from funding independent research on marijuana.

In the wake of the popular initiatives in California and Arizona in 1996 and 1998 supporting medical marijuana, the Clinton administration promised to prosecute any doctor who even qualifiedly recommends it to a patient. The *New England Journal of Medicine* responded with a lead editorial titled "Federal Foolishness and Marijuana." Even the stodgy American Medical Association (AMA) issued sharply worded appeals for the federal funding of therapeutic pot research.[20]

Medical associations rightly question the prohibition policy. The British Medical Association has urged the government to allow marijuana to be prescribed in a range of medical conditions and asked health officials to set up clinical trials to assess marijuana's therapeutic benefits. These efforts have the support of many doctors, including the president of the Royal Pharmaceutical Society and the previous president of the Royal College of Physicians. Some doctors in the United States are following the British lead. In 1997, the American Medical Association recommended a review of its policies on marijuana as a "medicinal remedy."[21] A report issued in December 1997 by the association's Council on Scientific Affairs recommended renewed research efforts to see whether the "potential benefits of smoking marijuana" outweigh the known risks.

The bottom health line: at worst, pot is like heavy cigarette smoking; at best, unlike tobacco, it has significant health benefits otherwise unattainable. Unlike many commonly used and often fatal substances sold over the counter without prescriptions—aspirin, rubbing alcohol, diuretics—marijuana is virtually harmless. Yet we criminalize it, without any fatal effects, while allowing carcinogenic, nontherapeutic tobacco to be sold without restriction.

THE "GATEWAY" DRUG?

The argument is often made that marijuana leads to harder drugs. Some writers even assert that most hard drug users began with pot as their first drug.

The argument is suspect on statistical as well as logical grounds. Its recent origin is a 1994 report by the National Center on Addiction and Substance Abuse at Columbia University, which did assert that juveniles who smoke marijuana are eighty-five times more likely to use cocaine than those who don't smoke it. The survey reported that 17 percent of the marijuana users interviewed said they had tried cocaine. Only 0.2 percent of those who had not used marijuana said they had tried cocaine. Put another way, 83 percent of the pot smokers, or nearly five out of six, said they hadn't tried cocaine, which undercuts the threat of marijuana as the "gateway drug."[22]

Another variation of another gateway argument is a University of Michigan survey in 1978, in which 72.1 percent of all seniors said they had had an alcohol drink in the past month, a figure double the number that had used pot; and 40.3 percent said they had engaged in binge drinking, with five or more drinks in one sitting, over the past two weeks—a figure four times the number who had smoked pot daily. Young beer drinkers were far more likely than pot users to get into fights, smash cars, or have illegal sex. Thus, in terms of the gateway argument, alcohol, not pot, is the greater social problem. Back in 1972, President Nixon's National Commission on Marijuana and Drug Abuse had found the same thing, concluding that "only a small portion of users" were likely to become persistent, frequent users of these other drugs because "the majority [of users] appear to experiment only."[23] In 1998 the World Health Organization found the gateway theory the least likely of all hypotheses for hard drug use.

Even if the overstated argument about the pot-cocaine connection were true, its logic is wanting. Not everything that precedes another is the cause of the latter; this is the classic *post hoc, ergo propter hoc* fallacy. If every predecessor were the cause of a subsequent event, the "gateway drug" argument would logically lead to the criminalization of all preteen food. After all, probably well over 90 percent of hard drug users at one time in their early years ate peanut butter and jelly sandwiches with gusto.

ECONOMICS AND POT PRICES

The long prison sentences now given to marijuana offenders have turned marijuana into a precious commodity whose pricing reflects stern enforcement efforts. Some marijuana is currently worth more per ounce than gold, now over $330 dollars an ounce. The price of an illegal drug reflects not only its supply, demand, and production costs but also the legal risks of selling it. As the risks increase, so does the profit. Marijuana prices have risen sharply since the War on Drugs began. In 1982 the street price for an ounce (adjusted for inflation) was about $75. By 1998 it had reached about $325; in some places it is twice that amount in 1999.[24] Although the costs of cultivating marijuana rose during that period, most price increases represent sheer profit, the reward for evading punishment. The risks of cultivation encourage more potent strains, which bring a higher price and, for a while, a lower volume of sales.

Large profit margins have transformed marijuana cultivation from a fringe economic activity into a multibillion-dollar industry. A quarter to half the marijuana used in this country is grown here, mostly in the nation's midsection. For the value of our annual marijuana crop plausible estimates start at $4 billion and range up to $24 billion, while the 1998 value of our largest legal cash crop, corn, was roughly $16 billion. The highest-quality marijuana grows indoors on the West Coast, but for sheer volume, the Midwest rules. New strains like "hydroponic," where the plants are grown without soil, and "wet"—marijuana soaked in formaldehyde—have increased the drug's potency to the point where it can earn as much as $6,000 a pound in parts of California—ten times the typical price for marijuana from Mexico.[25]

Part of the cultivation problem stems from government policy. During World War II our government encouraged the corn belt to plant marijuana to replace fiber supplies cut off by the Japanese. The program left marijuana growing wild as "ditchweed" over thousands of midwestern acres. The same growing conditions that are ideal for corn also nurture marijuana. In 1999 dollars, a bushel of corn sells nationally roughly for $2.50; a bushel of manicured marijuana sells for about $70,000. An acre of hemp in Pennsylvania in 1999 can bring upwards of $500, compared with the $375 that neighboring farmers get for an acre of feedcorn. Marijuana has become the largest cash crop in the United States. In Indiana the value of the annual crop now rivals that of corn. In Alabama it rivals that of cotton. The threat of long prison sentences has made some marijuana growers rich but has hardly affected its cultivation.

POT ERADICATION

Because of the extent of homegrown pot cultivation, especially in California, various law enforcement groups have tried to eradicate its cultivation by prosecuting the landowners involved. The northern California experience is instructive.

In 1983 then-state attorney general John Van de Kamp vowed that the aggressive, military-assisted Campaign against Marijuana Planting, or "CAMP" for short, would "run growers out of the state." Military helicopters began to swoop low on hillsides in northern California, particularly at harvest time. Lots of troops on the ground plus great sums of money were assigned to CAMP. But in the Emerald Triangle and the Silicon Valley, locations of high-potency cultivation, few growers got arrested, and only a tiny fraction wound up in prison. Sheriff David Renner of Humbolt County began as a dedicated advocate of CAMP and, in its military fashion, arranged for more than a decade of low-flying helicopters during annual autumn raids. After more than a decade, Humbolt County voters had enough and threw Renner out of office in 1994.

Though he had led the attack on marijuana, Renner now raises a white flag. "I say go ahead and legalize it," he now says, because pot has become a "black hole" for law enforcement because of mixed messages from government and ordinary citizens. One message is that marijuana is a dangerous drug that should be harshly suppressed. Another is that it's a minor matter best ignored. The emerging "hempster" movement promotes still another message: pot is environmentally friendly and a valuable natural resource with many beneficial uses.[26]

Elsewhere, efforts to eradicate marijuana cultivation have made that industry stronger than before. In Kentucky, where the state participates in a federally funded program to burn marijuana, eradication efforts have actually spread marijuana cultivation throughout the state and transformed a small industry into an organized criminal cartel with a high degree of community support—the exact opposite of the desired goal. In Arcata, north of San Francisco, the town's police in 1998 began to issue ID cards to users of medicinal pot as well as to approved growers of medicinal pot.

POT ENFORCEMENT

Our present penal policy is both draconian and checkerboard to an extreme. The 1986 Anti-Drug Abuse Act greatly increased the penalties for federal drug offenses, established mandatory-minimum sentences, and effectively transferred sentencing power from judges to prosecutors. The mandatory minimums reflected not an individual's role but the quantity of drugs involved. Prosecutors, rather than judges, acquired the authority to decide whether a mandatory-minimum sentence applies. The short-lived public health approach of the 1960s thus yielded to our present policy of criminal repression. All use of pot became a serious crime. In 1997, 695,201 people were arrested nationwide for violating marijuana laws, 87 percent of them for simple possession, a crime that does not generally lead to incarceration. Possession of more than an ounce is in many states a felony. Conviction may lead to a few months or years behind bars and the loss of a house or a job.

State marijuana laws now vary in an uneven checkerboard fashion in policy, enforcement, and severity. Between 1973 and 1978, eleven states reclassified marijuana possession as a misdemeanor, petty offense, or civil violation punishable by a $100 fine. Consumption trends in those states and in states that retained stricter sanctions are indistinguishable. A 1988 scholarly evaluation of the Moscone Act, California's 1976 decriminalization law, estimated that the state had saved half a billion dollars in arrest costs since the law's passage.[27] Nonetheless, public opinion began to shift in 1978. No other states decriminalized marijuana, and some, like Alaska, eventually recriminalized it.

Some states now classify marijuana with drugs like mescaline and heroin; others put it in a separate legal category. In New York possessing slightly less than an ounce of marijuana brings a $100 fine, rarely collected; in Nevada possessing any amount of marijuana is a felony. In Montana selling a pound of marijuana, first offense, could bring a life sentence. In New

Mexico selling 10,000 pounds of marijuana, as a first offense, can earn a prison term of no more than three years. In Idaho selling water pipes could lead to a prison sentence of nine years. In Arizona, if a death occurs for any reason (e.g., heart attack) during a marijuana offense, the offender merits the death penalty.[28] Ten states have largely decriminalized marijuana possession, thereby saving billions of dollars in court and prison costs without experiencing an increase in marijuana use.[29] Ohio currently has the most liberal marijuana laws: possession of up to three ounces is a misdemeanor punishable by a $100 fine. In 1996, Ohio decriminalized the cultivation of small amounts of marijuana for personal use.[30]

Although the penalties for buying, selling, or possessing marijuana are often severe, the penalties for growing can be even more severe. In Iowa cultivating any amount can lead to a five-year prison sentence; in Colorado, an eight-year sentence; in Missouri, a fifteen-year sentence. In Virginia the punishment for growing a single marijuana plant is five to thirty years. In Montana a life sentence can result from growing a single marijuana plant. Under federal law the death penalty applies for growing or selling a large amount of marijuana, even a first offense. The crime bills recently passed in 1996 by Congress specify the death penalty for any marijuana offender caught with 60,000 plants or more.

Opponents of our current policy point to the experience of the states that decriminalized the possession of small amounts of marijuana for personal consumption in the 1970s. In these states no increase in marijuana use took place. Indeed, marijuana consumption declined in those states, just as it did in states that retained criminal sanctions against marijuana. The Netherlands saw similar results when it decriminalized marijuana consumption in 1976.[31]

Permissive programs regarding pot use depend, at least partially, on law enforcement support. Unfortunately, such support is unlikely in the United States, since many of our law enforcement agencies fear that drug reform would endanger their jobs or funding. Both the law enforcement community and the traffickers thus oppose legalization in all its varieties, although for markedly different reasons. Checkerboard legislative and enforcement policies say much about inequality, inconsistency, and injustice, because in practice pot prosecution reflects location and status more so than conduct. Conduct condoned in one state may be severely punished just across the state line. It is an understatement to observe that our nation's fifty differing pot policies have created an extreme legal checkerboard.

SELECTIVE ENFORCEMENT

Courthouse observers, judges included, find that children of the upper- and upper-middle-class users are rarely charged and even more rarely sent to prison for marijuana. Instead, if they do happen to get caught, they enter private treatment programs before trial. Privileged young men and women receive more privileges in court. The son of Indiana congressman Dan Burton, an outspoken proponent of life sentences for some marijuana crimes, was arrested for transporting nearly eight pounds of pot to Indiana in the trunk of his car and months later was arrested again at his apartment with thirty marijuana plants. The Indiana prosecutor gained dismissal of the original charges, and a judge sentenced him to community service, probation, and house arrest.

Marijuana is popular with professional athletes, academics, scholars, and upper-class society—groups that, as a whole, rarely, if ever, appear in court or even in police dossiers. In nine years serving on a major urban trial court, I saw no member of these groups convicted of any marijuana sale or use. Instead, those prosecuted for pot are overwhelmingly isolated, lower-class blacks, whites, and Hispanics living in inner cities who use pot in places less privileged than faculty clubs and the locker rooms of the National Football League (NFL) and the National Basketball Association (NBA).

Contrary to the wholesome image marketed by the NBA, 60 to 70 percent of its 350-plus players smoke marijuana. "If they tested for pot, there would be no league," asserts Richard Dumas, the former Phoenix Suns guard now playing in Europe. "Weed is something guys grow up doing, and there's no reason for them to stop. Because almost everyone does it, no one wants to test for it. They're afraid to." The NBA's fourteen-year-old drug policy protects players despite behavior that is illegal and commonplace. Under the collective bargaining agreement, the league allows mandatory drug testing of rookies only and prevents teams from testing veterans for cocaine and heroin except under rare circumstances. The NBA has co-opted law enforcement of pot. "The policy is ridiculous," said Karl Malone, Utah's 1997 and 1998 All-Star.[32]

The result of this highly selective pot war directed largely at young people and minorities has been the exact opposite of what prohibitionist politicians intended. Pot now encourages individuality and protest. A drug culture once again flourishes on college campuses despite draconian, mandatory-minimum sentences. Fifteen years into our current War on Drugs, rough numbers show its cost-effectiveness: $30 billion spent so far at the state, federal, and local levels to fight marijuana; $2 billion worth of assets seized; 4 million Americans arrested; .25 million people convicted of marijuana felonies and sent to prison for at least a year, while the marijuana leaf increasingly becomes the rallying cry for disaffected youth and counterculture adults.[33]

Students increasingly disbelieve abstinence-based educational messages. When they try marijuana and find that it does not have the announced negative consequences, they tend to disregard more justified warnings regarding cocaine or opiates. Indeed, when they are taught that alcohol is a drug and then witness permitted adult alcohol consumption, they are left believing that in a matter of vital importance to them—drug use—they are being lied to. Our inconsistent policy tests their credibility.

SENTENCES AND PRISON

One of every six inmates in the federal prison system—roughly 15,000 people—has been incarcerated primarily for a marijuana offense. Other inmates are serving life sentences in state correctional facilities across the country for growing, selling, or possessing marijuana. Of the people recently convicted of violating federal marijuana laws, 56 percent had no criminal record deemed relevant at sentencing. The War on Drugs, which began as an assault on marijuana, now resonates counterproductively throughout our justice system. In 1980 there were almost twice as many violent offenders in federal prison as drug offenders; now, in 1999, more people are incarcerated in our nation's prisons for marijuana than for manslaughter or rape. Since 1992, some 21,424 Americans have been sentenced to federal prison solely for marijuana convictions.[34]

Attempts to reduce dangerous prison overcrowding suffer from our counterproductive drug laws. Prison cells across the country overflow with nonviolent drug offenders whose mandatory-minimum sentences do not allow for parole, while violent offenders routinely receive early release. In 1992 violent offenders on average were released after serving less than half their sentences. In that year the average punishment for a violent crime was forty-three months in prison, while the average punishment under federal law for a marijuana offender that same year was about fifty months in prison.[35]

The trend toward alternative sentences for drug offenders has lately gained support in some unexpected quarters. Arizona's recently passed Proposition 200 not only allows the medical use of marijuana but also has reformed the state's approach to drug control with mandatory treatment in lieu of prison. Arizona voters backed the initiative by a margin of two to one. The Clinton administration attacked Proposition 200 as a dangerous heresy and threatened to prosecute any physicians who recommend marijuana to patients. Clinton's drug czar, General Barry McCaffrey, called the Arizona initiative part of "a national strategy to legalize drugs."[36]

Secretary of health and human services Donna Shalala said that the successful California and Arizona pot initiates reinforce the belief that marijuana is not harmful. In her words, the Clinton administration remains "opposed to the legalization of marijuana [because] all available research has concluded that marijuana is dangerous to our health." No such danger has been mentioned. Shalala has not declared war on tobacco, whose dangers, like those of alcohol, are known to be fatal.

HAS PROHIBITION WORKED?

Teenage marijuana use has grown since 1992; by one measure it has doubled. That increase cannot be attributed to any slackening enforcement of marijuana laws. The number of Americans arrested each year for marijuana offenses has increased by 43 percent since President Clinton took office, to 695,201 marijuana-related arrests nationwide in 1997, an all-time record. More Americans were arrested for marijuana offenses during the first three years of the Clinton presidency than during any other three-year period in our history, and more Americans are in prison today for marijuana than at any other time in our history. Yet teenage marijuana use continues to grow. Schoolkids of the late 1990s are more likely to smoke pot than teens a decade ago. In 1998 *Time* magazine reported that urine tests show 13 percent of teenagers used the drug in 1997 compared to 2 percent in 1989.[37] In 1982, when President Reagan declared his War on Drugs, 88.5 percent of America's high school seniors said that it was "fairly easy" or "very easy" for them to obtain marijuana. In 1994, well after a decade of the War on Drugs, the proportion of seniors who said they could "easily" obtain it was 85.5 percent—marking no improvement in over a decade of expensive enforcement.

Pot enforcement is an enormous drain on police resources, not to mention the future of our youth. Between 1973 and 1989 the annual arrests on marijuana charges by state and local police ranged between 360,000 and 460,000. The annual total fell to 283,700 in 1991 but has since more than doubled. Of the 695,201 people arrested for marijuana in 1997, 87 percent of them were for possession, not sale, of the drug.[38]

In 1996 the U.S. Department of Health and Human Services surveyed almost 18,000 Americans and concluded that marijuana use among youths aged twelve to seventeen rose 105 percent from 1992 to 1994 and 37 percent between 1995 and 1998. At the Phoenix House Foundation ten years ago, 13 percent of adolescents sought treatment for marijuana; today that figure has jumped to 40 percent. Mark Kleiman, a UCLA professor who specializes in national drug policy, says, "It's destructive to focus the country on one small part of drug use. Focusing on marijuana ignores the rising use of methamphetamine and the fact that heroin appears to be coming back, and ignores the No. 1 drug of abuse among high school kids—alcohol."[39]

The number of high school sophomores who said they had used drugs rose to 37.5 percent in 1997, from 33.3 percent in 1995. Among eighth graders, the number climbed to 23.6 percent from 21.4 percent, confirming that experimentation is beginning at a younger age. Marijuana accounts for nearly 90 percent of such drug use.[40] Our pot law has given all these young people a lifelong criminal record as well as a potent rallying symbol to counter established adult values.

Prompted by concern over rising marijuana use among adolescents and fears of being labeled soft on drugs, the Clinton administration launched its own antimarijuana campaign in 1995. But the administration's claims to have identified new risks of marijuana consumption—including a purported link between marijuana and violent behavior—have not withstood scrutiny. Neither Congress nor the White House seems likely to put marijuana policy before a truly independent nongovernmental commission, given the consistency with which such commissions have reached politically unacceptable conclusions favoring decriminalization.

The European experience is a bracing message countering our pot policy. In the United Kingdom, where drug penalties are harshly enforced, the rate of marijuana use among fifteen- and sixteen-year-olds is the highest in Western Europe—one and a half times the rate in Spain and the Netherlands, where pot has been decriminalized. The U.K. rate is six times as high as in Sweden, which has pursued a public health approach to drugs. Sweden now has the lowest rate of marijuana use in Western Europe; under its law the rarely imposed maximum punishment for most marijuana traffickers of any quantity is a prison sentence of three years.

Cultural factors exert more influence on a country's rate of marijuana use than changes in the law. The Netherlands decriminalized marijuana in 1976. Teenage use there declined by as much as 40 percent over the next decade. The rate of use among American teenagers peaked in 1979 and was falling when Congress passed the Anti-Drug Abuse Act in 1986.[41] In contrast, governments in Europe and Australia, and notably, in the Netherlands, have reconsidered their former punitive cannabis policies. In 1976 the Dutch government adopted a policy of separating the "soft" and "hard" drug markets. Criminal penalties and police efforts against cannabis were relaxed. Marijuana and hashish can now be bought in hundreds of coffee shops throughout the country. Police close coffee shops caught selling hard drugs. Almost no one is arrested or even fined for cannabis possession, and the Dutch government collects taxes on the gray market sales.

In the Netherlands today cannabis consumption for most age groups resembles that in the United States. Young Dutch teenagers, however, are less likely to sample marijuana than their American peers; from 1992 to 1994, only 7.2 percent of Dutch youths between the ages of twelve and fifteen reported having tried marijuana, compared to 13.5 Americans in that age bracket. Far fewer Dutch youths, moreover, experiment with cocaine, buttressing the government's claims of success in separating hard and soft drugs. Many Dutch parents regard our "reefer madness," antimarijuana campaigns as simplistic and destructive.[42]

In the 1990s the European trend toward decriminalization of cannabis has accelerated. Across much of Western Europe possession and minor sales of the drug are effectively decriminalized. Spain decriminalized private use of cannabis in 1983. In Germany, the federal Constitutional Court effectively sanctioned a liberal cannabis policy. In 1996 Luxembourg decriminalized pot, as did three of the most populated Australian states. A recent poll showed that 51 percent of Canadians favored decriminalizing pot.

CONCLUSION: THE INJUSTICE

After some fifteen years of our hysterical war on pot, millions of ordinary Americans—excluding many important people like scholars and pro athletes—have been arrested for marijuana offenses. Hundreds of thousands have been marched into courts, imprisoned, and given lifelong criminal records. The result? Marijuana continuously enhances its status as a symbol of individuality, rebellion, and counterculture. Our ill-founded prohibition has canonized pot well beyond the likely effect of a more tolerant policy.

Our police and judges have become cultural arbiters, making selective judgments about which potheads to punish while remaining unconcerned about tobacco and alcohol addicts. Marijuana has not improved anyone's ability to pass a test or hit a curve ball, but it has defined millions of Americans, including many disfranchised youth, as criminals in a nation whose president admits smoking it but not inhaling—a defense available to no one else. Instead of debating the wisdom of our current policies and our obsession with ethnic symbols, Congress and the administration compete to appear tougher on pot.

Our war on pot has been driven by political and ethnic concerns without regard to social consequences. The repeated conclusions of the many commissions studying marijuana use are as effective—and ignored—today as when they first appeared. We have far more serious conduct to curtail than a drug whose negative health effects match those of tobacco and whose health benefits far surpass it. If we were serious about criminalizing pot for its negative health effects, we would begin, first, by knowing what these negative health effects are instead of desperately trying to find them *ex ante*. Then we would explore how these nonfatal effects merit the criminalization that known fatal drugs like tobacco and alcohol somehow escape. At bottom, our inconsistent pot policy shows not only tobacco and alcohol lobbying but also the fact that marijuana is really criminalized not for health reasons but rather because it symbolizes individuality, generational conflict, and unconventional lifestyles. Our pot policy achieves no social good and causes much harm. It defines many good people as criminals, discriminates selectively against lower-class users, and denies pot's medical benefits to the sick—all in the name of a capricious war whose enormous financial costs have increased the very problem it set out to correct.

The illogic of our anti-pot hysteria appears most clearly in a federally funded 250-page report issued in March 1999 by the Institute of Medicine, a branch of the National Academy of Sciences. The White House Office of

National Drug Control Policy, headed by drug czar Gen. Barry McCaffrey, commissioned and funded the two-year study after voters in California and Arizona endorsed medicinal marijuana in 1996 referenda. To insure its impartiality the Drug Policy office assigned the research to the independent, government-supported agency whose eleven medical experts would base their findings not on politics or policy but on undiluted medical data.

The conclusions of this latest report could not more fundamentally undermine our present national policy on pot. The institute found that marijuana helps patients with pain, nausea, and severe weight loss associated with AIDS and other serious illnesses. On the other side of the ledger, the researchers did find that smoking a joint of marijuana is more toxic than smoking a conventional tobacco cigarette and observed that an inhaler would serve as a safer delivery system. Most importantly, the report found no evidence that giving pot to sick people increases illegal usage generally nor, added the medical authors, is there any support for the popular notion that marijuana serves as a "gateway drug" to more serious drugs such as cocaine and heroin.[43]

General McCaffrey's response to his own commissioned research was to call for still "more research." Indeed, such dogged thinking pervades the topic of marijuana every time scientific research or voter wishes contradict official pot policy. The 1996 Republican Congress prevented the District of Columbia from releasing the results of a 1996 ballot question asking its residents if pot should be made legal for medical purposes, apparently fearing, notwithstanding the first amendment, that the voters' answer would be affirmative. The Clinton administration continues to shut down pot buyers' clubs and threatens to prosecute doctors who write prescriptions for a drug now found beneficial by the same administration's own sponsored research.[44]

Besides its illogic, our pot hysteria reflects one of the most obvious inconsistencies in our drug war, one which impairs areas of legitimate drug prohibition. Our government continues to prohibit a substance repeatedly found to have medical benefits while desperately seeking still more research to uncover a reason to justify its prohibition. The answer to this backward quest is not hard to find, but it is not to be found in the medical laboratory. We continue to penalize marijuana not for any medical or physiological reason but for cultural and ethnic reasons: we dislike the lifestyles of many of those who use it. Our prohibitionist pot policy thereby undermines itself because it reinforces a principle dating back to Adam and Eve: forbidden fruit tastes better simply because it is forbidden.

NOTES

1. E. Schlosser, "More Reefer Madness," *Atlantic Monthly*, 90 (Apr. 1997).
2. Id.

3. E. Schlosser, "Reefer Madness," *Atlantic Monthly*, 46 (Aug. 1994).

4. Id., 48.

5. Id., 49.

6. Id.

7. Id., 48–52.

8. Id.

9. Id., 49.

10. Id., 48–52.

11. *Arizona Republic*, AZ (July 1, 1998) See also the issue of July 3, 1998 A2.

12. "Pot Effects," *Arizona Republic*, B8 (Dec. 22, 1996).

13. "Pharmacopia," *Esquire*, 134 (Oct. 1997).

14. "Pot Effects."

15. L. Zimmer and J. Morgan, *Marijuana Myths, Marijuana Facts: A Review of the Scientific Evidence* (New York: Open Society Institute, 1997).

16. "Marijuana as Medicine: A Plea for Reconsideration," *Journal of the American Medical Association*, 1875 (June 21, 1995).

17. *Arizona Republic*, AZ (Oct. 27, 1997).

18. *Arizona Republic*, A26 (Aug. 10, 1997). See also W. Stempsey, S. J., M.D., "The Battle for Medical Marijuana," *America*, 14–16 (April 11, 1998).

19. L. Grinspoon, *Marijuana, the Forbidden Medicine* (New Haven: Yale University Press, 1993). See also his "Commentary: Marijuana as Medicine" in note 20.

20. See 273 *Journal of the American Medical Association*, 1875–1876 (June 21, 1995).

21. *Arizona Republic*, B7 (Oct. 1, 1998).

22. *New York Times*, E4 (Apr. 20, 1997). Citing research from the Office of National Drug Control Policy, "Drugs and Crime Data, Drug Use Trends" (June 1995), 3.

23. M. Massing, *The Fix* (New York: Simon and Schuster, 1998), 150–151.

24. W. Moyers, "America's War on Marijuana," *Front-Line*, PBS (Apr. 28, 1998).

25. *Arizona Republic*, A10 (Apr. 19, 1998). See also Schlosser (1994), 56.

26. *Arizona Republic*, A2 (Nov. 13, 1995).

27. E. Nadelmann, "Commonsense Drug Policy," 77 *Foreign Affairs*, 111, 122 (Jan.–Feb 1998).

28. *Ariz.* Rev. Stat. 13–1105 Cf. also E. Schlosser, "Reefer Madness," Atlantic (1994).

29. Schlosser, "Reefer Madness," 50.

30. Id., 55

31. J. Torruella, "One Judge's Attempt at a Rational Discussion of the So-Called War on Drugs," 6 *Public Interest Law Journal*, 1 (1996): 23.

32. "NBA's Uncontrolled Substance Abuse Policy," *New York Times*, A26 (Oct. 26, 1997).

33. Id.

34. U.S. Sentencing Commission, Washington, DC, 1998.

35. Schlosser, "More Reefer Madness," 92.

36. Proposition 200, adopted by Arizona, Nov. 9, 1996.

37. *Time*, 22 (Apr. 6, 1998). See also Editorial, *Wall Street Journal*, A10 (April 21, 1998).

38. Nadelmann, "Commonsense Drug Policy," 122.

39. Zimmer and Morgan, *Marijuana Myths*, 23.

40. Id.

41. Nadelmann, "Commonsense Drug Policy," 123.

42. *Time*, 29 (Dec. 9, 1996).

43. *New York Times*, A19 (March 19, 1999) (summarizing the Institute of Medicine Report).

44. Id.

6

THE DRUG WAR: TAKING MINNOWS FROM THE POND

Policy-makers, like addicts, are in denial.
                                        —Bill Moyers, PBS, Mar. 29, 1998

Mary and Cornelius Jefferson were turning in for the night on June 24, 1997, when they heard a battering ram tearing the front door of their Bronx apartment from its hinges. Not robbers but police officials burst in, armed with pistols and a search warrant. Based on the word of a paid informer with a criminal record, the warrant told of a young Hispanic man selling cocaine from the apartment. Instead, the police found this terrified couple in their sixties, in a meticulous apartment, plastic slipcovers protecting the sofas and diplomas lining the walls—and no drugs of any kind.

In 1992 a federal court convicted Paulita Cadiz, a nineteen-year-old pregnant woman with no prior record, of aiding drug dealers. Lazaro Delgado was driving through Boston when he saw Cadiz, then eighteen. When Delgado asked if she wanted a ride, she got in his car. He eventually stopped the car and told Cadiz to go around a corner, meet a woman, Mersky, and bring her back to the car. Cadiz walked Mersky to Delgado's car. Mersky then went to another nearby car and purchased crack cocaine. Unknown to Delgado and Cadiz, Mersky was an undercover drug agent who had recorded her conversation with Cadiz, in which Cadiz stated, "Just go to the car, it will go quickly." Despite her claim of being an unknowing participant, she was found guilty of a drug conspiracy from her ten-minute car ride with Delgado and her eighty-second conversation with the undercover agent and faced a mandatory ten-year prison sentence. Delgado was acquitted.

Another scenario: in late 1992, Los Angeles federal judge Spencer Letts sentenced first-time offender Johnny F. Patillo to a ten-year mandatory prison term for attempting to ship a package containing 681 grams of crack cocaine. He had been a "mule," a minor player in drug trafficking. A strong advocate of stiff drug sanctions, the judge lamented imposing the ten-year mandatory minimum, stating that "my conscience . . . requires that I avoid intentional injustice." The federal sentencing guidelines required imprisonment of twelve to fifteen years; the judge noted that a twelve-year sentence for a first-time offender with a spotless prior record "is worse than uncivilized, it is barbaric."[1]

A fourth scenario: On May 12, 1986, Michigan police stopped Ronald Harmelin for a red light violation. A search of the car revealed a gym bag with 672.5 grams of cocaine and $2,900, for which he was eventually convicted. A first offender, Harmelin was sentenced to mandatory life imprisonment without parole, a sentence affirmed by the U.S. Supreme Court.[2]

These four scenarios are not unusual in our nation's continuing drug war.

POLITICAL ADDICTION

An evil grips America, a life-sapping, drug-related habit that undermines authority, ruins lives, distracts police, and nourishes an insider's culture of winks and smirks. Our national addiction to drug prohibition is siphoning off resources needed for violent crime and drug treatment and prevention and in the process ruining lives and making the drug problem worse. Numerous authorities have tried to warn us, including President Clinton's former surgeon general. Drug prohibition rivals heroin and nicotine among the habits that are hardest to kick. We learn slowly, if at all. In baseball a player with three strikes is out. After repeated failures to stop drugs by expanding the war, our legislators and judges still wave their bats determined to smash the drug problem even at the cost of rationality and enormously increasing tax moneys. Unlike real ballplayers who learn from their strikeouts, our policymakers show dogged single-mindedness: if you can't see the ball, swing harder.

The issue is not whether hard drugs—heroin, cocaine, and their derivatives—are addictive and debilitating. They are both. The issue is not whether they ruin lives, cause health problems, and drain human resources. They do. The issue is the best way to combat their menace—or how to address the problem without making it worse.

A BRIEF HISTORY

People have used drugs for hundreds of years. Cocaine and morphine have long been available as coca leaves or poppy plants to be chewed, dissolved, or taken with alcohol or water. In the late 1600s European settlers brought crude opium to American colonists who used it for pain relief. Benjamin Franklin regularly took laudanum—opium in alcohol—to relieve kidney stones. The poet Samuel Taylor Coleridge began using laudanum as a painkiller while he was a student at Cambridge, where he developed a lifelong addiction to it. By the time of the Civil War, surgeons on both sides regularly dispensed morphine. In 1874 a pharmacist in London, searching for a nonaddictive alternative to morphine, boiled morphine with acetic anhydride, producing a substance with powerful narcotic properties. In 1898 a pharmacist at the Bayer Laboratories in Germany noted the powerful effects of the substance as a painkiller, which Bayer accordingly marketed under the name suitable for a drug of such heroic qualities—"heroin."

Politicians soon associated smoking opium with Chinese immigrants working on the railroads, an early example of a recurring phenomenon in our drug prohibition: the linkage between certain drugs and disfavored ethnic groups. Cocaine became linked with blacks just as marijuana was linked to Mexicans and opium with Chinese. State and national legislatures began to penalize the use of opium by the Chinese in the 1870s, cocaine use by African Americans in 1900, and marijuana usage by Hispanics in the depression. Our drug war continues this earlier ethnic war against those who get their highs without the protected, acceptable drugs of the upper class, such as tobacco and alcohol.

As early as 1884 purified cocaine became commercially available as a legal drug across the counter, first costing five dollars to ten dollars a gram—later twenty-five cents a gram until the price inflation of World War I. Coca-Cola appeared in 1886 with the advantages of coca but without the dangers of alcohol—supposedly a temperate substitute for alcohol. The cocaine was removed in 1900, a year before the city of Atlanta prohibited its use without a prescription.

Cocaine is one of the most powerful of the central nervous system mood elevators. Within a year of its introduction the Parke-Davis Drug Company produced coca and cocaine in some fifteen forms, including cocaine for cigarettes, for injection, and for sniffing. Parke-Davis even offered consumers a handy cocaine kit that, the company boasted, could take the place of food, make the coward brave and the silent eloquent, and render the sufferer insensitive to pain. In 1910 President William Taft reported to Congress that heroin and cocaine posed a serious addiction problem for the nation. Four years later President Woodrow Wilson signed the Harrison

Act, which permitted cocaine only through prescription and forbade private trafficking in both cocaine and heroin.

However well intended, drug prohibition was unnecessary. In 1900 the nation had no significant drug problem. The typical addict was a middle-aged southern white woman strung out on laudanum, and the total number of addicts was probably less than 1 percent of the nation's population. Addiction peaked around 1900, and decreased until reaching a relatively small number (about 100,000) in the 1920s. Both drugs and alcohol were frowned on at the turn of the century because the temperance movement had been so successful. Once moral suasion yielded to police power, we acquired an instant black market, organized crime, rampant corruption, and violence on a scale unimagined. After a decade of this, people got fed up with crimes and gunplay, and alcohol prohibition sank of its own weight in 1933.[3]

THREE COMPETING VIEWS

The current national debate on hard drugs presents three competing perspectives: prohibitionist, libertarian, and public health.

The drug warrior perspective, at the extreme of the prohibitionist mind-set, views a paternalistic state acting as a severe, protective parent to its child-like citizens. Emphasis is on law enforcement and control of drugs by legislation and harsh penal sanctions. Drug warriors, like former drug czar William Bennett, believe that drugs cause addiction and crime and that public policy should eradicate all drugs and punish violators severely in the traditional condemnatory court system.

The libertarian perspective is the polar opposite. Psychiatrist Thomas Szasz and economist Milton Friedman, two of many representatives in this group, see drug use not as a disease or a social problem but rather as a matter of personal values, an ethical, not a medical or social issue. To classical libertarians, drug use reflects a mind-set more so than chemistry or physiology. To libertarians like Friedman a free-market approach to illegal drugs reduces the lawlessness associated with abuse. To this group even medicalization appears paternalistic; instead, informal social control should be the appropriate focus.

The third view, the public health perspective, includes advocates for drug legalization and medicalization. The surgeon general, not the attorney general, should lead the War on Drugs; to this group addiction is a disease, and criminal sanctions are inhumane and wasteful. This group advocates treatment rather than punishment and invokes the ideal of harm reduction as the social goal and supports medical marijuana laws such as those passed in 1996 and 1997 in California and Arizona. Medically oriented advocates embrace the medical model of addiction: the best approach to drugs, like the best approach to cigarettes, is treating addiction as a disease rather than punishing it as a moral evil.[4]

THE DRUG WAR AS CIVIL WAR

Our national drug policy squarely fits the first of these positions: warfare. Our drug war first became a national fight under President Ronald Reagan, who once said, "In this crusade, let us not forget who we are. Drug abuse is a repudiation of everything America is. The destructiveness and human wreckage mock our heritage."[5] President Bush left no doubt about his similar position: "Speak the truth: that drugs are evil, that they ruin and end young lives . . . the drug dealers are murderers and should be treated as such."[6] "All of us agree that the gravest domestic threat facing our nation today is drugs," he announced. In a speech full of military metaphors ("If we fight this war as a divided nation, then the war is lost") with ringing calls to arms ("Victory. Victory over drugs is our cause") he pledged $8 billion on antidrug programs. Other officials echoed the cry. Speaking at Harvard in 1989, the then-drug czar William Bennett summed up our government's attitude toward drugs: "It makes a mockery of virtue." Building more prisons is "the morally right thing to do," former attorney general William Barr said in 1992. On *Larry King Live*, Bennett even suggested beheading drug dealers.

Such militaristic pomp permeates our drug crusade, which equates our drug-using citizens with contagious lepers. Since 1989 this crusade has imposed ever-tougher sanctions against users as well as against nonaddicted, nondealing consumers. "Who's responsible?" President Bush asked in 1989. "Everyone who uses drugs. Everyone who sells drugs. And everyone who looks the other way." Such rhetoric shows that it is easier to bring people to their feet rather than to their senses.

Unfortunate symbols surround the drug war metaphor, an image singularly unhelpful in our drug policy. Why such a divisive metaphor for the relationship of a government to its own citizens? Such an image suggests a new civil war of the powerful against the addicted, with heavy equipment, military curfews, interdictions, and prisoners of war (POWs)—blacks, Hispanics, and poor whites, our fellow citizens now targeted as the enemy. The drug war thereby becomes a race and generational war, an internal Vietnam. This war attacks drug user groups unevenly. Whites represent 80 percent of drug users but only about 12 percent of those arrested. Blacks make up about 13 percent of monthly drug users but are 90 percent of those arrested for drugs. Minorities generally constitute 90 percent of those arrested for crack cocaine. Because of this war prisons overflow with black and brown POWs, undermining decades of national and local efforts to improve their life chances in inner-city ghettos.[7]

This demonization has been very expensive. According to the Drug Policy Foundation, President Bush spent $45.2 billion in four years on the drug war, more than double the $22.3 billion President Reagan spent. Bush's drug war cost $32 billion in the first three years, of which about 80 percent was spent trying—without success—to cut the supply of drugs. Drug trafficking increased rather than declined. Bush spent $2.2 billion alone to stop cocaine production in South America. Cocaine production went up instead.[8] President Clinton has continued his predecessors' policies, allocating two-thirds of drug funding to enforcement and interdiction, with only one-third for treatment. Federal drug policy primarily focuses on supply control efforts via traditional law enforcement.[9] We forge ahead despite the facts and the waste of tax moneys, $17 billion in 1998 alone.

We cling to drug prohibition for the same reason we cling to other self-destructive habits: we like the way they make us feel. Prohibition makes its advocates feel powerfully righteous. But, as the same drug warriors know well, our War on Drugs has become a witless mission impossible. Challenging the economics of drugs by criminal weapons approximates repealing the law of gravity. Government militarism has generated a crescendo of massive but futile enforcement efforts—bumper stickers, no-knock entries, asset forfeitures, slogans, DARE programs, roadblocks, turf wars, cul-de-sacs, interdiction and eradication, school zones, parades and prisons, harsher sentencing, death penalty swooning, building razing, urine testing, crime patrols, loitering and nuisance abatement ordinances, evictions, and telephone-tampering—and still more tax money. None of them has—or can—hit the ball; nonetheless, we close our eyes and just swing harder.[10]

Much of this effort makes the drug problem worse. If the drug war's purpose is to make criminals out of one in four black males, it has succeeded. If it seeks to create a high crime rate and thus nurture political demagogues who promise to stamp it out, it is achieving that end. If the war desires de facto repeal of the Bill of Rights and the Fourth Amendment, victory is in sight. If its purpose is to transfer individual freedom to the government, it has succeeded as well as any real war. As it seeks to stamp out drug crimes, it succeeds in stamping out courtroom justice as well.

The unintended consequences of our drug war are everywhere: our courts, both state and federal, are jammed primarily with drug cases; civil cases take a back seat or none at all. Our prisons overflow with nonviolent drug users. Drug-infected families suffer twice with lifelong convictions and family disruption. Urban and ghetto children as well as adults are stigmatized as criminals, which makes recovery and employment far more difficult. Our institutions, as well as those of our South and Central American neighbors, totter under the immense wealth generated illegally under current drug policies.[11] Street sellers and mules, mostly minorities, thrash about in the law's tattered nets, while druglords and drug-using athletes, academics, and upper-class suburbanites generally remain unscathed. The costs of criminal prohibition are too high, its benefits too dubious, its enforcement too capricious, the criminal methods too blunt.

Necessary reforms to counter the present strikeouts cannot begin so long as our politicians see drugs primarily as a law enforcement problem. Recognizing this illusion opens the door to controlling them other than by warfare. The core question is not whether hard drugs are good or bad—they clearly are bad. The real issue is how the government can best deal effectively with their horrors. The debate in the medical, sociological, and law enforcement communities turns on whether drug control is more effective in the criminal or the health systems. Despite the political rhetoric, the question remains wrongly decided in favor of the former.

Politics is a major obstacle to rational drug policy. At its broadest, narcotics present more a political than a medical or legal problem. The impetus for hard drug prohibition comes, in good part, from tensions among socioeconomic groups, ethnic minorities, and generational conflicts. Its main impetus lies in shining politicians' moral halos. Our government got into this drug taffy pull in the first place less because of lapses in rational policy making than because of the political seductions of drug control. This war provides shiny badges of political opportunity at home and abroad: the rhetoric of the War on Drugs, like that of being tough on crime, brings out the vote. The unenlightened but politically astute response to drugs is to call for a continually expanded war, with more money, more police, longer sentences, bigger prisons. The law enforcement bureaucracy always responds by accepting this challenge because drug war expansion offers votes and empire—more money, more forfeitures, more personnel, more seizures, and greater power. The military-industrial complex pales in comparison to the host of industries now catering to our drug war. Researchers abound who tell the government what it wants to hear, prison builders, correction and parole officers' associations, drug-testing companies, private prison managers, and purveyors of antidrug education. War-room expansion constitutes a very attractive offer that legislators and criminal justice executives cannot refuse, especially coupled to a self-righteous halo. But it is an offer that finally needs refusing if for no other reason than to salvage the law's credibility.

Before the War on Drugs began, two federal agencies enforced the drug laws on a total budget of about $4 million. Today, there are fifty-four agencies involved in drugs, including the Drug Enforcement Agency (DEA), National Security Agency (NSA), Internal Revenue Service (IRS), Alcohol, Tobacco and Firearms (ATF), State Department, Pentagon, Customs, Coast Guard, army, navy, air force, and marines. The overall budget as of 1998 is $17 billion, with more than $8 billion going to the DEA alone.[12] None of this effort has had any noticeable impact on drugs. State and local law enforcement agencies now expend more than 20 percent of their total budgets on drug enforcement that otherwise could be devoted to schools or public works or against violent crime.[13] The United States now has the highest addiction rate in its history and, after Russia, the highest rate of imprisonment in the world, largely because of drug-related crime.[14]

PRISON STATE

One of the most measurable effects of the War on Drugs has been the creation of a prison state.[15] According to FBI statistics, 1 million arrests are made annually for violations of federal and state drug laws.[16]

From 1925 through 1973, our prison population fluctuated between 90 and 120 people in prison per 100,000 population; in 1973 the rate was 98 people in prison per 100,000; by 1986, following the start of the War on Drugs, the incarceration rate doubled to 200 per 100,000. In 1993, the rate of Americans serving prison time stood at 445 per 100,000; by 1999 that figure almost doubled again to 668 of 100,000 people.[17]

Since 1980 our prison population has more than tripled, from 500,000 to over 1.8 million. The big contributor is drug and alcohol abuse, which figures in the crimes and incarceration of 80 percent—some 1.4 million— of these 1.8 million prisoners. Those 1.4 million inmates violated drug or alcohol laws or were "high" at the time they committed their crimes or stole property to buy drugs or have a history of drug and alcohol abuse and addiction or some combination of these characteristics. Among these prisoners are the parents of 2.4 million children, many of them minors. If the current rate of prison increase continues, one in every twenty Americans born in 1998 will spend some part of life in prison, as will one in every eleven men and one in every four black men.[18] Our country is fast becoming what novelist Franz Kafka calls a "penal colony."

Conviction for drug offenses is the fastest-growing category in the federal prison population, accounting, as of 1998, for 61 percent of the total compared with 38 percent in 1986. One in four federal prisoners is a low-level, nonviolent drug offender with no previous record. Most receive mandatory-minimum sentences averaging six years before release, emerging often with a worse drug problem and more drug connections than before, thanks to ready drug contacts in prison. In state prisons the picture of drug availability is similar to that in federal prisons.[19]

Mandatory-minimum sentences ensure that many nonviolent, low-level drug offenders sit in prison for a long time, taking cells from violent offenders. In 1990, almost 90 percent of first-time drug offenders in federal courts went to prison. First-time violent offenders went to jail less often and for shorter periods. In 1991, there were over 6 million cocaine users, 5.7 million users of hallucinogens and inhalants, and approximately 700,000 heroin users. Today only about one-eighth of the hard-core cocaine and heroin abusers are incarcerated. If we add the nonusers to these

user offenders, there are so many drug offenders that it is fiscally and prac-
tically unrealistic to incarcerate more than a small number of them.

Tough sanctions do little to deter those who already have offended. Despite a high lifetime likelihood of arrest, the probability that an individual
will be caught committing a drug offense is very low. In a sample of 254
crack dealers in Miami, approximately 87 percent had been arrested at
some point, but of over 220,000 offenses, the likelihood of arrest for each
incident was less than 1 percent.[20] If we wanted to double the number of
traffickers now incarcerated, our prisons could not hold them. More cru-
cially, we can do nothing to prevent replacements from emerging on the
streets of otherwise unchanged communities to replace those behind bars.
Incarceration has little effect on the crime rate if we incarcerate the wrong
offenders. One major result of our drug myopia is the incarceration of
replaceable street offenders with little or no prior criminal history, no violent offense behavior, and no involvement in sophisticated criminal activity, while big-time drug importers and dealers remain untouched.

There are other consequences, too. The felonization of young male minorities only creates fodder for prisons, boot camps, and jails. Young offenders labeled as felons by the age of eighteen find themselves locked into
a criminal career track, making it much more difficult to secure education
or employment or mainline civic status. Felonization addresses the drug
problem by making civic recovery harder, resulting in increased welfare
needs. High levels of incarceration of poor minorities prevent involvement
in their families and communities.[21]

Among low-level drug offenders, sentences have increased 150 percent
above what they were prior to the implementation of the federal sentencing
guidelines and the antidrug abuse acts that established mandatory drug
minimums. Two-thirds of these low-level offenders receive harsh mandatory drug minimum sentences. In England drug offenders are *half* as likely
to go to jail or prison as Americans, and when they do, they are likely to
stay for shorter periods. They are *far* less likely to be sentenced to the
extraordinary long terms typical of our drug war. The proportion of American drug offenders sentenced to over ten years is more than triple that in
England and Wales, both of which are regarded by continental standards
as harsh on drug offenders.[22]

Criminal recidivism is very much a function of drug and alcohol abuse.
The more often an individual is imprisoned, the likelier the inmate is to be
a drug or alcohol addict or abuser. Forty-one percent of first-time offenders
in state prison have a history of regular drug use; the proportion jumps to
81 percent for those with five or more prior convictions. Regardless of their
crimes, individuals who test positive for drugs at the time of arrest have
longer criminal records and have been imprisoned more often than those
who did not test positive.[23]

Proponents of the War on Drugs often declare that our draconian pro-hibitionist laws cause a decline in drug use.[24] The evidence, however, shows that the number of heavy drug users in the United States is increasing rather than declining.[25] An increasing number of high school students use mari-juana and LSD.[26] Even proponents of the War on Drugs candidly admit drug abuse cannot be entirely eliminated.[27]

Part of the futility of the current war is its counterproductivity. A user must associate with criminals to get drugs. Many are driven to become criminals in order to finance their habits. Even an addict who seeks treat-ment must confess to being a criminal in order to qualify for treatment. Enforcement has thus been a stimulant. The government has spent close to $500 billion over the past twenty years to enforce drug prohibition. During the same period use levels rose, and the number of arrests and the amounts of drugs seized greatly increased, as did drug use itself. [28]

Although the vast majority of Americans would not take prohibited drugs if they were legalized,[29] many people fear that use would escalate sharply with legalization.[30] Implicit in the legalization argument is the as-sumption that current prohibitionist laws discourage people from using drugs.[31] The available evidence, however, shows the contrary.

IMPOSSIBLE STRATEGIC GOALS

Our government's drug strategy hinges on the three policies of eradica-tion, interdiction, and street-level enforcement. Interdiction, or border mon-itoring, has failed with heroin and cocaine. The only minor success involves marijuana, which is difficult to transport. Smugglers have moved to cocaine and heroin as substitutes for marijuana because pot can so easily be grown within our own borders. A Rand Corporation evaluation of interdiction concluded that "even massively stepped-up drug interdiction efforts are not likely to greatly affect the availability of cocaine and heroin in the United States."[32]

Mexican drug traffickers have now become almost as powerful as the Medellin and Cali drug cartels of Colombia that were at their height in the 1980s. Mexican syndicates now control a third of cocaine distribution in the United States, 20 percent of the heroin, 80 to 90 percent of the meth-amphetamine, and most of the marijuana. The Mexican cartels' reach has spread from their strongholds in the West and Southwest to major cities in the East, including Chicago and New York, which historically have been under the sway of Colombian and Dominican drug organizations.[33] These cartels respond to interdiction simply by moving their supply routes and points of entry to less targeted areas, moving regularly from Miami to New Orleans to Mexican border points. Interdiction is like slaying a hydra: many new heads replace the one cut off.

The same dynamics have made Caribbean countries like the Dominican

Republic and Haiti major transfer points for cocaine destined for our market. This ebb and flow of trafficking patterns underscore what DEA officials call the balloon effect: squeezing on one point of entry makes drug activity bulge in another. "Our current interdiction efforts almost completely fail to achieve our purpose of reducing the flow of cocaine, heroin, and methamphetamine across the [Southwest] border," according to a candid October 1997 internal memo from the office of drug czar General Barry McCaffery.

The balloon effect is not new. Drug control campaigns against heroin in Turkey in the 1970s stimulated heroin production in Southeast Asia, Afghanistan, and Mexico. In Peru, success in disrupting the air bridge to Colombia led to a switch to river routes. Our drug officials were proud of the drop in cocaine smuggling after intense interdiction efforts in southern Florida in the 1980s. Almost immediately, traffickers shifted to air drops over the Caribbean for pickup by boat. When enforcers caught up with this tactic, traffickers switched to routes through northern Mexico and new routes in the Pacific.

The federal government's obsession with interdicting drug supplies suffers from a basic fallacy. A true shortage would drive up prices and force addicts to commit more crimes to maintain their habits. But cocaine and most other illicit drugs are easy to smuggle across our porous borders, which is why every overpublicized drug seizure ends up having scant effect on the law of supply and demand that dictates street prices.[34] In theory, cocaine should be the easiest of the illicit crops to eradicate because it grows principally only in Peru and Bolivia. Almost all the world's cocaine supply grows on 700 square miles of land. It would still be prohibitively costly to eradicate the crop because cocaine could be grown on another 2,500,000 square miles of arable land in the world.[35] There is little incentive for dirt-poor countries like Peru or Burma to stop growing coca leaf or opium poppies when such crops make more economic sense than legal alternatives. By the same token, discouraging drug production by subsidizing alternative crops is a fool's game. Drug entrepreneurs can afford to pay more since the cost of the raw material is a minute fraction of the wholesale price of the delivered product.

Most of the price of drugs on our streets is the result of the value added to the drugs after they enter the country—the inflated black-market costs of distributing them here. At the point of export, the price of cocaine is still only 3 to 5 percent of the price a consumer will pay. Even the costs of smuggling the drugs from Colombia to the United States account for less than 5 percent of the retail price. An extremely successful crop eradication program that tripled the leaf price of coca would raise cocaine prices in the United States by 1 percent. The effect on our drug use would be barely perceptible.

Street-level drug enforcement efforts show little success because they reach only the replaceable last link in the distribution chain. Street enforcement efforts have not impacted drug availability. Crimes ancillary to drug trafficking have increased in almost every case where street enforcement strategies have increased. Recent police enforcement has sought to break up large-scale drug rings, arrest small-scale dealers when they sell drugs outside areas of endemic use, and punish users when they commit crime. Local police try to restrain street-level selling, and private employers have tried to restrain drug use among workers by random urine testing. The result has been a slow, but steady, loss of ground for law enforcement agencies. Street enforcement probably cannot do much better; the future probably holds a worse prognosis because of easy replacement of arrestees.

Easy replacement defeats enforcement. Large numbers of dealers, arranged in a hierarchy throughout our nation, take drugs from floating points of importation and distribute them down the chain to small-scale sellers who provide them to users. The high profits at every level of the trade guarantee a large reservoir of individuals "sitting on the bench" waiting an opportunity to take places vacated by those removed by arrest. If members of a drug ring are simply replaced when they are caught, the law's deterrent effect is virtually nil. If the person caught happened to be inept, adding a more cunning replacement increases, rather than reduces, drug crime. Effective law enforcement thus serves as a sorting mechanism to aid drug traffickers in their search for more competent suppliers than the unfit ones arrested.

A further flaw compounds the hydra effect. Our drug warriors aim to cut the foreign drug supply—and raise U.S. prices—with tough enforcement strategies that make production and trafficking more risky. Their very success in raising production costs and consumer prices radically inflates black-market prices for growers and traffickers. A pure gram of pharmaceutical cocaine that would cost about $15, for example, brings about $150 on the retail black market. Production costs are so low that the average drug organization can afford to lose 70 percent to 80 percent of its product and still be profitable. A startling table, drawn from the Department of Justice's Drug Enforcement Administration report of September 1993, presents the basic economic scenario of drug inflation: initial cost of raw opium as harvested by hand, from incised poppy pods, in the Shan territories of Myanmar, $66–$75 per kilogram (2.2 pounds); one kilo of prepared morphine base on the Thai border, $900–$1,000; one kilo of refined heroin in Bangkok, $6,000–$10,000; wholesale refined heroin cost in the United States, calculated by the kilo, $940,000–$1,400,000.

These black-market profits provide a steady incentive for drug suppliers to remain in the trade and for new suppliers to enter. So the stick (law enforcement) intended to discourage black marketeers creates the carrot (enormous profits) that ensures that producers and traffickers pursuing high profits will keep the supply of drugs up, and competition among them keeps prices from rising too high, undermining the aim of our enforcement policy. It is thus not surprising that heroin and cocaine prices have declined, not increased, over the past fifteen years. For supply-side policies to work, drug prices must rise. If, as most economists believe, the use of drugs is not particularly sensitive to price, the total value of drugs sold actually increases when enforcement is successful. This breeds ancillary crime as users steal to pay for their habits and dealers fight over turf. If supply-side antidrug policies create a vicious circle of higher prices and more crime, demand-side policies should lead to a virtuous one. Low demand means lower prices, lower revenue, and less incentive to steal and kill. However, the naive attack on drug supply through intense interdiction, eradication, arrest, prosecution, and punishment results in a "crime tariff"[36] that the seller charges the buyer in order to monetize the risk in breaking the law, in short, a premium for taking risks. Drug enforcement creates this tariff and thereby maintains inflated rewards for illegal drugs in the black market.

For example, an ounce of pure pharmaceutical cocaine at roughly $80, just under $3.00 per gram, becomes worth about $4,480 if sold in the black market at $80 per diluted gram (at 50 percent purity). The crime tariff is $4,400 per ounce. This type of law enforcement succeeds, to some unknown extent, in making drugs less available—to the extent (probably slight) that demand is elastic or sensitive to price. But because the crime tariff is paid to lawbreakers rather than the government, law enforcement pumps vast sums of money into the black market, which supplies incentive for homicides, street crime, public corruption, and international narcoterrorism. If these phenomena were costed out, one might well conclude that the War on Drugs makes a net negative contribution to the safety of our people.

The classic case study of draconian law enforcement efforts against drugs is New York's "Rockefeller drug law." In 1973, New York amended its laws as part of an all-out drug war with intense street enforcement and severe penalties so that drug sellers faced mandatory prison terms of fifteen to twenty-five years. In 1977, the New York Bar Association found that the state had spent $32 million in implementing laws resulting in a net effect described as "negligible at best." No reduction in drug-related crime or in heroin usage occurred.

As of 1999 New York's Rockefeller drug laws still require a minimum of fifteen years in prison for anyone selling more than two ounces or possessing more than four ounces of cocaine, heroin, or other controlled substances. They make no distinction between a drug kingpin and a street-level junkie. As a result, many first-time offenders serve longer prison terms than violent rapists and robbers. Another Rockefeller law increases sentences even more for second offenses, resulting in thousands of small-time offenders serving even more time than violent criminals. The 22,000 drug offenders of New York's 70,000 inmates as of 1999 could be rehabilitated with drug treatment for far less than the $30,000 annual prison cost per inmate.

The New York Bar Association found the Rockefeller laws an expensive failure.[37] Drug use actually increased during periods when criminal penalties were harshest and enforcement most vigorous. In 1997, the Human Rights Watch found that New York's continuing disproportionate mandatory sentences for drug offenders violate international law and the Universal Declaration of Human Rights.[38]

Drug wars have created serious problems that would not exist without intensive enforcement efforts. Closely related to drug-related corruption is the impetus the drug war gives organized crime. Intensified enforcement has created organized crime groups. Enforcement targets only those easiest to catch and most visible to the police—minority users and sellers on street corners and parking lots. Arrested dealers are the most visible, the least important, and the smallest operators. Enforcement weeds out inefficient and slothful neighborhood dealers while ignoring widespread drug use among upper-class athletes and academics. Organized crime strongly supports drug prohibition because it realizes enormous profits in the drug market precisely because the drugs are illegal.[39] The actual cost of producing illegal drugs is modest; the surcharge added by organized crime is great. Drug laws act like a government-sponsored subsidy providing organized crime with billions of dollars.

Drug policy has not failed for lack of resources, funding, legal powers, or adequate manpower but because the problem is not amenable to a criminal justice solution. As the Pennsylvania Crime Commission astutely concluded in its 1987 report on organized crime: "Short of creating a police state, there is no evidence to suggest that vast expansion of investigative efforts would lead to the eradication of illegal drugs."[40]

COUNTERPRODUCTIVE EFFECTS

Recent innovative drug control programs have failed. The much ballyhooed DARE Program, which costs upward of $400 million annually in federal funds, has no long-term effect on children's use of drugs and, among some populations, seems to have increased drug use. DARE effects a transfer of responsibility from parents to government with a not so subtle suggestion that parents can't do their parenting job. In suburban Chicago schools, students who attended seventeen weekly one-hour DARE sessions reported more drug use than those who did not take the classes. By the end of the study, 74.8 percent of the DARE students reported having used alcohol at some point in their lives, compared to 70.3 percent who did not take DARE classes, and 77.4 percent of DARE students, compared to 73.4 percent of non-DARE students, reported some illegal drug use. According to Dennis Rosenbaum of the University of Illinois, who directed the study,

"DARE may have given students some ideas about experimenting with drugs."[41]

Current draconian laws have created incentives for juveniles in competing for drug-dealing jobs. In money and penal terms, a juvenile is less risky to hire than an adult. The longer the sentences imposed on adults, or the more intense the adult enforcement effort, the greater the advantage to drug traders of hiring juveniles. Indeed, one of the contrary effects of New York's Rockefeller laws was to spur employment of juveniles in what previously was an adult trade. Longer adult sentences and more intense adult enforcement create this transfer by increasing the wage gap, by increasing the risk that an adult will inform, and by increasing the consequences of being informed on.[42]

When drug prices increase, drug consumers may be forced, because of the decline in real income, to begin dealing drugs to support their habit. Some of this increase in dealing takes the form of exposing neophytes to the drug, thereby increasing horizontal consumption. High drug prices increase, rather than reduce, drug use. Proponents of the drug war correctly argue that high monetary prices could deter new users from taking heroin, but they err in extrapolating their analysis to addicts. An optimal deterrence strategy would prevent new users from being exposed to the drug and simultaneously ensure that prices are low for those already addicted. In economic terms, the goal is to create price discrimination.

Mandatory-minimum drug sentences have been hailed as the penal solution. The independent Rand Corporation has studied their efficacy, focusing on cocaine, the most problematic drug. Rand took two approaches to model the market and arrived at the same conclusion: mandatory-minimum sentences are not justifiable on the basis of cost-effectiveness at reducing cocaine consumption or drug-related crime. They reduce cocaine consumption less per million taxpayer dollars spent than spending the same amount on enforcement under the previous nonmandatory sentencing regime. Either enforcement approach reduces drug consumption less per $1 million spent than putting heavy users through treatment programs. Mandatory minimums are also less cost-effective than either alternative at reducing cocaine-related crime.

A principal reason for these findings is the high cost of incarceration, now averaging between $25,000 and $30,000 per year per inmate. Caulkins, Rydell, and their Rand colleagues first estimated the cost-effectiveness of additional expenditures on enforcement against the average drug dealer apprehended by federal, state, or local authorities. Increased enforcement places additional costs on dealers, which they pass along to cocaine consumers in the form of higher prices. Higher cocaine prices discourage consumption. By mathematically modeling how cocaine market demand and supply respond to price, Rand researchers estimated the changes in total cocaine consumption over fifteen years for an additional $1 million invested in different cocaine control strategies.[43] Spending $1 million on mandatory-minimum sentences for higher-level dealers does, indeed, have a bigger effect on cocaine consumption than spending the same amount on either enforcement approach against typical dealers. Nonetheless, against any given type of dealer or at any level of government, mandatory minimums are less cost-effective than conventional enforcement. Moreover, although federal mandatory minimums do better relative to treating heavy users than do longer sentences for all dealers, treatment is still more cost-effective. Rand concluded, again, that the government would have to spend an additional $783 million to reduce cocaine consumption by 1 percent. Relying on interdiction, it would need to spend $366 million more for the same benefit, and on domestic law enforcement, $246 million more. Relying solely on treatment would cost just $34 million more. Treatment, then, is seven times more cost-effective than domestic enforcement, ten times more effective than interdiction, and twenty-three times more effective than attacking drugs at their source.[44]

Why is conventional enforcement more cost-effective than mandatory minimums? Drug enforcement imposes costs on dealers through arrest and conviction, which include seizure of drugs and other assets, and through incarceration, which involves loss of income. Per dollar spent, the cost burden from seizures is greater. A million dollars spent extending sentences thus imposes less cost on dealers—and consequently reduces cocaine consumption less—than a million dollars spent on conventional enforcement, which includes asset seizures.[45]

According to Rand, treatment should reduce serious personal and property crimes the most per $1 million spent, on the order of fifteen times as much as would incarceration. Why is treatment so much better? Most drug-related crime is economically motivated, undertaken to support a habit or to settle scores between rival dealers. The level of economically motivated crime relates to the amount of money flowing through the cocaine market, which is a function of strict law enforcement.[46]

INCONSISTENCY: THE ALCOHOL AND TOBACCO EXAMPLES

Today our nation's two most dangerous drugs—tobacco and alcohol—remain freely available, while less dangerous drugs lead to felony convictions. We learn, as of 1998, that the tobacco industry spikes cigarettes with nicotine and seeks to habituate smokers. Yet tobacco still remains a legal drug wholly inconsistent with our policy of drug prohibition for health reasons.

Each year, nicotine kills about 450,000 of our citizens, mostly via cancer. Alcohol kills about 100,000. The so-called hard drugs kill about 5,000 from overdosing. Tobacco and alcohol far outdistance the other drugs in social suffering and fatalities. For every person who dies from cocaine poisoning, 37 people die from the direct effects of alcohol and 132 from tobacco-related illnesses. No deaths from marijuana have ever been reported. Our policy inconsistency between alcohol and tobacco, on one hand, and hard drugs, on the other, weakens respect for hard drug prohibition. The effort to explain to youngsters the inconsistency between these drugs based on their health and social consequences leaves the young in awe at the law's caprice.

The tremendous economic and manpower investments in the War on Drugs have resulted, at best, in modest reductions in use compared to the results of the relatively insignificant educational investments made by the government to discourage tobacco and alcohol use. Although the social costs of tobacco and alcohol use are many times greater than those of illicit drugs, government spending related to the use of illegal drugs is twice that spent for alcohol and tobacco abuse. Though ten times more tobacco and alcohol users exist than users of illegal drugs, government spending on the users of illegal drugs is twice the amount spent on tobacco and alcohol users. Where, then, is the logic in prohibiting drug use but not alcohol or tobacco use?[47]

One prevailing argument against marijuana, cocaine, and heroin is that they are gateway drugs, leading users to progressively more dangerous drugs. Our government fails to see the logic of that same argument regarding tobacco. Young people ages twelve to seventeen who smoke tobacco are eight times more likely to use illegal drugs than are their nonsmoking peers.[48] Even conservative senator Jon Kyl (R., AZ) sees tobacco as the true gateway drug:

Cigarette smoking is often the precursor to drug addiction. A survey by the Substance Abuse Mental Health Administration reported that almost 75 percent of teens surveyed had tried cigarettes before marijuana. Moreover, a 1996 National Household Survey on Drug Abuse showed that current smokers are more likely to be heavy drinkers and illicit drug users. Equally disturbing is the apparent innovation by youth in combining tobacco and drugs. For example, some teens smoke cigarettes after they smoke marijuana to enhance their high. This behavior illustrates the undeniable connection between tobacco and drugs.[49]

In April 1999, Pride (National Parents' Resource Institute for Drug Education) in its first national drug abuse survey found that grade- and middle-school youngsters abuse cigarettes and alcohol far more than marijuana or harder drugs, roughly by a factor of seven times. Though that figure varies as students progress through high school, alcohol and cigarettes remain in far greater use than pot or hard drugs.

Though cigarettes and alcohol are the true gateway to hard drugs, no wars on these drugs have been declared. The question is not whether illegal drugs are dangerous but whether their damage can be lessened by our present militaristic approach. Tobacco and alcohol are far greater health and social threats than illegal drugs, and tobacco is far more lethal than alcohol. Alcohol is a factor in more than half of all robberies, homicides, and rapes, as it is in many cases of child abuse and wife battering. Fetal alcohol syndrome is the leading preventable cause of birth defects in the Western world. "Binge" drinking is the single most serious problem on college campuses. Overall, some 14 million Americans suffer from alcohol abuse or alcoholism. According to the National Institute on Alcohol Abuse and Alcoholism, alcohol causes "more economic and social damage than any other public-health problem."[50] Yet we declare no war on alcohol.

Hard drugs are less a health threat than either tobacco or alcohol. Conservative William Bennett's book *Body Count*, addressing the fight against drugs and crime, includes a thirteen-page section on "Liquor, Disorder, and Crime." "Make no mistake," the book asserts, "liquor is as much a part of the problem as drugs, perhaps a bigger part." The book calls for measures aimed at reducing alcohol consumption, including stricter zoning codes and limits on advertising—but not for the declaration of an alcohol war.[51]

Contrary to popular myth, alcohol is more tightly linked to violent crimes than are crack cocaine, heroin, or any other illegal drug. In state prisons, 21 percent of the inmates convicted of violent crimes were under the influence of alcohol—and no other substance—when they committed those crimes. In contrast, at the time of their crimes only 3 percent of violent offenders were under the influence of cocaine or crack alone, and only 1 percent were under the influence of heroin alone. In local jails, 26 percent of the inmates incarcerated for violent crimes were under the influence of alcohol alone at the time of their offense. In contrast, at the time of their crimes only 4 percent of violent offenders were under the influence of cocaine or crack alone, and none were under the influence of heroin alone.[52] We are targeting the wrong drugs: alcohol and tobacco are far greater social ills than hard drugs.

PRISON-ONLY POLICIES

As though these inconsistencies were not enough, the futility of the War on Drugs appears directly in the fact that judges and other criminal justice practitioners grease a mindless drug turnstile. These officials typically wash their hands of addicts once they are sentenced to prison, where they are quickly forgotten, and the substance abuse problems that caused their imprisonment are ignored. In prison addicts find other addicted companions and often a ready supply of drugs as well. Why then should we be surprised that released inmates return to drugs? In the words of Joseph Califano, the head of Columbia University's National Center on Addiction and Substance Abuse,

The most troublesome aspect of all these grim statistics is that the nation is doing so little to change them. From 1993 to 1996, as the number of state and federal inmates needing substance abuse treatment climbed from 688,000 to 840,000, the number of these inmates in treatment hovered around 150,000—and much of the treatment they received was inadequate. From 1995 to 1996, the number of inmates in treatment actually decreased as the number in need of treatment rose.[53]

Changing one's residence from the street to a jail causes no automatic reformation. If the objective of our prison system is to protect the public safety by keeping incorrigible offenders off the street, the prevailing prison policy of punishment only, with no treatment or preparation for becoming law-abiding in the community, is shortsighted to the point of myopia. Treatment is seven times more cost-effective than prohibition. One dollar spent on treatment of an addict reduces the probability of continued addiction seven times more than one dollar spent on incarceration. Unfortunately, treatment for addicts is currently unavailable to almost half of those who would benefit. Yet we are willing to build more and more jails, even though at one-seventh their cost we could subsidize effective medical care and psychological treatment.

The medical profession now agrees. Medical treatment for drug addiction works as well as treating diabetes or other chronic diseases, dramatically reduces crimes, and is a lot cheaper than jail, according to a study released in March 1998 by bipartisan public health experts. "We've been telling people to 'just say no' when addiction is a biological event," said Dr. June Osborn of the new Physician Leadership on National Drug Policy, speaking for prominent physicians and public health leaders from the Clinton, Bush, and Reagan administrations that commissioned the research from half a dozen universities. The medical scientists concluded that:

- Jailing a drug addict costs $25,900 per year. Residential drug-treatment programs range from $4,400 to $6,800 a year.
- Drug treatment can cut crime by 80 percent, according to Brown University addiction director Norman Hoffman.
- Long-term drug treatment is as effective as long-term treatment for chronic diseases, according to Dr. Thomas McLellan of the University of Pennsylvania.[54]

CONCLUSION: THE INJUSTICE

In 1988 Congress passed a resolution proclaiming its goal of "a drug-free America by 1995," a panacea yet to happen, indeed, unlikely ever. Our drug policy has preferred such rhetoric to reality and moralism to pragmatism. Drug control officials make medical assertions with no basis in fact or science. Police officers, generals, politicians, and guardians of public morals qualify as drug czars—but not, to date, a single doctor or public health figure. Independent commissions are appointed to evaluate drug policies, only to see their recommendations ignored as politically risky. Our War on Drugs has made matters worse, not better.

In 1998 over 500 health officials, politicians, and educators, including former Secretaries of State Elliot Richardson and George Schultz, sent a letter to UN secretary-general Kofi-Annan declaring, "The global war on drugs is now causing more harm than drug abuse itself," noting that annual revenue generated by illegal drugs is about $400 billion, or the equivalent of roughly 8 percent of total international trade. "This industry," the letter said, "has empowered organized criminals, corrupted governments at all levels, eroded internal security, stimulated violence and distorted both economic markets and moral values. These are the consequences not of drug use per se but of decades of failed and futile drug war policies." In 1980 our country spent $4 billion fighting the drug war. Every year since, drug warriors have told the government's money changers that the current sum is not enough. Now, as of 1999, we spend eight times more, and the drug warriors repeatedly tell us we need to spend still more—and the end is not yet in sight, despite an eightfold increase in drug incarcerations.

Our American economic system relies on a theory that profit motives ultimately control enterprise. During the four decades of the Cold War, we Americans told communist countries, "Black markets are the only thing working in your economies and no matter how severely you oppress people you cannot overpower the profit motive." Now we ignore our own advice. Our drug laws actually provide remunerative training in entrepreneurship for minority youth. Our drug war theory holds that harsh punishments can make students accept minimum wages rather than drop out and clear $1,500 a week selling drugs. It assumes Colombians will give up $500 an acre for producing coca leaves and accept $5 for growing coffee beans. It speculates that enlarging prisons and filling them to overflowing will crush a very profitable industry. Capitalist theory and drug war theory are mutually exclusive. Capitalism has worked; drug prohibition has not. The profit motive explains both.

Drug prohibition has ignored the truly fatal drugs, alcohol and tobacco. Ever harsher sentences for drug trafficking have led only to drug substitution and replacement of adults with juveniles in drug sales. Felonization of adults oils judicial turnstiles, cycling and recycling the poor in and out of their communities to courts and prisons and back again. Felonization ends when our nation's youngest reach adult incorrigibility—a process that pits white Americans and their legal drugs—alcohol and tobacco—against young, poor minorities and their criminalized drugs.

Our War on Drugs has been a civil war, a race war, and a generational war. Demonizing the enemy into POW status only makes the problem worse. If we were fighting a real war that, like Vietnam, strengthened rather than weakened the enemy, we would come to our senses, declare

victory, and abandon the punitive cause for some other approach. Why do
we do differently in this domestic war?

NOTES

1. *New York Times*, A1 (May 26, 1998).

2. 501 U.S. 957(1991).

3. M. Grey, *Wall Street Journal*, A23 (Aug. 26, 1998).

4. J. Schaler, ed., *Drugs* (Amhurst, NY: Prometheus, 1998), 11–13.

5. M. Lyman and G. Potter, *Drugs in Society* (Cincinnati: Anderson, 1991), 23.

6. Id., 62.

7. M. Tonry, *Malign Neglect: Race, Crime and Punishment in America* (New
York: Oxford University Press, 1995), 81–82. See also J. Torruella, "One Judge's
Attempt at a Rational Discussion of the So-Called War on Drugs," 6 *Pub. Int. L.J.*
1, 19 (1996): The war on drugs has had a lopsided impact on minorities. Through-
out the drug war, "non-whites [have been] arrested and imprisoned at four to five
times the rate of whites, even though most drug crimes are committed by whites."
The racist impact of prohibition is further seen when one considers that one in four
African American males is imprisoned or under penal supervision for drug offenses.

8. *San Jose Mercury News*, A12 (Sept. 28, 1992).

9. *Keeping Score: What We Are Getting from Our Federal Drug Control Dollars* (New York: Carnegie Foundation, 1995), 5.

10. Bar of the City of New York, "A Wiser Course: Ending Drug Prohibition,"
June 1994, 2. See, for example, "And Still the Drugs Sit There," *The Economist*,
27 (May 21, 1994) ("Since 1980 America has spent more than $100 billion in the
war on drugs. Despite that, cocaine, heroin and marijuana are as available and as
inexpensive as ever. Drug use fluctuates but is not going away. Indeed, surveys
show that young people now seem increasingly tolerant of drugs and less worried
about the health effects of them, if used in moderation"). Despite law enforcement
efforts, use of even the so-called hard drugs, like heroin, has failed to disappear.
T. Gabriel, "Heroin Finds a New Market along Cutting Edge of Style," *N.Y. Times*
1, (May 8, 1994) (reporting that "high-grade heroin that can be smoked rather
than injected has caught on, both coasts, in circles whose habits often set trends—
young people piloting the fast lane in the film, rock and fashion industries").

11. See James Brooke, "In Colombia, One Victory in a Long War," *New York
Times*, A12 (Dec. 3, 1993) (quoting Bogotá prosecutor as saying, "It is a secret for
no one that 99 percent of official [Colombian] institutions have problems with
[drug] infiltration"). Faced with the devastation wrought by the "War on Drugs,"
Colombians are calling for drug legalization. James Brooke, "Colombians Press for
Legalization of Cocaine," *New York Times*, 6 (Feb. 20, 1994) (reporting that "influential opinion makers in Colombia, the world's largest cocaine producer, are
increasingly backing . . . legalization"). Joseph B. Treaster, "Use of Drugs Is Legalized by Colombia," *New York Times*, 3 (May 7, 1994). But see James Brooke,
"Colombia Reimposes Curbs on Marijuana and Cocaine," *New York Times*, A14
(June 2, 1994) (reporting that Colombian president Trujillo used his powers of
decree to impose "a series of restrictions that essentially limit drug consumption to
private residence where children are not present").

12. *Keeping Score.*

13. E. Nadelmann, "Drug Prohibition in the U.S.," 245 *Science*, 940 (1989).

14. *Keeping Score.*

15. Grinspoon and J. Bakalar, "The War on Drugs—A Peace Proposal," 330 *New Eng. J. Med.*, 357 and n. 2 (1994) (citing Federal Bureau of Investigation, *Crime in the United States* (1991). Almost one-quarter of these arrests is for simple possession of marijuana. Id. Indeed, being arrested for simple possession of marijuana is "the fourth most common cause of arrest in the United States." Id. Ironically, studies indicate that marijuana is the number one cash crop in the United States. Katherine Bishop, "Front in Marijuana War: Business Records," *New York Times*, B6 (May 24, 1991). See also, re the Rand study, M. Massing, *The Fix* (New York: Simon and Schuster, 1998), 50.

16. Drugs and Crime Data Center and Clearinghouse, *Fact Sheet: Drug Data Summary* 1, April 1, 1994.

17. Telephone interview with Todd R. Clear, professor of criminal justice, Rutgers University (Apr. 28, 1994).

18. Joseph A. Califano, Jr., "A Punishment-Only Prison Policy," *America*, 3–6 (Feb. 21, 1998).

19. "Department of Justice Report: Two-Thirds of Non-Violent Offenders Serving Mandatory Minimum Sentences," *The Drug Policy Letter*, 28 (Spring 1994); Todd R. Clear, "Tougher Is Dumber,"*New York Times*, A1, 21 (Dec. 12, 1993); Michael deCourcy Hinds, "Feeling Prisons' Costs, Governors Weigh Alternatives," *New York Times*, A17 (Aug. 7, 1992). See also N. Morris, "Teenage Violence and Drug Use," 31 *Valpo. L.R.* 547, 548 (1997) (describing the "ready availability" of drugs within prisons).

20. J. Inciardi and W. Pottieger, "Kids, Crack and Crime," 21 *J. Drug Issues*, 266–267 (1991).

21. T. Meares, "It's a Question of Connections," 31 *Val. L.R.*, 579, 589 (1997).

22. E. Currie, *Crime and Punishment in America* 19 (New York: Holt, 1998).

23. Califano, "Punishment," 3.

24. See, for example, H. Kleber, "Our Current Approach to Drug Abuse—Progress, Problems, Proposals," 330 *New Eng. J. Med.*, 361 (1994) ("Some drug-abuse experts and historians agree that we are in the declining phase of a drug epidemic that began about 30 years ago"). But see "Drug Use Increasing despite Federal War," *Gannet Suburban Newspapers*, 16A (May 12, 1994) (quoting White House drug policy director Lee Brown as saying things are "not getting any better").

25. See Douglas Jehl, "Clinton to Use Drug Plan to Fight Crime," *New York Times*, D20 (Feb. 10, 1994) (reporting that experts estimate that 4 to 6 million Americans are heavy drug users); "Drug Use Increasing Despite Federal War" (reporting that recent federal report found heroin use has increased in the Southwest, West, and part of the South, marijuana use continues to rise nationally, cocaine use remains stable; reporting that "the number of people using drugs monthly dropped about 21 percent from 1991 to 1992—from 14.5 million to 11.4 million" but that "the number of hard-core users—about 2.7 million people who consume the bulk of the nation's $49 billion worth of drugs annually—hasn't changed much since 1988").

26. Joseph B. Treaster, "Survey Finds Marijuana Use Is Up in High Schools," New York Times, A1, A14 (Feb. 1, 1994).

27. Kleber, "Approach," 361.

28. Letter to the Editor, "Put Drug War Price at $500 Billion," *New York Times*, A22 (July 1, 1992) (Ernest Drucker and Peter R. Arno, respectively, professor and associate professor of epidemiology and social medicine at Albert Einstein College of Medicine); see also Joseph P. Treaster, "Echos of Prohibition: 20 Years of War on Drugs, and No Victory Yet," *New York Times*, sec. 4, 7 (June 14, 1992); James Ostrowski, "Thinking about Drug Legalization," Cato Institute Policy Analysis No. 121, May 25, 1989, 6 ("there is a real danger that escalating the war on drugs would squander much of the nation's wealth").

29. Grinspoon and Bakalar, "War on Drugs," 358 ("Public-opinion surveys also suggest that few people who do not now use illicit drugs would use them if the laws changed. . . . Only 2 percent of people who do not use cocaine say they might try it if it were legalized, and 93% state vehemently that they would not").

30. See, for example, David T. Courtwright, "Should We Legalize Drugs? History Answers No," 44 *Amer. Heritage* 41, 50 (1993); Joseph A. Califano, Jr., "Battle Lines in the War on Drugs: No, Fight Harder," *New York Times*, A27 (Dec. 15, 1993). Many proponents of the current prohibitionist laws argue that users of psychoactive substances would not be able to control their consumption if such substances were legalized and readily available. For example, Letter to the Editor, "Can Drugs Be Used Only in Moderation?" *New York Times*, A28 (Feb. 25, 1994) (Philip J. Pauly, associate professor of the history of science at Rutgers University, argues that it is unlikely that "recreational users of cocaine and heroin could indulge 'moderately' as a part of genteel social behavior"); see also Letter to the Editor, "Why Marijuana Should Remain Illegal," *New York Times*, sec. 1, 22 (Feb. 26, 1994) (Stephen H. Greene, acting administrator of the DEA, argues that marijuana should continue to be prohibited, in part because users would not be content with marijuana distribution by a "health regulator").

31. For example, Letter to the Editor, "Can Drugs Be Used Only in Moderation?"

32. P. Reuter, G. Crawford, and J. Case, *Sealing the Borders* (Santa Monica, CA: Rand Corp., 1998). See also S. Rotella, *Underworlds and Politics at the U.S. Mexican Border* (New York: Norton, 1998).

33. E. Bertram and K. Sharpe, "The Drug War's Phony Fix," *The Nation*, 18–19 (Apr. 28, 1997).

34. Id.

35. E. Nadelmann, "Drug Prohibition," 945.

36. H. Packer, *The Limits of the Criminal Sanction* (Stanford, CA: Stanford University Press, 1968), 277–282.

37. "The Nation's Toughest Drug Laws: Evaluating the New York Experience," Report of the Bar Association of New York (1978). See also V. Kappeler, et al., *The Mythology of Crime* (Prospect Heights, IL: Waveland Press), 178.

38. Human Rights Watch Report, No. 2, Mar. 1997.

39. Nadelmann, "Drug Prohibition, 941.

40. Pennsylvania Crime Commission Annual Report (1987).

41. *Crime Control Digest*, 2–3 (Apr. 3, 1998).

42. M. Kleiman, "Reducing Dealing Among Adolescents," 31 *Val. L.R.*, 551, 556 (1997).

43. Rand Drug Policy Research Center, "*Are* Mandatory Minimum Sentences Cost Effective?" (Santa Monica, CA: Rand Corp., 1997), 1–2.

44. Grinspoon and Bakalar, "The War on Drugs." See also, re the Rand study, M. Massing, *The Fix* (New York: Simon and Schuster, 1998), 50.

45. Massing, *The Fix*, 50.

46. Rand Corp., "Mandatory," 3.

47. J. Torruella, "One Judge's Attempt at a Rational Discussion of the So-Called War on Drugs," 6 *Pub. Int. L.J.*, 1, 12 (1996).

48. Shepherd Smith, "Controlled Substance War Needs Best Fighters: Parents," *Arizona Republic*, B7 (May 15, 1998).

49. Jon Kyl, "White House Drug Policy," *Arizona Republic*, B4 (May 29, 1998).

50. "Strong Stuff," *New York Times Magazine* (Mar. 22, 1998). See also W. Bennett, *Body Count* (New York: Simon and Schuster, 1996).

51. *New York Times Magazine* (Mar. 22, 1998). See also Bennett, *Body Count*, 1996.

52. Joseph Califano, "A Punishment—Only Prison Policy," *America*, 3 (Feb. 21, 1998).

53. Id.

54. "Treating the Addict Works," *Arizona Republic*, A4 (Mar. 18, 1998).

7

PRISONS AND COUNTERPRODUCTIVITY

Prison building is not Nation building.
—Daniel Feldman, Assemblyman, New York

In *Bonfire of the Vanities*, Tom Wolfe describes a criminal court in the Bronx that could be anywhere in America in the year 2000:

Every year forty thousand people, forty thousand incompetents, dimwits, alcoholics, psychopaths, knockabouts, good souls driven to some terminal anger, and people who could only be described as stone evil, were arrested in the Bronx. Seven thousand of them were indicted and arraigned, then they entered the maw of the criminal justice system. . . . And to what end? The same stupid, dismal, pathetic, horrifying crimes were committed day in and day out, all the same. . . . One thing was accomplished for sure. The system was fed, and those vans brought in the chow.

All judges have seen this recurring scenario. Frustration can lead to recourse to lengthy prison sentences as a supposed remedy for this turnstile. In *State v. Mitcham*, a child molestation case, where an Arizona trial judge sentenced the defendant to 142 years in prison, the majority of appellate judges rejected a claim of excessive sentence. I wrote separately, in part, as follows:

From one perspective, this sentence length is not on its face disproportionate to other draconian sentences already approved on appeal in this state. *See e.g. Taylor,*

(2,975 years); Rice, (525 years); Williams (95 years). However other considerations point in another direction. This sentence is well beyond the life sentence for first degree murder, a crime one class more severe than the crimes here. . . . Unlike a homicide inmate, Mitcham cannot be released on any basis, so he will die in prison long after he has ceased to be a criminal threat. Criminality, largely a matter of youth, declines dramatically after age 30. Prison terms extending beyond criminality effectively render inmates permanent residents in a state-supported old folk's home.

Warehousing these elderly criminals is expensive. Statistically, Mitcham can expect to live to age 67. If so, he will remain in Arizona's prison system for another 37 years. At a conservative 1996 figure of $20,000 for his maintenance, the cost to taxpayers of his confinement will greatly surpass $740,000. Our penal policy may soon require fencing the Grand Canyon.[1]

Arizona is not unusual in looking primarily to prisons to solve the crime problem. Our entire country now indulges in prison as the prime solution to crime. Albert Blumstein, one of our foremost criminologists, observes that our mind-set regarding crime and prisons reflects a "pre-Galileo, prison-centric" universe, where incarceration has become the chief and only recourse to the crime problem.

While prison is appropriate for most violent criminals, its ability to reduce crime is overrated to the point of myth. Here are some of the myths.

MYTH 1: High imprisonment rates produce low crime rates.

Actually, states with the lowest crime rates have lowest imprisonment rates. Conversely, states with the highest crime rates have highest imprisonment rates.

MYTH 2: Crime rates are high because we have not been locking up enough criminals.

The number of prisoners has more than doubled in the past decade. The United States now vies with Russia as the world leader in incarceration rates.

MYTH 3: Longer prison sentences reduce recidivism.

Lengths of imprisonment and inmate recidivism rates are unrelated. Inmates released early from prison have the same or lower recidivism rates as those who serve full terms. Offenders placed on probation instead of prison have lower rearrest rates.

MYTH 4: Inmates are now serving shorter prison terms than before.

From 1923 to the 1970s the average national length of stay for all prisoners for all crimes collectively was about two years. Because of harsher sentencing policies adopted in the 1980s, the average length of stay has risen threefold and will continue to rise over the next years.

MYTH 5: Offenders released from prison are responsible for most of the serious crimes committed each year.

Inmates released from prison in any given year account for only 3–5 percent of all arrests for serious crimes.

MYTH 6: Most offenders sentenced to prison are violent and dangerous criminals.

Only 25 percent of all imprisoned offenders have been convicted of a violent crime. Most prisoners have committed nonviolent crimes with little financial loss. In most prison systems, fewer than 20 percent of inmates require maximum custody.

MYTH 7: The murder rate is at an all-time high.

Although the United States has a high murder rate compared to other industrialized nations, the rate has not fluctuated much in the past twenty years. The current rate of 9.3 murders per 100,000 population is almost identical to the rate of 9.4 in 1973.[2]

Our most enduring myth is that prisons hold the singular answer to crime. They don't. At best, prison is a costly after-the-fact reaction to crime largely incapable of preventing it and uniquely able to make it worse. Building more prisons as the main way to address crime is like building more graveyards to address a fatal disease.

HISTORY OF THE PRISON MOVEMENT

Our prison system shows volatile swings in public mood. We have long been ambivalent about its purposes. We want a penal system that visits harm upon the guilty (*retribution*); makes offenders law-abiding (*rehabilitation*); dissuades would-be offenders (*deterrence*); protects the innocent (*incapacitation*); and enables criminals to become productive citizens (*reintegration*). We have wanted these goals without violating our social conscience (*humane treatment*), jeopardizing law (*constitutional rights*), or emptying the treasury (*cost-effective*). Because these competing public expectations cannot be met all at once in a penal panacea, first one and then the others dominate policymakers' attention.

Our first citizens saw colonial criminal laws as actually contributing to criminal behavior. They believed that making those laws more humane would diminish crime and also believed that extreme British punishments encouraged crime. The colonists decided that punishments should be more temperate and proceeded under this premise until by the 1820s they concluded that less brutal punishment, including imprisonment, did not eliminate crime either.

Imprisonment played a minor role until the mid-nineteenth century. Colonists initially used fines, whippings, branding, letter wearing, ear cropping, the pillory stocks, banishment, and the gallows. Many contrary factors shaped the emerging nineteenth-century prison. Revulsion toward hangings, whippings, mutilation, and other extreme punishments grew as the community questioned their deterrent effect. People who believed that criminals failed to be socialized by family and church assumed they could be redeemed in a well-regimented, corruption-free environment.

Pennsylvania led the way in building a new kind of prison—a monastery for convicted criminals—by turning part of Philadelphia's old Walnut Street jail into a "penitentiary," a place of penance, with solitary confinement cells for serious offenders, with a goal of moral and spiritual reform where prisoners, like monks, lived alone day and night. In the 1820s, rival prison systems sprang up. Under the New York or Auburn plan, prisoners slept in solitary cells at night and labored together during the day. Auburn's organized prison labor served as a model for later European and American prisons.

The nineteenth-century prison saved few souls and spared few bodies. Some wardens came to rely heavily on the whip. Others resorted to harsher disciplines like hanging prisoners by their thumbs or squeezing them into metal yokes. After the Civil War many prisoners came from new immigrant groups, notably, the Irish. Legislators with no sympathy for foreigners saw little reason for making prisons anything but custodial. As bad as conditions were, they seemed good enough for the Irish. The last third of the nineteenth century saw a new prison trend that continued through the first two-thirds of the twentieth: individualized punishment, rehabilitation and innovations such as the indeterminate sentence, parole, probation, and flexible release, all motivated by a rehabilitative goal.[3]

THE REHABILITATIVE GOAL

Postwar treatment interest led to reform-oriented correctional institutions emphasizing rehabilitation. The low crime rate in the 1950s, declining for some types of crime, engendered rehabilitative optimism. Psychological treatment, influenced by psychoanalytic professionals from Europe, increased the role of behavioral experts working with the assumption that offenders are psychologically disturbed and need therapeutic treatment for the emotional roots of their crime.

By 1965 the major purpose of the prison was accepted as rehabilitation. Through a variety of reeducative programs the prison was expected to turn the malefactor into a productive citizen. Legislatures set the maximum prison term for a particular offense and, rarely, also the minimum. Within that range the sentencing judge would order an indeterminate sentence of the maximum years that the prisoner could be imprisoned. A parole board based its release decisions on gravity of the crime, behavior in prison, and prediction of likely success after release. Early parole became the norm. Most prisoners served approximately one-third the indeterminate sentence imposed.

Indeterminate sentencing reflects a belief in this rehabilitative possibility. Incarceration in this theory would train prisoners for a life free of crime, with educative and vocational training and psychological techniques to turn them into lawful citizens once and for all time. This idealistic view is now decidedly on the decline.

INCAPACITATION

By the 1960s staggering criminal caseloads prevented meaningful probation and parole, and limited resources prevented true prison reformation. A ratio of one psychiatrist per 1,000 prisoners dashed any realistic chance of rehabilitation. The "Big Houses" holding between 2,000 and 4,000 inmates showed the impotence of the rehabilitation goal.

During the late 1960s a full-scale attack began to challenge this rehabilitative ideal, led by research maintaining that "nothing works," that rehabilitative purposes, fine in principle, fail in practice. This depressing view reflected difficulties of testing the conduct of discharged offenders in relation to their prison experience, but it had much popular appeal. Rehabilitative sentencing reform accordingly became a focus of political and academic unrest, though for sharply different reasons.[4] As Chapter 1 shows in detail, in 1984 Congress passed comprehensive federal sentencing reforms with guideline sentences for all federal offenses, with specific criteria limiting judicial discretion to rigid ranges, reflecting a shift from rehabilitation to retribution. Parole was effectively eliminated. Prosecutors for the first time could appeal sentences falling short of the guidelines.

By the mid-1970s, faith in rehabilitation had almost totally collapsed. The death knell came in a 1974 study by sociologist Robert Martinson, whose examination of 200 prison programs found little value in rehabilitation.[5] In its place came the thinking exemplified by criminologist James Q. Wilson: the purpose of prison is not to rehabilitate but to isolate and punish—in a word, incapacitation.[6]

Beginning with the law-and-order emphasis of the Nixon administration and continuing under the Reagan, Bush, and Clinton administrations, an ambitious and expensive incapacitative prison construction boom swept the country and continues into our new century. Our former rehabilitative aspirations have waned to the point where it is fashionable to say "nothing works" to reform criminals. The fact of the matter is that it is difficult to measure reformation. Some prisoners mature to a conforming life, others are confirmed in their criminality, and the line—and the time spread—between the two is unclear.

Despite the explosion in prison population in the last quarter century, despite an incarceration rate five to ten times greater than that of other industrialized nations, and despite the fact that California, New York, Texas, and Florida each has a prison population among the world's seven largest penal systems, the popular assumption still stands that our courts treat convicted criminals too leniently. This assumed leniency continues to incite more prison construction. Rehabilitation has lost credibility, and incapacitation has become our dominant justification for imprisonment, pushing successive decades of rampant prison construction. Now the primary penal goal is simply to distance the offender from the community without efforts at rehabilitation or reformation. Our dominant national penology now is atomistic. The walls of prison stand as a black box into which citizens disappear for a time and later emerge, changed or not. The number of black boxes and the potential reformation within them are relatively unimportant to justice officials; they are important only for the individuals in the process—a perspective that ignores the impact of indiscreet incarceration upon families, communities, economics, and recidivism rates.

Prisoners have their own views of current incapacitation practices:

The idea is to make prison a secular hell on earth—a place where the young potential felon will fear to go, where the ex-con will fear to return. But an underlying theme is that "these people" are irredeemable "predators" (i.e., "animals"), who are without worth. Why, then, provide them with the opportunity to rehabilitate—or give them any hope? Still, what really bothers me is knowing that many thousands of the young men entering prison now may never get that "last chance to change." And more disturbing to my mind are the long "no hope" sentences given to so many young men entering prison now—they can be given to people as young as thirteen and fourteen.[7]

PRISON DEMOGRAPHICS: WHO IS BEHIND BARS

In his 1831 visit to our country, Alexis de Tocqueville observed that American social reformers were in a grip of a "monomania" belief that prisons were a "remedy for all the evils of society." Our monomania has only worsened. The 1998 report from the Bureau of Justice Statistics shows that our prison population continues to grow steadily despite the fact that rates of reported crime have fallen for each of the last six years, with our prisons holding more people than any other country of the world. One of every 150 American residents in 1999 is behind bars, and our incarceration rate of 668 inmates per 100,000 residents is 5 to 10 times the rate in Canada and nearly 20 times the rate in Japan. Our inmates have quadrupled since 1980 and doubled since 1985; only Russia imprisons at a higher rate than we do.

There is good reason to question whether this policy of mass incarceration has produced our decline in crime. In some places like New York where crime has dropped most, the incarceration rate is relatively low, and in many Southern states generally high incarceration rates coexist with high crime rates. The level of our violent crime in 1999 is still about the same as 15 years previous, when far fewer inmates were in jails and prisons. Those populations have soared not because the police are catching more violent criminals but because of mandatory and generally longer sentences. The single largest imprisoned crime class—drug offenders—has quadrupled at a rate nearly twice the imprisonment rate for violent criminals. More than 400,000 Americans are now imprisoned simply for non-violent drug offenses, a number greater than in the prisons in England, France and Germany combined, without any decline in the overall number of drug users, whose population has stayed constant since 1988.

Prison's toll on the black community has been especially severe. Though they comprise only 12 percent of the entire population, they constitute nearly half the total number of inmates. One in every 12 black men aged between 25 and 29 is behind bars, 10 times the rate for whites, and most of that black population is imprisoned not for violence but for drugs, a disparity compounded by disparate penalties for blacks' crack cocaine by comparison with the powdered cocaine preferred by whites. By 2000 roughly 1 in 10 black men will be in prison, unable to work, pay taxes, care for their children, or vote, with one in seven permanently disenfranchised.

These data suggest that our policy of mass incarceration has substituted for public social policy in urban neighborhoods. Our politicians have dealt with difficult social and economic problems with the sledgehammer sensitivity of the criminal justice system, as though incarceration could solve inner city economic and social problems. The cost of solving social problems by imprisonment has been high for all citizens even beyond the inner city. Ballooning prison budgets have taken money from education, job training and other social programs which address crime causes more economically and permanently than imprisonment.[8]

One of every twenty U.S. residents born today will spend time in prison if our crime, incarceration, and death rates remain constant. For minority males, the risk of prison is much greater. Every black male in our country in 1999 has greater than a one-in-four chance of prison during his lifetime. The chance for Hispanic males is 16 percent, compared with 4.4 percent for Anglo males. These projections by the Bureau of Justice Statistics show the fate of a hypothetical population of newborns. Under present policies an estimated 5.1 percent of those born today—9 percent of males and 1.1 percent of females—will serve time in a state or federal prison.[9]

The average age of inmates coming into prison is thirty, although criminal activity peaks between the ages of sixteen and twenty-two. As criminals age, their crimes decrease. One way to observe this phenomenon is to compare recidivism rates and age. About 21.8 percent of those eighteen to twenty-four years old at release return to prison within the first year.

Prison Populations (the highest- and lowest-ranking prison populations by number of inmates and incarceration rate, as of June 30, 1998)[10]

Number of Inmates		Incarceration Rate*	
Highest		Highest	
1. California	158,742	1. Lousiana	709
2. Texas	143,299	2. Texas	700
3. Federal	118,908	3. Oklahoma	629
4. New York	70,723	4. Mississippi	547
5. Florida	66,280	5. South Carolina	543
Lowest		Lowest	
1. North Dakota	883	1. Minnesota	117
2. Vermont	1,312	2. Maine	121
3. Wyoming	1,424	3. North Dakota	126
4. Maine	1,634	4. Vermont	170
5. New Hampshire	2,165	5. New Hampshire	183

*Note: Sentenced prisoners per 100,000 state residents.

Source: Bureau of Justice Statistics.

About 49.9 percent of those eighteen to twenty-four years old at release return to prison within seven years. The statistics drastically differ for older inmates. For released prisoners above the age of forty-five, only 2.1 percent are back in prison within the first year, and 12.4 percent return within seven years. Avertable recidivists, or inmates who would not commit their recidivist act had they served their full initial sentence, are young; 66.1 percent of them are twenty-nine or younger. Only 3.3 percent of recidivists are older than fifty years. Criminality is then mostly a matter of youth rather than age. But if males fifteen to twenty-four years old commit the largest age-related crime, and the average prison inmate is thirty years old, we are presently incarcerating offenders on the downside of their criminal careers.

Prisoners are poorly educated. Most of them do not have high school degrees. The average inmate left school in the tenth grade and tests at the 6.7 grade level. Fully 42 percent of inmates are functionally illiterate, reading at or below the fifth grade level. They are also poor and under-employed. One-third are unemployed when arrested. More than half have annual incomes less than $10,000. They abuse alcohol and drugs. More than half are under the influence of drugs, alcohol, or both at the times of their crimes. More than 40 percent used drugs before committing the crime leading to their incarceration, but alcohol is a far greater factor than drugs. Most prisoners grew up in less-than-ideal environments; single mothers raised the majority. Many inmates were sexually abused as children.

These statistics outline the typical prisoner: a poor young male from a troubled home, black or Hispanic, lacking a high school diploma and steady employment, with an alcohol or drug problem and an unsteady childhood. Whatever the cause, our prisons and jails, particularly the larger, maximum-security institutions, now effectively segregate from society the young, disturbed black and Hispanic male underclass.

PRISON COSTS

Nationwide spending on corrections has increased faster than any other government category in the past decade. Many states now spend more on corrections than any other single budget item. Prison has become not only our ersatz social policy but also our modern public works program. National spending on corrections has risen three times as fast as military spending over the last twenty years. Seventy percent of all the prison space in use today was built since 1985. By contrast, only 11 percent of our nation's classrooms were built during the 1980s.[11]

To fund jails and prisons, state and local governments have diverted money from education. California is typical. Fifteen years ago, 3 percent of its budget went to prisons, with 18 percent for higher education. In 1994, it spent 8 percent of its budget on prisons and 8 percent on higher education. Between 1994 and 1995 the overrun in corrections spending was more than the entire increase in higher education.[12] Since the passage of Proposition 13, California has had to curtail its capital investments in everything except prisons. Since 1984, the state has opened twenty-one of them, bringing its portfolio to thirty-three. A prison guard in 1999 makes about $51,000 a year in California, while a first-year professor in its once famous university system earns $41,000. In the national rankings of state education spending per pupil, California has slipped to forty-third. In 1994, the National Assessment of Education Progress found that only 18 percent of California's fourth graders could read proficiently, placing the state just ahead of Louisiana.[13] Prison spending has impaired education, our best anticrime strategy.

The average cost of building a new cell in 1999 dollars is $54,000. Because states usually pay for prison construction by borrowing money, debt service often doubles or triples the original costs. With interest on the debt, the real cost of a new cell exceeds $100,000. The capital outlay represents a long-term financial commitment. Every $100 million of new prison construction entails $1.6 billion in expenditures over the next three decades. Operating a state prison cell averages a minimum of $25,000 per prisoner per year in 1999 dollars. The federal prison system uses all of the taxes paid each year by three average families to keep one inmate in prison for a year. In Delaware, the annual taxes of eighteen average residents are needed to house one prisoner for a single year.

Already, California and Florida spend more to incarcerate people than to educate their college-age populations. In California, where the number of prisoners has grown from 19,000 two decades ago to 150,000 today, the state confronts voters' refusal to approve more money for prison construction and an expected huge influx of inmates as tougher sentencing laws take effect. The California Department of Corrections has projected that it will run out of space by 2001.[14]

OLDER PRISONERS

Because of ever-lengthening sentences our nation's prisons are becoming old folks' homes. The graying prison population doubles every four years. By 1996, prisons housed almost 30,000 prisoners over age sixty. With the passage of mandatory sentences and "three strikes" laws, the number of elderly inmates is rising sharply. Between 1986 and 1995, the proportion of prisoners serving life sentences or sentences of twenty years or more increased by nearly half, from 17 to 25 percent. By the year 2000, there may be more than 90,000 prison inmates over the age of sixty-five, with correspondingly greater—and more expensive—medical needs.[15] In California alone, the "three strikes" law will increase the number of geriatric inmates from 5,000 in 1994 to 126,400 in the year 2020.

The statistical chance that a typical elder prisoner will commit a violent crime upon release is extremely low. One factor consistently associated with criminal behavior is age, which is the surest predictor of recidivism. The two variables vary inversely. Criminal behavior is heavily hormonal: it begins at age sixteen and peaks by age twenty-three. The probability of a person's committing a crime and being sentenced to prison for the first time declines steadily with age. About two-thirds of all arrests occur for persons under the age of thirty. The majority of violent crimes as well as property crimes occurs in the late teenage years and early twenties. The criminal cohort begins to desist from property crimes after age eighteen and from violent crimes after age twenty-two. By the time they become high-rate serious offenders, many will have reached ages where they will quit offending even without incarceration, so their extended confinement in prison results in little but very expensive crime prevention. Life imprisonment for a person aged fifty is a senseless waste of tax money. Because the average age of a person first admitted to prison is thirty and increasing, a substantial proportion of incoming prisoners is incarcerated well beyond the peak of their criminal behavior. Their lengthy incarceration therefore has little effect on the crime rate but great effect on the public treasury.

Because of health care costs and inmates' general poor health, the upkeep of an elderly inmate can triple that of a younger inmate. At the Louisiana State Penitentiary in Angola, which has an old folks' ward for inmates, warden Frank Blackburn says he personally knew of "25 to 50 longtermers that I would release immediately because there is no doubt they are rehabilitated. . . . There are just too many people in prison today as tax burdens who do not need to be there."[16] According to the Criminal Justice Institute, the annual cost for maintenance of inmates over sixty in 1998 dollars is almost $69,000, compared to the national average of $25,000 for other inmates. The tax cost of maintaining a graying prison population will eventually become staggering.

Wholesale incarceration of aged inmates involves high expense and small return in prevention. Typical young adult offenders in their twenties are particularly unsuitable for a long prison sentence: left to their own devices, most will quit offending soon independently of imprisonment. Efficiency suggests that we concentrate scarce prison resources on confirmed violent offenders, twenty-five years and over, who have survived the shakedown period of their early twenties.

LENIENCY?

Tough-on-crime politicians call for still more prisons, longer sentences, and harsher treatment of juvenile offenders, based on a widely accepted fiction, fanned by media crime saturation, that goes like this: the reason violent crime continues to plague us is that our justice system is far too lenient. Locking up more people for longer terms, the theory runs, reduces crime dramatically. The justice system lets criminals off too easily and puts them back on the streets to plunder with impunity. In his late 1996 presidential campaign, Bob Dole described the American criminal justice system as a "liberal-leaning laboratory of leniency."

The only answer from this perspective is simple: we must greatly increase the number of people behind bars, and we should make life harder for them while they are there. The National Rifle Association, for example, says we need 250,000 new prison cells to "build our way out of the crime problem," which means cracking down especially hard on juvenile offenders, now "coddled" by a justice system that clings to a discredited belief in rehabilitation.[17]

Many uninformed Americans conclude, in this same vein, that convicted criminals get off easily. They are partially right but for other reasons. Some offenders get off lightly for serious crime, while others pay too great a price for lesser offenses, as can be seen by comparing the federal time served by murders to that of first-time drug offenders. In 1992, federal prisons held about 1,800 inmates convicted of murder, serving an average time of 4.5 years. That same year the same federal prisons held 12,727 nonviolent, first-time drug offenders, serving an average actual sentence of 6.5 years. That disparity continues.

In the last decade the rate of incarceration nearly doubled. By the end of 1998, one of every 150 Americans was in prison or jail, compared to one of every 320 a decade earlier. The rate of incarceration has grown from 313 inmates per 100,000 U.S. residents in 1985 to 668 inmates per 100,000 in 1999. Our imprisonment rate now vies with Russia to lead the world. It is five times the rate of Canada and Australia and seven times the rate of most European democracies. The population of Americans incarcerated on any given day would constitute the sixth largest city in the country, equal to the total combined populations of Seattle, Cleveland, and Denver. Although the conservative coalition blames our court system for being soft on criminals, no other country except Russia uses prisons so harshly. Apart from Russia, Americans punish crime, particularly property and drug crimes, more severely than any other country. The 1.8 million Americans in prisons and jails in 1999 represent an increase of about 300 percent since the early 1970s.[18]

Contrary to the leniency claim, no other nation treats people who commit nonviolent crimes as indiscriminately as we do. In a national survey, prison wardens felt that, on average, half of the offenders under their supervision could be released without endangering the public.[19] Politicians have not heard their message. Over the past two decades we have hosted the biggest prison construction boom in history, to the point where, in the past decade alone, the number of federal and state inmates has doubled, to nearly one million, and the local jail population has nearly tripled. Washington state, for instance, has witnessed a 79 percent increase in prison capacity, though the state population has grown just 18 percent. "At that rate," says Governor Mike Lowry, "everyone in Washington State will be working—or in—prison by 2056."

Our War on Drugs has spurred most of this prison growth. A recent Texas study of its sentencing patterns found that 77 percent of all prison admissions were for nonviolent crimes such as drugs. Indeed, the most frequent crime resulting in a prison sentence today is simple drug possession. For such an offender the rehabilitative value of a prison cell is questionable given the prevalence of drugs inside prison. Incapacitation requires that prisoners take their crimes off the street, but in the case of drugs, prisons do little or nothing to reduce their availability. In most other countries, a criminal who commits a nonviolent offense such as drug possession receives a shorter prison term or a noncustodial sanction such as a fine or community service.

Violent offenders cause little of the recent prison increase. Fully 84 percent of the increase in prison admissions since 1980 is for nonviolent offenders. A person arrested for a drug offense in 1995 was five times more likely to go to prison than a similar person arrested in 1980. So are we too lenient? Not regarding our incarceration rate or the severity of the sentences imposed, but only regarding the sentences actually served by violent offenders.[20]

THREE STRIKES AND THEIR EFFECTS

Many states have adopted "three strikes and you're out" laws, with a third felony conviction resulting in life imprisonment, as well as mandatory lengthy prison sentences for nonviolent crimes like drugs. Both these innovations are counterproductive. The first downside is proportionality. Three-strikes laws reflect the deterrence-incapacitation trend, which abandons proportionality between the harm caused and the punishment prescribed. When this law addresses relatively minor property offenders sent to prison for twenty-five years to life, the proportionality claim evaporates. The major policy goal of the three-strikes law was to decrease serious crime, a goal achieved, in theory, by long-term incapacitation of hard-core offenders. Yet a small percentage of offenders commits a disproportionately large number of major crimes. Logically, these offenders, rather than nonviolent first offenders, should be the primary targets of a strict penal policy. But a large percentage of the present prison population, including three-strikers, is incarcerated only for nonviolent property crimes.

Waiting until someone has been convicted three times means punishing too many older criminals and too few young predators, who pose the greatest threat. The more strictly these laws are enforced, the more that violent inmates get pushed out of prisons. As of 1990, almost forty states were under court order to relieve prison overcrowding by releasing prisoners. At the end of 1996, state prisons were operating from 16 to 24 percent over capacity; federal prisons were 25 percent above capacity. One in seven state facilities is overcrowded. In California, convicted prisoners in county jails serve only 25 percent of their sentences because jails overflow with people awaiting trial. Though such revelations cause understandable public outrage, the public doesn't understand that the partisan debate is largely symbolic.

Treating petty thieves and drug users as if they were killers results in killers being treated too leniently. The conservative Cato Institute concluded that mandatory sentences, like three-strikes laws, are the best thing for violent criminals, from their point of view, because overcrowding forces their early release. Typically, mandatory sentences apply to drug users and petty thieves instead of dangerous predators. Upward of 70 percent of the third strikes in the first two years of the California three-strikes law were nonviolent. The proportion of *violent* offenders sentenced has been relatively low. As of 1995, more people had been sentenced under California's three-strikes law for simple marijuana possession than for murder, rape, and kidnapping combined and more for drug possession generally than for all violent offenses.[21] More than twice as many marijuana possessors (192) have been sentenced for second and third strikes in California as for murder (4) rape (25) and kidnapping (24). Eighty-five percent of all offenders sentenced under this law are sentenced for nonviolent offenses. When the final version of the three-strikes law included burglary as one of the crimes eligible for three-strikes treatment, the statute tripled the scope of the law and extended long mandatory sentences to a population consisting of two-thirds nonviolent offenders.[22]

Drug use is the most common third strike; nationally, nearly a third of those in prison are held for drug offenses, as compared to less than 10 percent in 1980. Time served for violent crimes has decreased with mandatory drug minimums. Dangerous criminals are regularly released to make room for far less serious offenders incarcerated under burgeoning mandatory sentences. The most studied case is Florida, where—despite the addition of 25,000 new prison beds—a huge influx of drug offenders during the 1980s caused massive prison overcrowding, forcing an early-release program that deposited tens of thousands of offenders without mandatory sentences onto the streets, including many violent criminals, even robbers and rapists.[23]

In Florida, as the number of drug offenders serving mandated sentences has increased, the average prison stay for all prisoners has dropped to sixteen months. Judge Lawrence Irving, a Reagan appointee who quit the bench in frustration over the sentencing laws, has complained, "You've got murderers who get out sooner than some kid who did some stupid thing with drugs." Every time a nonviolent third-striker goes to jail or prison for twenty-five years to life, other criminals, younger than the third-striker and more prone to violence, must be released to make room. According to Judge Burton Katz, young, violent, and dangerous felons are being paroled because their early release frees the space required to incarcerate, for twenty-five years to life, the pizza thief and the department store thief and the drug addict on the corner. As a group, according to Katz, the three-strikes population is less dangerous than the young men who have committed violent first felonies.[24]

The basic issue in addressing a three-strikes rule from the viewpoint of incapacitation should be the anticipated future duration of the criminal career of offenders after they commit their third strike. A three-strikes offender in his or her twenties is very unlikely to continue as a threat beyond age fifty, when the prisoner still has a future life expectancy—and future prison occupancy—of more than twenty-five years. That represents a cost to the taxpayers of about half a million dollars for each such offender, who is—at that time—almost certainly no longer a threat to anyone.

Such long criminal careers are even more unlikely for property offenders, whose careers tend to be shorter. It is important to resist the temptation to add additional offenses to three-strikes legislation. It is even more inappropriate to include drug offenses as strikes, as Congress has done. Most candidates for three-strikes punishment would face a sentence of at least ten or twenty years or more for that third offense anyway. If even that threat fails to inhibit that third crime, how much greater an increment of deterrent threat will these individuals—not well known to engage in careful, long-range planning—see when the threat is extended to life in prison?

For imprisonment to deter offenders and potential offenders, it must stigmatize. Prison is most likely to deter if the prisoner's social standing is injured by being excluded from a group he or she cares about. But many of an offender's peers and relatives have also done time. About one-quarter of all males living in our inner cities will be jailed at some point in their lives, so the stigma attached to having a prison record in these neighborhoods is not as great as it was when prison terms were relatively uncommon. In some inner-city areas imprisonment is merely a rite of passage, even a badge of honor. Having a parent behind bars is the single most criminogenic factor in becoming a criminal; half of all juveniles in custody in 1999 have a close relative who has been in prison. The prison stigma is fast disappearing.

Laws requiring long sentences for three-time violent offenders have had no apparent success in reducing the volume of crime. From 1994 to 1995, both violent and overall crime rates dropped more in the thirty-seven states without such three-strikes laws than in the thirteen that had them, according to the Justice Policy Institute. Violent crime fell 4.6 percent in states without the laws, while it fell 1.7 percent with them.[25]

DO PRISONS MEAN LESS CRIME?

Getting tough has always been a "silver bullet," a quick fix for crime. Each year in Louisiana and many other states lawmakers try to outdo each other in legislating harsher mandatory penalties and in reducing avenues of release. This state, along with Texas, boasts one of the highest lockup rates, imposes the most severe penalties, and vies with Texas to execute more criminals per capita than anywhere else. If getting tough resulted in public safety, Louisiana citizens would be the safest in the nation, but Louisiana, in fact, has the highest murder rate among the states. The threatened punishment is hardly ever a factor in the equation. But its lawmakers, like the incorrigible criminal, are unable to learn this message.

To support more prisons, the Department of Justice in 1992 cited data from a 1987 government study that claimed that the imprisonment of one inmate "saves" society $430,000 per year. If this figure were true, society would be getting a 17-to-1 return on its investment in prisons based on how much it costs to incarcerate one person for one year. The study arrived at the $430,000 figure by assuming that each prisoner, if not incarcerated, would commit 187 street crimes per year at a "cost" to the victim of $2,300 per crime. Criminologists Franklin Zimring and Gordon Hawkins, who analyzed the government's claim of $430,000 in cost saving, concluded that if the assumptions underlying the study were true, all crime in our country would have disappeared several years ago.[26]

In the past fifteen years prison time has dramatically increased. While average prison time served per violent crime roughly tripled between 1975 and 1989, reported levels of serious violent crime varied around the level of about 2.9 million per year. If tripling the average length of incarceration per crime had a strong preventive effect, violent crime rates should have declined. While rates declined during the 1980s, they generally rose after 1985, suggesting other factors. While incarceration does affect some crime and recidivism rates, adding more prisons does not necessarily make for beneficial effects. States with high rates of imprisonment may or may not have high rates of crime, while states with low rates of crime may or may not have high rates of imprisonment. North Dakota and South Dakota, virtually identical in demographics and geography, provide a telling example: South Dakota imprisons its citizens at three times the rate of North Dakota, but the crime rates between the two states nearly match. Homicide and incarceration rates show a similar pattern. Louisiana puts more of its citizens in prison per capita than almost any other state besides Texas, yet it also had the highest homicide rate in 1994. Oklahoma, with the third highest incarceration rate, ranked twentieth in its rate of homicide. As these examples show, dramatically increasing incarceration rates does not cause a decline in crime.

Moreover, crime rates show no consistent correlation with incarceration rates. New York was one of the ten states with the lowest rate of increase in prison populations between 1990 and 1995, and yet New York City enjoyed the largest decline in homicides of any major city. Despite predictions that doubling the nation's prison population would produce a 15 percent to 18 percent drop in robbery, the prison population has quadrupled since 1996, and robbery rose by twice the predicted rate. Why? Because young, first-time offenders replace those taken off the streets and because sooner or later most offenders are released and, with nothing but hard time behind them, revert to crime.[27]

California illustrates this phenomenon. After embarking on the largest prison construction program in the history of the country and spending $3.8 billion, California had twenty-five prisons by 1992, a 300 percent increase in capacity. By 1992, 562,000 people (or 2.2 percent of all Californians eighteen years of age or older) were either in jail or prison or on probation or parole. Although its prison population quadrupled in size, the overall per capita crime rate in California remained essentially the same. The message appears in another way by comparing California and Texas. In the 1980s the two states experienced similar crime and incarceration patterns until a depression forced Texas to reduce prison construction, while California continued to build prisons and increase inmates. The much higher imprisonment rates in California had no appreciable effect on its violent crime rate and only slight effects on its property crime rate. Despite reduced prison construction and incarcerations, the Texas crime rate remained constant.

Because increasing rates of imprisonment can occur at the same time as declining rates of crime, using the data selectively, as the National Rifle Association does, can make it seem that prisons lower crime. In California, the prison population rose in nineteen of the past twenty-one years. In fifteen of those nineteen years, violent crime rose as well, indicating that massive prison growth did not reduce its violent crime. Yet some elected officials point to the four years that crime fell and claim that additional prison construction is the cause of the decline.

One of the reasons for the inefficiency of prison is that prison touches only a few criminals. The criminal justice system is like a large funnel. At the top is a huge flood of crimes: federal victimization surveys estimate that 34 million offenses are committed each year nationwide, with some 22 million of them "serious" because of involving violence or significant property loss. Only about half of the 34 million are reported to the police, and only about a fifth of those reported result in an arrest for a serious crime. Of these, ultimately, only about 2 percent of total crimes result in conviction. A large majority of those who *are* convicted are incarcerated. But enacting harsher sentencing policies has no impact on those 98 percent who are never convicted. As the earlier *Bonfire of the Vanities* quote suggests, in the end only a few hundred thousand crimes result in someone's being punished by prison.[28]

These figures of reported crime and arrest rates cannot be altered by penal policy. Judicial sentencing can hardly be taken as a major impediment to crime control when it impacts only 2 percent of the entire criminal volume. If 34 million serious crimes are being committed in this country, and 31 million are never solved, the only way to truly reduce crime is to find some way to stop some of the crime from being committed in the first place before police and courts come into play. The deterrent value of threatened long sentences is questionable, given the odds against arrest and conviction. The only effective way to curb such crimes is not by punishment but by "front end" deterrence. Though it is gratifying to see crime drop, it is impossible to point to an increase in the prison population as the primary explanation. The decline seemingly results from a combination of demographic changes (fewer criminally active young males), more effective law enforcement, and greater stability in the drug trade, which leads to less violence among drug gangs.

MAKING IT WORSE?

Hard time doesn't always pay the anticipated dividends. More than nine out of ten inmates currently in prison will be released and will return to society. If the characteristics that landed them in prison in the first place are not fixed in prison, they return to society no better for their prison experience. In an important 1992 Rand study, recidivism rates of prison inmates with an identically matched group of probationers show that prisoners had higher recidivism rates than similar offenders placed on probation, suggesting that the prison experience itself can be criminogenic. Although such studies do not conclude that prisons cause recidivism, prisons are hardly our panacea. If we incarcerate without self-improvement, the prisoner is unlikely to acquire the skills to enter mainstream society, which partly explains why longer incarceration periods correlate to higher recidivism rates.

Undeniably, incarceration reduces recidivism among some offenders. It is equally undeniable that it *increases* recidivism among others because it makes some criminals worse. In a study of delinquent youth in Massachusetts, John H. Laub and Robert Sampson show that going to prison often increases the chances of committing further crimes as adults, mainly because it reduces prospects of getting a stable job.[29] Although prisons cannot become country clubs, making them gulags jeopardizes public safety. Ideal correctional facilities would balance punishment and self-sufficiency, particularly as inmates get closer to release.

Lawyer Louis Nizer once wrote: "Nothing is more ungainly than a fisherman pulled into the water by his catch." A corrections system that makes problems worse is equally ungainly. According to Jeff Bingaman, former attorney general in New Mexico: "Prisons simply do not deal with the basic problems of crime in our society. Prison is a dehumanizing experience, and most persons come out the worse for being in. Nearly all young criminals, even under the strictest sentencing practices, will return to society."

Our prison gates have become revolving doors. In most states nearly two-thirds of all young released convicts are rearrested within three years of their release. Grady Wacaster, a prison warden in Spooky Hollow, North Carolina, observes: "People say we go to lock 'em all up and teach 'em a lesson. So we put them in prison and they get out and commit another crime and go back in. It looks to me like we ought to teach ourselves a lesson."

The problem goes beyond three-strikes policy to mandatory sentences as well: they, too, are counterproductive. When penal resources are scarce, the priority given to more serious offenses means that life-threatening violence receives a large share of the most serious punishments. No matter how small the prison, we make room for Timothy McVeigh types. But expanding punishment resources directly impacts cases of marginal seriousness more so than violent crimes. When fear of lethal violence translates into a general campaign against all crime, the extra penal resources focus disproportionately on nonviolent behavior.

The relatively modest impact of California's crime crackdown on three-time offenders is not a result of lenient attitudes toward robbery and murder. Quite the opposite. Since robbery and murder are seriously punished in California, a smaller number of robbers and killers spared by the previous regime were available to be swept up by the three-strikes crackdown. Sixty percent of all California prison inmates in 1980 had been committed for offenses of violence; only 27 percent of the additional prison space added between 1980 and 1990 increased the number of violent inmates. If the efficiency of anticrime policy reflects the proportion of violent offenders imprisoned, the prison resources available in 1980 merit a 60 percent efficiency rating, while the additional resources committed to imprisonment during the 1990s show a 27 percent efficiency rating.[30]

Under our present penal policy, we spend more and more money locking up fewer violent people and more nonviolent ones. The Cato Institute concludes that the single biggest reason for our expanded prison population has been the decision to send to prison offenders who would otherwise, fifteen years ago, have received a nonprison sentence, most of them drug users. One out of five federal prisoners is in jail for what the Justice Department classifies as low-level activity involving no violence, no serious prior criminal record, and no sophisticated criminal activity.[31] When most of the persons who go to prison are violent offenders, the distinctiveness of violent crime is enhanced. However, as more nonviolent offenders go to prison, the distinction between the violent and the nonviolent becomes blurred. If the punishments for both robbery and burglary increase, but the punishments for burglary increase more so than those for robbery, the gap between the punishments for robbery and for burglary narrows. Blurring the line diminishes deterrence.

Such "scaling" prevents increases in penal severity from reducing lethal violence. To the extent that killing is deterred by threatening the maximum punishment with much lesser punishment for nonlethal acts, the incentive to avoid killing is reduced as the severity of the punishment for nonlethal crime increases, simply because the gap between the two punishments diminishes. If the threatened punishment for theft is two years and that for a killing is fifty years, the difference between those two penalties may act as a strong incentive against killing. But if theft evokes the maximum penalty in the first instance, there can be no room for further recourse to a higher punishment. Like a building where the ceiling's height cannot be increased, raising the level of the floors by remodeling only decreases the distance between the floor and the ceiling. The irony of our crime war has been that the largest increases in punishment affect non-violent offenses of lesser seriousness, that is, those crimes like drugs on the margin between prison and nonprison sanctions.[32] A recent study of imprisonment in California between 1980 and 1991 makes this point dramatically. From 1980 to 1991, the number of prisoners imprisoned for all offenses increased by almost 80,000. The number of robbers in prison in California grew by 104 percent during the decade, less than one-third the general increase in prison population. The number of burglars in California prisons grew at a rate just equal to the general increase in prison population—a rate of 335 percent. Larceny inmates expanded by 565 percent, and the number of people in prison after conviction for drug offenses expanded fifteenfold. Stated differently, violent criminals fell to 42 percent of the prison population in 1997, from 57 percent, while drug inmates grew to 27 percent, up from 8 percent.[33]

The severity with which we view murder means that the murderer will already be in prison before a crime crackdown, and the bulk of other prison space goes to offenses of less seriousness than murder. In this special sense, cracking down on all crime without distinction because of concern about violence is self-defeating.[34] The additional prison space is taken up by nonviolent, not violent, offenders.

NO TREATMENT

Not surprisingly, many young individuals released from prison are unsuccessful on the outside. A Department of Justice follow-up study of 108,580 young inmates released from prison to parole in eleven states in 1983 found that 63 percent of these individuals faced arrest again within three years for either a felony or serious misdemeanor. Most of those who stay out of prison do not live successful or gratifying lives. They remain dependent on others or the state, drift back and forth between petty crime and subsistence, menial, dependent living, or gravitate to the new urban underclass—the homeless. Many die relatively young. That revolving door helps explain the seeming contradiction that many states with high incarceration rates also have high violent crime rates. Florida has the twelfth highest lockup rate among states, and it ranks first in violent crime. Conversely, twelve of the fifteen states with the lowest incarceration rates also score low on violent crime.

If prisons only punish and offer no inducements or opportunities for rehabilitation, they simply produce tougher criminals. When prisoners have no constructive way to spend their time, they fill the hours building resentment, not to mention a grab bag of criminal tricks to take back to the streets. "All we do," says Dr. John May, one of the ten doctors who service the 9,000 inmates at Chicago's Cook County Jail, "is produce someone meaner and angrier and more disillusioned with himself and society."[35]

Mandatory sentences without rehabilitation obstruct crime control. In an important study of federal and state prisoners, "Behind Bars: Substance Abuse and America's Prison Population," the National Center on Addiction and Substance Abuse at Columbia University announced in 1998 that mandatory sentences without mandatory rehabilitation result in returning inmates to society with the same problems as before they were incarcerated. Joseph Califano, its director, stated:

If . . . the objective of our criminal justice and prison system is to protect the public safety by incarcerating incorrigible offenders and rehabilitating as many others as possible, the prevailing policy of prison only—with no treatment or preparation for return to the community—is, as Brooklyn District Attorney Charles J. Hynes puts it, "lunacy." For treatable alcohol and drug abusers, mandatory sentences (particularly those which require convicts to serve their entire time in prison with no parole) endanger rather than protect the public safety.[36]

Califano's plea for an end to mandatory sentences and reintroduction of rehabilitation, especially for addicts, is supported by William Murphy, president of the National District Attorneys Association, and by General Barry McCaffrey, White House drug policy director, neither known for being soft on crime. If prisons only warehouse inmates without inducements for rehabilitation, they simply produce worse criminals on release. Drug clinics do more to rehabilitate drug addicts than prison, job training does more to reduce recidivism than jails, and early childhood prevention programs do more than any other factor to reduce a propensity to crime. This message falls on deaf ears in anti-rehabilitation, pro-incapacitating, tough-on-crime demagoguery.

CONCLUSION: THE INJUSTICE

At our millennium, prison dominates our society to an extent unparalleled in our history. Mass incarceration has been our most implemented and most expensive social policy. The fact that we imprison our population at a rate six to ten times higher than that of other advanced societies means that we rely primarily on our penal system to maintain social cohesion. We are engaged in repressive experiment to test the degree to which our society, for the first time in its history, can maintain its national bond through punishment rather than through shared civic values. Under this ideology our unity as a nation increasingly comes not from shared community virtues but from a shared fear of punishment. This positivist penal policy has made our country safe only for demagogues.

The past twenty-five years tell us that we have paid a steep price for an approach to violent crime badly out of civic balance. We have relied on expensive jails and prisons as our first defense against crime, yet we still maintain the developed world's worst level of lethal violence. We have depleted other public institutions, like education, drug treatment, and job training, in order to pay for incarceration—a self-defeating course that ensures that violent crime will remain high despite ever more drastic efforts to contain it. We have put our bricks, mortar, and tax money at back-end strategies rather than at cheaper, more effective front-end strategies.

Diminishing vocational training in many prison systems means that inmates leave prison today even less fit for an ever more demanding labor market than they were when they went in. They have acquired the stigma of prison without increasing their capacity to function on the outside—a true "incapacitation." To the extent that incarceration aggravates the already severe labor-market problems of mostly low-income, poorly educated inmates, it eventually dramatically increases the costs to the public sector of welfare, indigent medical care, and homelessness.

The fact that prisoners represent only a fraction of a much larger pool of offenders, most of whom are not caught, greatly limits incapacitation's effect on crime rates. Our failure to match the increasing rates of imprisonment with corresponding programs to reintegrate offenders means that we are steadily producing ever-larger armies of unreformed ex-offenders whose chances of success in the legitimate world diminish precisely because of their prison experience. We incapacitate them in the traditional sense of the word—reducing their capacity to function effectively in society. Our "get tough policies" have disproportionately incarcerated nonviolent offenders, caused early release of violent offenders, and kept many aged inmates in prison long past their crime-prone years. Our penal fires, à la Shakespeare, are being consumed by their own ashes.

We could learn from others. Scandinavian institutions lack the racial polarization, the ever-present threat of violence, and the serious overcrowding that characterize our prisons. The contrast with our prisons was dramatized in 1979, when Sweden's Supreme Court refused to extradite a convicted American sex offender because by Swedish standards our prisons appeared inhumane and the fifty-nine-year mandatory sentence was considered to be excessive. Sadly, at our millennium, our criminal justice has learned, to the dismay of probation founder John Augustus, only how to "punish maliciously [and] from a spirit of revenge."

Perceptive foreign observers are appalled by our current prison conditions and sentencing practices; they cannot believe that we could be so regressive. Nils Christie, an eminent Norwegian criminologist and author of *Crime Control as Industry*, has found U.S. prisons so repellent that after opening his analysis with the apologetic phrase: "Whom one loveth, one chasteneth," he draws an analogy with Nazi Germany: "The extermination camp was a product of industrialization . . . a combination of thought patterns. The prison system in the USA is rapidly moving in the same direction."[37]

American critics display less hyperbole but no less indignation. Human Rights Watch, having investigated prison conditions throughout the world, finds in our penology "numerous human rights abuses and frequent violations of the UN Standard Minimum Rules for the Treatment of prisoners." Our effort to punish so as to make an example of criminals has resulted in making our penal system itself an example of values opposite to what we profess.

NOTES

1. *State v. Mitchum*, 1CA-CR 94–0757 (May 2, 1996).

2. S. Donziger, ed., *The Real War on Crime* (New York: Harper, 1996), 48–75.

3. N. Morris and D. Rothman, eds., *The Oxford History of the Prison*, 2d ed. (New York: Oxford University Press, 1998), 210–212.

4. Id., 202ff.

5. R. Lipton, et al., *The Effectiveness of Correctional Treatment* (New York: Praeger, 1975).

6. J. Wilson, "What to Do about Crime," in *What to Do about Crime*, ed. N. Kozodoy (New York: Harper, 1996), 296. See also J. Wilson, *Moral Judgment* (New York: Basic Books, 1997), 3–4.

7. *New Yorker* (Feb. 28, 1998), 6.

8. 1998 Annual Prison Report, Department of Justice, Bureau of Justice Statistics, Washington, D.C., 1998. See also *New York Times*, A14(Aug. 9, 1998).

9. As reported in the *Arizona Republic*, A15 (Mar. 7, 1997) (commenting on 1996 Department of Justice prison statistics).

10. 1998 Annual Prison Report, Department of Justice, Bureau of Justice Statistics, Washington, D.C., 1998. See also *New York Times*, A14 (Aug. 9, 1998).

11. 59 Fed. Probation 3 (1996).

12. *The New Yorker*, 28.

13. Donziger, *The Real War on Crime*, 48.

14. F. Butterfield, "Punitive Damages," *New York Times*, sec. 4, 1 (Sept. 28, 1997).

15. E. Currie, *Crime and Punishment in America* (New York: Holt, 1998), 12–14.

16. Donziger, *The Real War on Crime*, 23ff.

17. Currie, *Crime*, 4.

18. D. Rothman, "The American Way of Jail," *New York Times Book Review*, 18 (Mar. 1, 1998).

19. T. Goins, *Institutional Research* (Richmond, Va.: Branch Cabell, 1994).

20. Currie, *Crime*, 38–43.

21. Id., 49.

22. Id., 64, citing research by Frank Zimring, *Estimating the Effect of Increased Incarceration on Crime in California* (Berkeley: University of California Press, 1995).

23. Currie, *Crime*, 49.

24. B. Katz, *Justice Overruled* (New York: Warner Books, 1996), 252.

25. *New York Times*, A7 (Mar. 7, 1997).

26. Donziger, *The Real War on Crime*, 75.

27. N. Morris, *The Future of Imprisonment* (New York: Oxford University Press, 1974), 212.

28. D. Anderson, *Sensible Justice* (New York: New Press, 1998), 9.

29. Currie, *Crime*, 74.

30. S. Estrich, *Getting Away with Murder* (Cambridge: Harvard University Press, 1998), 17–18, 76.

31. Id., 74.

32. F. Zimring and G. Hawkins, *Crime Is Not the Problem* (New York: Oxford University Press, 1997), 181–182.

33. Id., 32.

34. Id., 182.

35. *Time*, 28 (Feb. 7, 1994).

36. Press Release, "Behind Bars: Substance Abuse and America's Prison Population," National Center on Addiction and Substance Abuse (New York: Columbia University Press, Jan. 8, 1998).

37. N. Christie, *Crime Control as Industry* (New York: Routledge, 1994).

8

THE POLITICIZATION
OF CRIME

A memorial urging the United States ambassador to the USSR to convey the recommendation of the Senate of the State of Arizona that the
government of the Soviet Union be exiled to Siberia and thereafter go
straight to hell
— Memorial Resolution adopted by the Arizona Senate, 1983

Since the collapse of the Soviet Union and the loss of such a useful enemy,
crime has emerged as our nation's major rallying cause. Our politicians
now demonstrate their toughness by invoking the death penalty, longer
sentences, and harsher prisons. Those who question the wisdom, cost, and
effectiveness of such measures become "soft on crime," the new analogue
to being soft on communism. Though the enemy now is internal rather
than external, this demonization of thoughtful dissent serves the same
goals: votes and political power, but only rarely improvements in the war
on crime.

A century ago House Speaker Thomas Reed rose and declared to his
colleagues: "Gentlemen, we have decided to perpetuate the following outrage." Politicians are not so candid today. Instead, at every level—federal,
state, and local—they have capitalized on our fears, campaigned on "get
tough" platforms, and won. Their victory is often the defeat of principled
justice.

PRESIDENTIAL CRIME POLICIES

The politicizing of crime as a national issue stems from the 1964 presidential election, when Barry Goldwater promoted the theme of law and order and challenged Lyndon Johnson's War on Poverty as a softheaded response to crime and urban disorder. Even though Johnson won the election, the nationalization of the issue began a new era of political involvement in crime control.

Richard Nixon's victory over Hubert Humphrey in 1968 reflected Nixon's hard-line approach, which painted liberals as naïve social do-gooders. When Nixon won, the moral/punitive theory of crime emerged as a political alternative to liberalism: the decline in moral values must be reversed; punishment should follow any rule breaking; and the justice system must punish as many lawbreakers as possible by making law violations costly enough to prevent their occurrence. Nixon accordingly promised to replace Democrat Ramsey Clark as attorney general, whose defense of civil liberties and procedural safeguards made him seem soft on crime. Nixon told campaign crowds, incorrectly, that crime was rising nine times faster than the population. When Clark responded, accurately, that "there is no wave of crime in this country," he became a prime target of the campaign.

Since Nixon's era, fear of crime has prompted both major political parties to target suburban swing voters, who have the lowest risk of being victims of street crime but vote more than do inner-city residents. Presidents and other elected officials have tried to convince suburbanites and the general public that Washington remains tough on crime via repeated showcase strategies.[1] As a prime example, George Bush became president by criticizing Michael Dukakis for the conduct of Willie Horton, who committed a rape while on a weekend furlough from a Massachusetts prison. A convicted first-degree murderer serving a life sentence without parole, Horton received a forty-eight-hour pass under the Massachusetts prison furlough program supported by Governor Dukakis. During that furlough, he took a young suburban couple hostage, tortured the man with a knife, and tortured and raped the woman. Bush related the nightmare:

What did the Democratic Governor of Massachusetts think he was doing when he let convicted first-degree murderers out on weekend passes? Why, even after one of the criminals that he let out brutally raped a woman and stabbed her fiancé, why won't he admit his mistake? Eight months later he was still defending his program and only when the Massachusetts Legislature voted by an overwhelming majority to abolish the program for murderers, did he finally give in. I think that Governor Dukakis owes the people of the United States of America an explanation as to why he supported this outrageous program.[2]

The Horton story became central to the 1988 presidential campaign. Horton reminded Democrats that appearing to be soft on crime was politically incorrect. The 1990s thereafter saw get-tough sentencing enhancements implemented throughout the country. Penalties increased, mandatory sentences reappeared, and prisons became overcrowded as politicians discovered that being hard on crime was the next best vote-getter to being hard on communism.

In 1992 presidential candidate Bill Clinton scheduled the execution of a brain-damaged man shortly before the New Hampshire primary. Rickey Ray Rector, an African American sentenced to death by an all-white jury, had destroyed part of his brain when he turned the gun on himself after killing the police officer for whose murder he received the death sentence. In the days before his execution, he was howling and barking like a dog, dancing, singing, laughing inappropriately, and saying that he was going to vote for Clinton, who denied clemency, allowed the execution to proceed, and personally viewed it. Clinton's first three television advertisements in his bid for reelection focused on expanding the death penalty. His State of the Union address in 1995 promised the death penalty for over sixty new federal crimes. His 1994 crime bill even made the murder of poultry inspectors a capital crime. The death penalty thereby became our nation's litmus test for measuring suitability to handle all the delicate affairs of high office.

GOVERNOR CAMPAIGNS

By 1994 crime had so dominated other national issues that an official of the National Governors Association observed that the "top three issues in the gubernatorial campaigns this year are crime, crime and crime." Many gubernatorial candidates then, as now, campaigned as if they were running for the office of public executioner.[3] Here are some examples of the public executioner rhetoric as governors tried to mine political gold in the death penalty vein:

New York

In 1996 New York governor Mario Cuomo was attacked for his vetoes of death-penalty legislation during twelve years in office and his refusal to return a New York prisoner to Oklahoma for execution. He defended himself by proposing a referendum on the death penalty but nonetheless lost to George Pataki, who promised to reinstate capital punishment and to send the prisoner back to Oklahoma for execution. Although Cuomo built more prisons than all other New York governors, the irony of his twelve-year tenure as governor was that no matter what he had done on crime issues, he became judged only by his opposition to the death penalty, even though crime rates were down, jail time was up, and police forces had grown.[4]

Texas

Candidates for governor of Texas in 1990 debated about who was responsible for the most executions and who could execute still more people. One candidate ran television advertisements showing photographs of executed prisoners with the boast that he had "made sure they received the ultimate penalty: death." An opponent ran advertisements taking personal credit for thirty-two executions. Crime in Texas dropped in 1992 and 1993, but that did not stop candidate George W. Bush, Jr., from attacking incumbent governor Ann Richards for being soft on crime. Bush ran an ad on television showing a man abducting and killing a woman in a parking garage and blasting Richards for releasing 7,700 offenders before their terms expired. Exit polls showed that Richards lost the election partly because of these ads. A Bush spokesperson admitted the ad was dishonest, but Bush insisted it was a good way to "elevate" the public discussion of crime.[5]

In Texas, which has executed three times as many prisoners as its closest competitors since 1976 and four times more than any other state, the murder rate as of 1999 remains one of the highest in the country. Since 1990, when the pace of executions began to accelerate, more law enforcement officers have been killed in Texas than in any other state, raising the possibility that police officers may be at greater risk of being killed in states like Texas with high execution rates.[6]

Florida

In Florida in 1990, the incumbent gubernatorial candidate, the late Lawton Chiles, ran television advertisements showing the face of serial killer Ted Bundy, who was executed during his tenure as governor. The governor boasted that he had signed over ninety death warrants in his four years in office. Bob Graham demonstrated in two terms as Florida governor and senator that nothing sells on the campaign trail like promises to accelerate the death penalty. Graham's signing of death warrants enabled him to escape the moniker of "Governor Jello." He increased the number of execution warrants he signed when running for reelection as governor in 1982, even though he knew they would not be carried out.[7]

George Bush's younger brother Jeb ran a television advertisement in his 1994 campaign for governor in which the mother of a murder victim blamed incumbent governor Chiles for allowing the convicted killer to remain on death row for thirteen years. Bush privately admitted that there was really no way Chiles could speed up the execution because the case was pending in federal court. He also argued that Florida's eight executions since Chiles' election in 1990 were not enough executions; a civilized state like Florida should have more. Chiles narrowly survived.[8]

California

In the 1994 California gubernatorial race, Kathleen Brown's personal opposition to the death penalty was a major liability to the point that she had to defend herself against Governor Pete Wilson's charges that she would appoint liberal judges like former justice Rose Bird. Desperate, Brown produced a late advertisement proclaiming willingness to enforce the death penalty. She lost to Wilson.

Although the U.S Supreme Court has made it clear that capital punishment may not be invoked for crimes not involving death, politicians find no hesitation in campaigning directly to the contrary. Al Checchi, a Democrat running in 1998 for governor in California, regularly gave campaign speeches demanding the death penalty for rapists and child molesters who, as he put it, "kill the spirit."[9]

Massachusetts

During his tenure as governor, William Weld repeatedly proposed showy and expensive death penalty legislation. "You can't put a price on justice," he once said in defense of a costly death penalty bill. Of course, Weld regularly put a price on justice anytime he urged funding social services or welfare programs. Any state puts a price on justice, even when it sets salaries for court officers or corrections officials, diverts juvenile offenders, or establishes shelters for battered women. Weld simply meant—but didn't say—that he was willing to pay the enormous price for a pervasive death penalty, however excessive it might be.[10]

Electoral Death Penalty Swooning

Examples of distortion of public duty in the name of capital punishment abound. In California's 1994 election, Republican candidates for insurance commissioner and state superintendent of schools ran television advertisements painting themselves as tough on violent crime, even though neither of those offices deals with criminal justice, and neither has any influence at all on death penalty policy. In the 1998 campaign for Arizona attorney general, both Republican candidates endorsed the death penalty and promised to invoke it liberally despite the fact that Arizona capital punishment decisions rest in the county attorney rather than in the attorney general's office.[11]

SHERIFF BRUTALITY

Toughness also occurs in other official venues. Maricopa County (Phoenix), Arizona, sheriff Joe Arpaio, self-proclaimed as the "toughest sheriff in America," has carried out his electoral promises of toughness on crime by a series of unusual jail innovations: hog-tying inmates; using restraint chairs as punishment; ordering his deputies to use pepper spray and stun guns on inmates; dressing inmates in pink underwear; using chain gangs wearing black and white stripes; denying inmates television, coffee, and cigarettes; serving green bologna sandwiches as basic food; and housing inmates in huge circus tents with holes in the roofs allowing rain to enter. His jailers have illegally opened privileged mail, "lost" legal papers, and kept targeted inmates in twenty-four-hour lockdown for months, in cells with no clocks, a blacked-out trapdoor, and a covered window. Inmates have been denied the use of a telephone and telephone book, the right to contact an attorney, and the use of a day room and held in solitary confinement. Jailers have listened to, and taken notes on, their telephone calls.

After several inmates were brutalized and killed by guards, the Justice Department filed a civil rights lawsuit against Arpaio for gross mistreatment of his inmates, the majority of whom are awaiting trial and therefore legally presumed innocent. The suit resulted in a consent decree where Arpaio promised to remedy his more outrageous practices. His stated explanation for his harshness was political image: to send a tough message to criminals and thereby reduce recidivism by 10 percent. Professor John Hepburn of the Arizona State Center for Justice Studies in a follow-up investigation discovered that, instead of reducing recidivism, Arpaio's jails registered a recidivism rate of 62 percent—that is, almost two of every three inmates, despite their tough treatment, returned to his jails within a short time after release, apparently learning nothing from their abusive treatment other than how to be abusive to others. Sheriff Arpaio's legal problems have not prevented him from writing his glowing autobiography, *The Toughest Sheriff in America*.[12]

COURTS AND JUDGES

The public's dissatisfaction with the courts rests on the belief that judges are soft on crime: 81 percent of people surveyed recently by Time/CNN agreed that "courts do not deal harshly enough with criminals." The incorrect perception that a great many violent felons are serving very little prison time thus drives the crime debate.[13] Contested elections hamper a judge's ability to be an impartial, unbiased adjudicator when such elections turn not on qualifications or jurisprudence but on enthusiasm for toughness at all costs.[14]

Capital cases have become campaign fodder in some contested judicial elections. Judges have come under attack for their decisions in capital cases, with the most notable examples in southern states with the largest death rows. Unpopular decisions in capital cases, even when compelled by law, may cost a judge the bench or promotion to a higher court.

Justice Stevens perceptively warned judges about caving in to such political pressure:

The "higher authority" to whom present-day judges may be "too responsive" is a political climate in which judges who covet higher office—or who merely wish to remain judges—must constantly profess their fealty to the death penalty.... The danger that they will bend to political pressures when pronouncing sentence in highly publicized capital cases is the same danger confronted by judges beholden to King George III.[15]

This voice of higher authority echoes loudly today in our judicial chambers particularly in contested elections. In many states judges who do not bend to political pressure on toughness lose their positions for no other reason. California has the largest death row of any state in the nation. In 1986, Governor George Deukmejian warned two justices of the state's Supreme Court that he would oppose their retention unless they voted to uphold more death sentences. He had already announced his opposition to then-chief justice Rose Bird because of her votes in capital cases. Unsatisfied with votes of the other two justices, the governor succeeded in defeating the two other justices as well as Justice Bird.[16]

The single county in America responsible for the most death sentences and executions—a veritable human-rendering plant—is Harris County, Texas, which includes Houston, where Judge Norman E. Lanford, a Republican, was voted off the court in 1992 after he recommended that a death sentence be set aside due to prosecutorial misconduct. A prosecutor who specialized in death cases and kept a hangman's noose over her office door defeated him in the primary with radio advertisements attacking her Democratic opponent for having once opposed the death penalty.

Justice James Robertson was voted off the Mississippi Supreme Court in 1992 by an opponent in the primary who ran as a law-and-order candidate with the support of the Mississippi Prosecutors Association. Robertson's opponent attacked him for expressing the view, correctly, that the Constitution did not permit the death penalty for rape where there was no loss of life. Indeed, the U.S. Supreme Court itself had held ten years earlier that the Eighth Amendment did not permit the death penalty in such cases.

Robertson was the second justice to be voted off the court in two years for seeming soft on crime. Joel Blass was defeated in 1990 by a candidate who promised to be a "tough judge for tough times" and to put more criminals behind bars. Justice Blass expressed concern during the campaign that his opponent was misleading the public, explaining: "Neither a Supreme Court judge nor the whole court can send a person to prison."[17]

In 1997 New York federal district court judge Harold Baer was soundly criticized for initially suppressing evidence in a criminal case due to an unconstitutional search and seizure. Vitriolic calls for his resignation or impeachment ensued. Even President Clinton questioned the judge's ruling and fitness to serve on the federal bench. On a motion for rehearing, the judge reversed his ruling, creating the distinct impression that he succumbed to political pressure over his initial ruling.[18]

In Tennessee, former Supreme Court justice Penny White was voted out of office in a 1996 retention election after she concurred with her colleagues' order for a new sentence hearing for a convicted murderer. The controversial ruling prompted public and political outrage, which fueled an active campaign against Justice White in her upcoming retention election. The Tennessee electorate voted not to retain her. Her defeat clearly resulted from the capital punishment decision in which she joined.[19]

A recent speech in Congress is a telling example of crime rhetoric that impugns the independence of the judiciary. In introducing the judicial Improvements Act of 1998 on June 11, Senate Judiciary Committee chair Orrin Hatch said that one of the sections of the bill would ensure that "tough sentencing laws . . . will not be ignored by activist judges who improperly use complaints of prison conditions filed by convicts as a vehicle to release violent offenders back on our streets." As an example of "this activism," he cited U.S. District judge Norma Shapiro of Philadelphia, who, according to Senator Hatch, "jumped at the chance . . . to impose her activist views and wrestle control of the prison system by setting a cap on the number of prisoners that can be incarcerated in Pennsylvania." He went on to ask, "How can we expect law enforcement to provide protection and safe streets if at every turn there is a Judge Shapiro waiting anxiously for the chance to release lawlessness on our communities?" Far from jumping at the chance to take over the prisons, Judge Shapiro initially dismissed the lawsuit because there was related litigation pending in state court. In addition, when required by the U.S. Court of Appeals to hear the case, Judge Shapiro reluctantly approved and then sought faithfully to enforce a consent decree to which the city of Philadelphia had agreed. The litigation quickly became a political football in Philadelphia, with Judge Shapiro a convenient target of blame and a source of cover for local politicians.[20]

Legislators have also distorted judicial sentencing figures for political gain. In 1993 Senator Phil Gramm, later to run for president, wrote an article in the *New York Times* entitled "Don't Let Judges Set Crooks Free." America was "deluged by a tidal wave of crime," and the "main culprit" was a justice system that fails to deter potential criminals. "Soft sentencing" had brought "a dramatic decline in the cost of committing a crime and a dramatic increase in crime." According to Gramm, a murderer could expect to spend just 1.8 years in prison. A rape earned sixty days. A robbery resulted in twenty-three days behind bars, and a car theft just a day and a half.

However measured, the average time offenders spend behind bars then and now bears no resemblance whatsoever to the numbers cited by Gramm, which were distorted out of all proportion for his political goals.[21] Gramm's figures came from Morgan Reynolds, a Texas A&M economist, who arrived at them by dividing the average time served by rapists into the total number of rapes committed. Thus, those who never got arrested or convicted bring down the average time served. The real figures for homicide including involuntary manslaughter are more than ten years, according to the U.S. Bureau of Justice Statistics. The Justice Department also says that seven years—not sixty days—is the average term for a convicted rapist.

Judicial toughness invites exaggeration as well as distortion. Alabama circuit judge Mike McCormick ran electoral advertisements proclaiming: "Some complain that *he's too tough on criminals*, AND HE IS . . . we need him now more than ever." Proclaiming that one is "too tough" on crime is incompatible with holding the balance between the state and the accused. Such ads also may violate the code of judicial conduct, which prohibits preelection pronouncements impairing judicial impartiality.[22]

Distortion can also involve judicial qualifications. Texas has the nation's second largest death row. After a decision by the state's highest criminal court, the Court of Criminal Appeals, reversing the conviction in a notorious capital case, a former chairman of the Republican Party called for Republicans to take over the court in the 1994 election. One of the Republicans elected to the court was Stephen W. Mansfield, a member of the Texas bar only two years, who campaigned on promises of using the death penalty, greater use of the harmless-error-doctrine, and sanctions for attorneys who file frivolous appeals in death penalty cases. Mansfield misrepresented his prior background, experience, and record, had been fined for practicing law without a license in Florida, and, contrary to his assertions of extensive writing on criminal and civil justice issues, had virtually no experience in criminal law. His legal writing consisted of a guest column in a local newspaper. Mansfield defeated the incumbent judge, a conservative former prosecutor. Among his responsibilities now is the review of every capital case in Texas.[23]

DRUGS AND MANDATORIES

During the 1980s and 1990s political figures of both parties repeatedly campaigned on tough-on-crime platforms involving mandatory sentences. A *New York Times* headline captures the climate: "Senate's Rule for Its Anti-Crime Bill: The Tougher the Provision, the Better." The Anti-Drug Abuse Act of 1986 required mandatory-minimum sentences for most violent drug offenses. After Maryland basketball star Len Bias died with crack cocaine in his system, mandatory-minimum sentences, based only on the amount of drugs, were set at five years, ten years, and twenty years, without discussion or insight into how such mandatories undermine sentencing guidelines, ignore individual circumstances, and impose wider effects on justice and taxes and their inability to reduce replacements in the drug trade.[24]

The $1.7 billion plan passed the House 392–16 and the Senate by a voice vote. The media coverage of the Anti-Drug Abuse Act scarcely mentioned its enduring legacy: the "mandatory minimums" that fill the federal prisons with small-time dealers, especially those who deal crack. A crack dealer caught with 5 grams—a handful of "rocks" worth roughly $500—automatically gets five years in federal prison, the same as for selling 500 grams of powdered cocaine. In 1988 the mandatory-minimum requirement was amended, again without real debate, to include drug coconspirators or those who attempt to traffic drugs. Advertised as a tool that would help federal drug agents nab ranking members of the Medellin cartel, it has been used in practice to nab the girlfriends of petty drug dealers, occasionally for doing nothing more than telling an informant they thought was a friend where to go to meet the boyfriend-dealer.

These laws have had no demonstrable effect on drug- or gun-related violence, but they have greatly increased the political halo of tough-on-crime politicians.[25] A Congress genuinely interested in truth in sentencing would admit how erratically and arbitrarily mandatory minimums are enforced, that they promote plea bargains, that serious crimes are already subject to very tough sentences, that convicted drug traffickers are quickly replaced, and that defendants are not faceless or fungible.

Nonetheless, the Senate passed new mandatory minimums again in 1993 with no opposition from the Clinton administration. "Mandatory minimums are a political response to violent crime," Senator Orrin Hatch then conceded. Congress and state legislators have enacted new mandatory-minimum sentencing laws not because they are effective in controlling crime—their primary effect has been to crowd prisons with nonviolent, low-level drug offenders—but because they are effective rhetorically. Like capital punishment, mandatory-minimum sentencing has become a political symbol for toughness on crime.[26]

Our War on Drugs illustrates the politician's role in crime myth construction. In 1990, President Bush's administration arranged for the Drug Enforcement Administration (DEA) to conduct a high-profile drug arrest. Since public focus on the drug war was waning due to concern over other social problems, the administration needed to refocus public attention on the drug war. Following a DEA drug bust, the president made a national television address concerning drugs. The DEA went to considerable means to persuade the drug dealer to meet the agents at their desired location for publicity—just outside the White House.[27]

Drug-control legislation has appeared like clockwork during almost every congressional election year since the 1980s, with more drug-control schemes but without crime- or cost-effectiveness research. On September 25, 1996, Speaker of the House Newt Gingrich introduced legislation demanding either a life sentence or the death penalty for anyone bringing more than two ounces of marijuana into the United States. Gingrich's bill attracted twenty-six cosponsors. In the same session Senator Phil Gramm proposed denying federal welfare benefits, including food stamps, to anyone convicted of a drug crime, even a misdemeanor. Gramm's proposal, endorsed by many other senators, limited the punishment to people convicted of a drug felony. It was incorporated into the welfare bill signed by President Clinton.

Historically, this is the way the endless debates about criminal justice work. If an approach proves to be based on faulty premises, lawmakers assume that the law can be simply changed at a later date. That once happened, in fact, with mandatory minimums in drug cases, which were passed in 1950 and repealed in 1970, when the federal prisons were filling up with minor drug offenders. That year, George Bush, then a congressman representing Texas, stood in the well of the House and noted that federal judges were almost unanimously opposed to the minimums. "Practicality requires a sentence structure which is generally acceptable to the courts, to prosecutors and to the general public," Bush then said.[28] But repealing inept tough-on-crime laws involves the risk of appearing soft on crime, and so it rarely occurs.

THE 1994 CRIME BILL

The centerpiece of the 1994 bill championed by President Clinton was an array of traditional crime-fighting techniques with $10 billion for new prisons, $8.8 billion for 100,000 new police, and some sixty new federal death penalties for crimes, including train sabotage, sexual abuse, or obstructing poultry inspectors.[29]

The sixty new death penalties show the triumph of symbol over research. With one exception, all were penalties for murder and thus already covered by state homicide statutes. But Democrats and Republicans wanted them to appear to be an entirely new set of severe punishments promising many new executions. The new death penalties had no relationship to the crime problem at either the state or federal levels. As Senator Joseph Biden grimly joked, their proposals "did everything but hang people for jaywalking."[30]

Successful Republican amendments to the bill included the extension of the death penalty to drug kingpins engaged in dealing in large quantities of illegal drugs. This provision had been added to the 1991 crime bill by Senator Alphonse D'Amato (R-NY) but had been omitted from the Biden bill. On its introduction, D'Amato committed himself and other Republican supporters to pressing it again. Here is the flavor of his rhetoric:

I am outraged that despite all the talk of getting tough on crime, the administration has shown itself, in fact, to be soft on crime. By deleting two provisions that I added to the 1991 crime bill, the new bill will not be the one that cracks down on crime, but one that gives criminals a break—a break they do not deserve and should not get. . . . It cannot be wrong to require the death penalty for large-scale drug enterprises. Those who sell death should receive death. How many people have to die before we come to the realization that we need a greater sanction against those who head the criminal drug enterprises? Killing people by selling them drugs has the same result as killing them with a gun. The death penalty for drug kingpins . . . provides the ultimate sanction.[31]

According to a *New York Times* article about mandatory proposals offered by Senator D'Amato, "Mr. D'Amato conceded that his two successful amendments, which Justice Department officials say would have little practical effect on prosecution of crimes, might not solve the problem. 'But,' he said, 'it does bring about a sense that we are serious.' "[32]

The rhetoric in the 1994 crime bill outweighed its real impact on crime, but that message was obscured. "This could be one of those turning points in our history in terms of positions of the parties and their public perceptions," then Senate majority leader George Mitchell said triumphantly after passage of the crime bill. "I think the time is over when in fact or in perception the Republicans are seen as the party that's tougher on crime. It's the Democrats."

The courts have ruled that capital punishment is unconstitutional for crimes in which no life is taken, but that ruling has not given politicians any pause. In 1995 House Speaker Newt Gingrich demanded death for drug smugglers, as, again, did Senator D'Amato. Gingrich even suggested that mass executions—"27 or 30 or 35 people at one time"—would make an excellent deterrent.[33] The sixty new federal death penalties were touted as the linchpin in the new crime war. Only a few legislators had the courage to speak out. "If you can show me how adding 50 more death-penalty provisions is going to deter one person, then I am for it," said Michigan congressman John Conyers. "Why not 100 more? How about I reach your 100 and I bid 110, and someone else that's tougher on crime is for 150? So what? The one thing that's been proved in my 30 years in this business is that you can't deter people by guaranteeing them that they will go to jail or be executed."[34]

Most of these measures, including the proliferating new death penalties, were purely symbolic. "We are going to show everybody how tough we are," Senator Biden, sponsor of the Senate bill, admitted. "Maybe these provisions will have some effect. But I want to advertise as the author of the underlying bill, as the author of the death penalty amendments, they are not going to have much effect." Senator Hatch agreed: "It's no use kidding ourselves; some of these tough on crime amendments may not have tremendous effect." Nonetheless, Hatch also remarked, "We are sending a message across this country that the Congress had finally awakened," in time, of course, for the midterm elections.[35] The $30 billion crime bill passed in 1994 contained money for a pilot prison so that nonviolent female offenders with infants and toddlers can be housed with their children. Like most of the other prevention programs in the law, the pilot prison has not been funded, and the facility has never been built.

Of all the lessons to be drawn in the 1994 crime legislation and the lesser measures in the 104th Congress, at the top of the list is the way so many provisions derive from manipulating public opinion rather than from practical experience or careful crime research. On most important issues, crime policies owe more to pollsters and campaign consultants than to the expertise of criminologists.[36]

THREE STRIKES

The most recent sentencing obsession for politicians has been "three strikes and you're out." As first enacted in California, the law did not require that the third felony be violent, nor did it take into account the time period between the felonies, nor did it allow for any assessment of the dangerousness of the offender. Every single candidate running for statewide office in the 1990s supported it, notwithstanding its flaws.[37] Governor Pete Wilson called for even harsher sentences. "Not three strikes you're out, not two strikes you're out, but one strike you're out," he once declared to an exuberant crowd.

During his 1994 State of the Union address, President Clinton told the nation: "Those who commit crimes should be punished. And those who commit repeated, violent crimes should be told, 'When you commit a third violent crime, you will be put away, and put away for good. Three strikes, and you're out.' " It was the biggest applause line of the night. But in the end the law signed by Clinton later that year doesn't require that all three felonies be violent crimes for the perpetrator to be put away for life. Sometimes, one will suffice, and the felonies are broadly defined to include much nonviolent conduct. Five years after "three strikes" laws to put repeat criminals away swept the country, most states have left the statutes in mothballs. Most of the twenty-three states that adopted such laws in the mid-1990s have each put a half dozen or fewer people behind bars under the statutes, which create long and usually mandatory sentences for criminals who commit new offenses. In many states, for a third offense the laws send defendants off to prison for life without parole.

There are, of course, some big exceptions: California is packing its prisons, putting away more than 40,000 people for second and third strikes since the law passed in 1994—a quarter of the state's prison population. Of these 4,400 were sentenced to twenty-five years to life. Georgia has sentenced nearly 2,000 under its law. But in most places, the laws are written more narrowly and rarely are applied. "It went a long way on a catchy title," says D. Alan Henry, a criminal justice authority on the three strike movement. "Contrary to what legislatures thought, there weren't awful numbers of people who had committed heinous crimes and who were released and then came back and were treated lightly." E. Michael McCain, a prosecutor from Milwaukee County in Wisconsin, astutely says the laws don't deter criminals and instead spend money keeping them behind bars long after they've passed their criminally active years.[38]

The popularity of three strikes legislation in no way relates to its success. Few people sentenced under the new California scheme are repeat violent offenders. Fully 70 percent of all second- and third-strikes cases have been nonviolent and nonserious offenses. In Los Angeles County, only 4 percent of second and third felony convictions were for murder, rape, kidnapping, or carjacking. A pizza thief, an employed, middle-aged man who stole a piece of pepperoni pizza from another table on a dare, ended up in court charged with his third strike and a lifelong sentence.[39]

President Clinton's major contribution to this debate in his State of the Union speech in 1994 was to endorse vigorously a federal provision for three strikes that would require a mandatory life sentence for a third felony. Yet only a tiny number of violent offenders on federal property would be affected by the federal statute. Life in prison without parole is a senseless waste of thousands of dollars of federal money for those who will never commit another robbery after the age of fifty. None of these questions became the subject of serious political discussion.[40]

The major weakness of the third-strike movement is that the third strike, which triggers a mandatory sentence of twenty-five years to life in prison, could include a lesser offense if prosecuted as a felony. Thefts of a slice of pizza, a pound of meat, a shirt from a store have all been actual cases. Unlike the prior two strikes, the third felony does not have to be either violent or serious.[41] In August 1998, Phillip Sanders, a forty-three-year-old ex-con from West Palm Beach, Florida, was sentenced to life in prison under Florida's three-strikes law for shoplifting—$49.73 worth of boxer shorts and cigarette lighters, to be exact.

"If someone came to the Senate floor and said we should barbwire the ankles of anyone who jaywalks, I suspect it would pass," Senator Biden quipped in 1994 shortly after voting with ninety of his colleagues to impose mandatory life sentences on people with the bad judgment to commit a third felony on federal property. This provision would not have affected the vast majority of offenders nationwide. The Senate proposal would cover someone whose first two strikes were relatively minor property crimes involving threat of force—shoplifting or holding up a sandwich shop with your finger in your pocket—if those crimes were defined as violent felonies by the state in which they were committed.[42]

Unlike a gullible public, knowledgeable justice administrators readily see through this legislative posturing. "I feel that we're pulling one over on the public," Chase Riveland, director of Corrections for Washington state, remarked on the *MacNeil-Lehrer Newshour* in 1994, asserting that three-time loser laws were "not really dealing with violence on our streets."[43]

Shortly after the enactment of its three-strikes law, violent crime in California showed a downturn, which supporters of the three-strikes policy quickly attributed to the new law. "There is just no way to ignore the positive impact of the three strikes law," boasted Attorney General Daniel Lungren, one of its strongest proponents. "California's drop in crime (a decrease of 6.6 percent in reported offenses of violence over the first six months of 1995) is outperforming similar downward trends in other parts of the nation." More detailed research showed the inconvenient pattern that in 1994–1995 violent and overall crime rates dropped more steeply in states *without* three strikes than in those that had adopted the policy. Of the thirteen states that had the three-strikes laws in 1994, California was by far the most significant because of its size. In eight of the others increases, rather than decreases, in violent crime appeared over the same period. According to a non-partisan Rand study, if the three-strikes law remains in force unamended by 2002, California will be spending more money keeping its 40,000 strikers in prison than putting people through college.[44]

Capital punishment and long mandatory prison terms for a wide range of offenders are only symbols of toughness. The utter failure of every administration's antidrug policies and harsh sentencing laws to stem drugs in the inner cities and to prevent gun violence, particularly among juveniles, has been unable to tarnish our politicians' image as cynosures on law and order. Seasoned law enforcement administrators know that there are no sweeping solutions to violent crime. Any progress we make will be discrete and incremental; only the symbols have effect—but that is enough for lawmakers.[45]

Former Democratic Congressman Dan Rostenkowski of Illinois truly learned what crime policies he'd been voting for only after he saw the inside of prison himself after being convicted on corruption charges. He was stunned by how many low-level drug offenders were doing fifteen- and twenty-year stretches. "The waste of these lives is a loss to the entire community," Rostenkowski said in a May 1998 speech. "That's not a problem many people spend much time thinking about. . . . Certainly, I didn't give these issues a lot of thought when I was a member of the civilian population." The chagrined former Ways and Means chairman went on to express guilt for voting for these "misguided" policies. "I was swept along by the rhetoric about getting tough on crime," he said. "Frankly, I lacked both expertise and perspective on these issues. So I deferred to my colleagues who had stronger opinions but little more expertise."[46]

CONCLUSION: THE INJUSTICE

The emotional furor generated by crime myth creates political grandstanding by proposing new crimes and sentences. Political leaders advocate the most severe sanctions, such as the death penalty, at the pinnacle of media sensationalism. Though, in fact, there has been a marked downturn in our crime rates for the last twenty years and notably in the last six, there has also been an accompanying increase in punitiveness. At our millennium we lock up more people for longer sentences for more offenses than any nation on the face of the earth, after Russia.[47]

A criminal conviction no longer inspires the awe it once did partly because of the tendency of politicians, Zeus-like, to hurl penalty thunderbolts to disapprove any and all conduct, as if throwing a law at conduct will eliminate it. As Professor Herbert Packer once noted, some of this thunderbolt tendency reveals two kinds of triviality: triviality of object and triviality of intention. Triviality of object refers to selecting behavior for which criminal punishment is disproportionate, such as including marijuana as one of the predicates for felony murder, as in Arizona and elsewhere. Triviality of intent means an attitude of political indifference toward actual enforcement of their ornate enactments. Conscientious legislators would not vote to penalize conduct without knowing both that law enforcement had the resources to apprehend violators and, more fundamentally, that society truly needed such protection via its police powers.[48]

Criminal legislation is rarely motivated by aims loftier than appearing tough on crime and fueling political careers. Politicians rarely win constituent support for principled reform because uninformed voters seem to demand toughness no matter the price to principle or taxes. Much crime legislation thus becomes mulch intended to nurture political image rather than to improve justice. As in *Les Miserables*, political careers are borne aloft on the excessive pains of criminals.

Political distortion can involve crime statistics. Many lawmakers and allied groups focus falsely on crime rates. The National Rifle Association (NRA) tries to convince the public to support prison expansion. Known primarily for its vigorous opposition to gun control legislation, the NRA's legislative agenda has been to divert public fear of violent gun crime with distortion of crime rates by lying with truncated statistics showing, falsely, that increased imprisonment causes a decline in crime.[49]

Recent national drops in crime to 1973 levels have criminologists searching for causes in the same way they sought reasons for increases in crime during the previous decade. The waning of the crack cocaine epidemic, the improving economy, aging baby boomer populations, and law enforcement policies aimed at guns seem to be the consensus factors. Oddly, the most costly and widespread solution—the explosion in the prison population—doesn't seem to top anyone's list, with good reason. The preponderance of research shows no connection between incarceration rates and crime rates. New York, which is experiencing its lowest homicide rate since 1964, has also had the country's third slowest rate of prison growth over the last five years. In searching for solutions to violent crime, policymakers need to give prison growth low rank in their lists.[50]

Wars on crime and drugs involve powerful rhetoric promising the enemy's surrender. But there are no victory and no armistice. Instead, another new war is declared, as if the previous war had never taken place—but the rhetoric rarely changes. Political irresponsibility generates the cancerous growth of imprisonment and false solutions to a falsely defined problem. We place bets on measures we know work poorly while shortchanging those that work well, like drug treatment. We lurch down a path that increasingly departs from both social science research and common sense. No other area of social policy, with the possible exception of welfare, exhibits such a great divergence between competent social science research and legislative action.[51]

Pretending to fight violence by locking up mostly nonviolent criminals is an inefficient use of taxpayer resources. In the classic "bait and switch" marketing ploy, customers are baited into a store by an advertisement for an item at a very low price, and, once in the store, are switched to a higher-priced product. In the justice field, the bait is citizen fear of violent crime, and the switch occurs when politicians build more prisons but then fill them with nonviolent offenders or pass three-strikes laws that imprison minor, nonviolent felons for life. This deceptive scheme profits only politicians who wish to appear tough rather than smart. We thus spend billions of tax dollars on prisons and executions and then underfund effective and cheaper drug treatment, education programs, and violence prevention programs by asserting a lack of money.

Another form of bait and switch lies in endless legislative tinkering with court rules and procedures in hopes of reducing crime. If only some rights were stripped away, some assert, we will better fight lawlessness. If only the police had more powers, they might not have to beat on people who insist on their rights. If only judges were denied control of cases and evidence, then guilty people would not escape being found guilty. If prisoners could be housed four to a cell and death row inmates killed off speedily, all criminals could be taken off the street. This endless tinkering amounts to rearranging the deck chairs on the *Titanic*. As administrators within the system know, these changes have no impact on crime because of the funnel effect described in the prior chapter.[52] The promise that crime will decrease because of rearranging court rules cannot be delivered any more than changing the music selections could save the *Titanic*.

To this mindset, hard research is irrelevant. Why is there such a gulf between what criminologists know and what policymakers do? One reason is the failure to consider social science research, coupled with lack of political nerve, which ensures little informed debate in electoral campaigns about the roots of crime or the justice system.[53] Neither presidential candidate in 1996, for instance, spoke to the issues raised by the mushrooming of our prisons or offered an articulate response to lethal violence among our inner-city youth. Instead, Clinton and Dole reached for the most symbolic and least consequential issues: extending the death penalty, victims' rights, boot camps, and school uniforms. That none of this pabulum makes any difference in the rate of crime didn't deter either candidate from eulogizing it at enthusiastic length.[54]

Our nation's legislative debates about crime have little to do with crime. Crime is a values issue; the only value is toughness, not smart, solid social science research. In 1997 Georgia governor Zell Miller, proudly proclaiming his intention to ignore criminological research on boot camps, said, "Nobody can tell me from some ivory tower that you take a kid, you kick him in the rear end and it doesn't do any good." Speaking of criminologists' research he added "I don't give a damn what they say."[55]

Profound questions arise about the wisdom of crime policies divorced from empirical data and rooted, instead, in political image. Individual justice, distortions of process, and indefensible practices are the legacies of such head-in-the-sand policies.[56] The very failure of these inept but well advertised policies encourages a new round of political demagoguery, followed by still more attention-getting nostrums of still greater impotence. As automobiles once had built-in obsolescence, our politicization of crime is largely both self-defeating and for that reason self-perpetuating.

Former deputy attorney general Philip Heymann, an experienced criminal lawyer and administrator in the Department of Justice, has observed that our lawmakers are "swept far from common sense by the heavy winds of political rhetoric about crime." Much crime policy, in his view, only addresses citizens' fear rather than real solutions. "Pretending to retaliate fiercely against the source of fear," in his mind, has been "politically popular in every country for a very long time, but the pretense achieves nothing more than a sham": "There is less of a market for real remedies [for crime] than for patient medicines. Thus, there are dozens of new death penalties in [new crime legislation] but they are largely irrelevant to any realistic law enforcement effort. . . . The only problem is that the prescription won't improve the patient's condition."[57]

Politicians' conflict between toughness and smartness too often results in the triumph of the former over the latter. In Heymann's eyes the truly effective but difficult task is "how to be smart as well as tough" in a political environment that applauds toughness rather than smartness. He perceptively notes that it takes but a little while to explain why one solution is smart and another is not, but "it doesn't take any time at all to explain why one thing's tougher than the next."[58]

Harold Pepinsky and Paul Jesilow open their book *Myths that Cause*

Crime with a powerful statement: "The sooner we recognize that criminal justice is a state-supported racket, the better." This hyperbole is close to the truth. At bottom our politicians have a vested interest in loud symbols of crime toughness and draconian prescriptions for crime ills.[59] In fact, most crime legislation of any year is irrelevant to crime and very relevant to vote-getting, while some of it is very detrimental to our citizenry. To justify the suffering caused by the Bolshevik takeover of Russia in 1917, Trotsky once observed that making omelets requires breaking eggs. At our millennium a good number of our political and popular judicial elections similarly can only be won by harming people, breaking pocketbooks, and ignoring hard data.[60]

NOTES

1. S. Donziger, *The Real War on Crime* (New York: Harper, 1996), 80–81 (hereafter, *Real War*).

2. S. Boyd, "Bush Challenges Dukakis to Explain Stand on Crime," *New York Times*, A20 (June 19, 1988).

3. *Real War*, 81.

4. Id., 80–81. See also "Cuomo Takes Anti-Crime Stance," *Washington Post*, A9 (Jan. 6, 1994).

5. *Real War*, 80.

6. Lord Windlesham, *Politics, Punishment and Populism* (New York: Oxford University Press, 1998), 217 (hereafter, *Populism*). See also the brutalization argument in Chapter 3, this book, regarding the increased homicide rates subsequent to executions.

7. *Real War*, 80.

8. Id. In 1996 Governor Gary Johnson of New Mexico urged judges to impose more death penalties and recommended it for juveniles as young as 13. Lubbock *Avalanche-Journal*, 3A (January 16, 1996).

9. S. Bright and P. Keenan, "Judges and the Politics of Death," 75 *B.U.L.R.*, 759, 774 (1995) (hereafter, "Death Politics"). See also J. Rauch, "Death by Mistake," *National Journal*, 1225 (May 30, 1998) (hereafter, "Mistake").

10. W. Kaminer, *It's All the Rage* (New York: Addison Wesley, 1996), 77 (hereafter, *Rage*).

11. "Death Politics," 775. See also *Real War*, 80, regarding the tendency of noncriminal justice officials to jump on the crime-toughness bandwagon.

12. *Arizona Republic*, A1 (Apr. 3, 1998). See also J. Arpaio, *The Toughest Sheriff in America* (Arlington, VA: Summit Publishing, 1996).

13. *Rage*, 219.

14. "Death Politics," 785, dealing with the tendency of judicial candidates to make "tough" promises impairing partiality.

15. *Harris v. Alabama*, 115 S. Ct. 1031, 1039 (Stevens, J. dissenting).

16. "Death Politics," 760. See also Stephen B. Bright, "Political Attacks on the Judiciary," 80 *Judicature* 165 (1997); Michael F. Colley, "In Defense of the Bench," *Voir Dire*, 3, 3 (Fall 1997); N. Lee Cooper, "On Independence, Once and for All," 8 *A.B.A.*, 8 (Aug. 1997).

17. "Death Politics," 786ff.

18. Henry J. Reske, "Where to Draw the Line," *A.B.A.J.*, 99 (Dec. 1996).

19. See Bright, "Political," 165–169; Colley, "In Defense," 3.

20. Editorial, 82 *Judicature*, 52 (Sept.–Oct. 1998).

21. E. Currie, *Crime and Punishment in America* (New York: Holt, 1998), 43–44 (hereafter, Currie). See also C. Cannon, "America All Locked Up," *The National Journal*, 1910 (Sept. 15, 1998).

22. "Death Politics," 823.

23. Id., 763, 785–786.

24. M. Tonry, *Sentencing Matters* (New York: Oxford University Press, 1994), 146.

25. *Rage*, 208.

26. Id., 218.

27. V. Kappeler et al., *Mythology of Crime and Criminal Justice* (Prospect Heights, IL: Waveland Press, 1993), 248ff.

28. Cannon, "America," 1912.

29. *Rage*, 194.

30. As the *Washington Post* noted in 1992, "In good times and bad, Americans rate crime among their top five concerns. Senators and House members long ago began reading the polls, and since 1980 anticrime legislation has been passed by every Congress." Guy Gugliotta, "Crime Bill a Hostage of Politics," *Washington Post*, A1 (Aug. 5, 1992). Since 1973, over 65 percent of Americans have consistently believed that the nation should spend more money to halt the rising crime rate. Ben Wattenberg, *Values Matter Most*, 119, 124 (1996) (graphing National Opinion Research Poll). See also H. Chernoff et al., "The Politics of Crime," 33 *Harv. J. Legislation*, 527, 537 (1996).

31. *Populism*, 54.

32. Tonry, *Sentencing*, 171.

33. *Rage*, 195. See also "Mistake," 1225.

34. *Time*, 25 (Aug. 23, 1993).

35. *Rage*, 196.

36. *Populism*, 222.

37. S. Estrich, *Getting Away with Murder* (Cambridge: Harvard University Press, 1998), 73 (hereafter, Estrich).

38. M. Boorstein, "Three Strikes Laws Mostly Ignored," *Arizona Republic*, A14 (Jan. 3, 1999).

39. Estrich, 74.

40. *Rage*, 33.

41. *Populism*, 72.

42. *Rage*, 197.

43. Id., 180.

44. *Populism*, 69, 72. See also M. Boorstein, "Three," A14.

45. *Rage*, 7.

46. Cannon, "America," 1913.

47. See Alfred Blumstein, "Violence by Young People: Why the Deadly Nexus?" *Nat'l Inst. Just. J.*, 3 (Aug. 1995).

48. H. Parker, *The Limits of the Criminal Sanction* (Stanford, CA: Stanford U. Press, 1968), 272.

49. A. Blumstein, "Seeking the Connection between Crime and Punishment," 4 *Jobs and Capital*, 23 (1995).

50. V. Schiraldi, Letter to Editor, *New York Times*, A11 (Jan. 4, 1999).

51. Currie, 6.

52. See Chapter 7.

53. Currie, 7.

54. Id., 6.

55. *Rage*, 225.

56. *Populism*, 216.

57. Id., 77.

58. Id.

59. H. Pepinsky and P. Jesilow, *Myths That Cause Crime* (Cabin John, MD: Seven Locks Press, 1985), 10.

60. As quoted in Tonry, *Sentencing*, 118.

CONCLUSION: IN SEARCH OF PRINCIPLED JUSTICE

Reform, reform—don't speak to me of reform; things are bad enough
as it is.

—Victorian legal reformer

The preceding analyses describe our justice system's repudiation of some
established legal principles and many social science findings. Why this disregard? In part, because of the opposition of two competing views regarding how criminal law achieves civic compliance. The two views could be
called "positivist" and "magisterial."

"Positivism" reveals these implications:

1. The citizenry serves the law, not vice versa, and the law views the
citizenry as a mass rather than as individuals.

This principle holds, with Thomas Hobbes and others, that the law's
sanctions promote political cohesion, a goal achieved via universal penal
consequences imposed on a compliant citizenry, whose collective obedience
serves the state's interest in harmony and control. The citizen's highest role
is to follow the law.

2. Efficacy of criminal law depends on police powers; the law acquires
more deterrent effect as it becomes more severe.

This principle reflects John Austin's view and that of the tradition of
legal positivism generally that the law's claim to efficacy lies in the strength
of the enforcement powers that back it up. In this view, the citizenry obeys

the criminal law not out of respect for its moral authority but from fear of penal consequences.

3. Criminals calculate crime in advance by a utilitarian calculus, weighing expected pleasures of crime against the likelihood and severity of punishment.

This axiom reflects the view of Jeremy Bentham, John Stuart Mill, and other utilitarians that human beings calculate expected gains and losses from behavior in general and criminal choices in particular. A citizen's degree of obedience thus turns on whether pleasures seem to outweigh pains of anticipated conduct. Punishments that are most severe, such as imprisonment and death, most effectively deter because they cause the greatest pain. Hence, an authoritarian government able to communicate and to inflict great pain best achieves legal compliance.

4. From an enforcer's perspective, punishment proceeds via the behavioral practice of negative reinforcement; crime must be followed reflexively by uniform, inescapable, and severe punishment.

This principle reflects the view of B. F. Skinner and other behaviorists, artfully displayed in Skinner's novel *Walden II*, that legal compliance results from systematically visiting unacceptable behavior with deprivation. Criminal behavior will diminish under a regime of uniform, negative reinforcement applied equally to all same-crime offenders.

5. By breaking the law, criminals lose any expectation of being treated by legal principle; they do not deserve principle because they do not live by it.

This norm reflects the view of some political and legal philosophers from Machiavelli to Rousseau that those who break the law also break the social compact uniting them to that society's legal system. As outcasts, they have no claim on its laws because the law grants its benefits only to its adherents.

6. In the fight against crime, enhancing political image as an authoritarian crime fighter is more important to public security than reacting to empirical criminological data.

This principle reflects the notion that crime is primarily a perception problem addressing the citizenry's need to feel secure. Hence, empirical data or views from experienced workers in the field yield to authoritarian devices that augment the sense of citizen security in, and dependence on, their political leaders.

Another competing view, not arbitrarily called "magisterial," shows the following contrasting traits:

1. The law serves the citizenry, not vice versa, and views them as individuals rather than as a group.

This principle holds, with Aristotle, Jacques Maritain, and others, that the best law serves the individual interests of the citizenry, who, in turn, respect it when they discover that its authority rests on moral principle rather than on police power.

2. Efficacy of law depends not on civic fear but moral authority, namely, adherence to fair principles in whatever particularized laws the community demands. Government achieves legal observance best by exemplifying in its laws principles of fairness, desert, and proportionality.

This principle echoes a natural law message that law arises not primarily from written enactments but from moral obligations implanted within each human being prior to, and independent of, legislation. Obedience to such law betters the individual. Legal observance results for this reason rather than from fear of being caught and punished.

3. Criminals, for the most part, commit crime without calculating the expected pains and pleasures of its consequences; to the extent that they do (rarely) calculate, deterrence via imposing or publicizing severe sanctions has little success in reducing such behavior.

This principle reflects much criminological research showing that almost all crime, particularly street crime, is an impulsive, ill-considered decision of the moment only rarely considerate of penal consequences. In the rare case when penal consequences are anticipated, they are simply disregarded as unlikely to occur.

4. Compliance with the law results best not from a behavioral regime of classical or operant conditioning where negative reinforcement shapes reflex behavior but, rather, from the pedagogical example of laws teaching moral principles.

This norm follows the extensive research of Thomas Tyler, Georg Simmel and others[1] to the effect that people obey the law not because they fear punishment but because they respect principles that all the citizenry, including criminals, are expected to adopt. The law's highest function, then, is not to punish but to teach, and its highest pedagogy lies in exemplifying its teachings in its own workings.

5. Justice does not punish by the *lex talionis*—we do not rape the rapist or steal from the thief—because such practices exemplify the very behavior we need to extinguish. Offenders deserve to be treated by principle just as much as law-abiders because offenders need to learn to restore these same principles in their own lives. For the law to act otherwise teaches otherwise.

This axiom also follows the research of Tyler and others that the law is not primarily a machine for punishing but a teaching and transmitting agent. It announces and transmits fundamental values via the behavior of police, courts, and corrections; civic observance results more effectively when citizens come to learn these values rather than fear arbitrary or authoritarian punishment.

6. Empirical data about penal effectiveness as well as about the extent of society's need for protection from crime work better in shaping criminal policy than the need of authorities to appear punitive.

This principle reflects with less eloquence Norval Morris' reminder: "Punishment cannot remake man; it can to a degree influence his behavior but it is very easy to exaggerate its effect; man can be more easily led to decency than whipped to it."[2]

This magisterial view reflects considerable social science research. Tyler finds that litigants are not as concerned with whether they have won or lost as with the fairness of legal procedures. Compliant civic behavior does not result primarily from reward and punishment but from the law's example of legitimacy, morality, and fairness. Fair treatment matters in this view more than coercion. People come to obey the law because they admire its modeling of fairness.

This view echoes today, in part, in the "broken windows" view of policing, which postulates, correctly it seems, that a climate of neglect of minor violations encourages disregard of major matters. If a window in a building is broken and left unrepaired, others soon follow; similarly, if the police ignore small-time violators, more serious offenses result.[3] The "broken windows" policing philosophy reflects a practical, grassroots application of the magisterial concept of law: if the law teaches by example, what it ignores promotes a climate of imitation in the citizenry. Put affirmatively, people live up to what the law models, for good or ill.

The impact of magisterial fairness on legal observance differs strikingly from the positivist model in classical criminology and economic theory.[4] Creating a moral climate for law alters compliance more effectively than altering the certainty or severity of punishments. Paul Robinson and John Darley put it well: "Most people obey the law not because they fear punishment but because they see themselves as persons who want to do the right thing."[5]

These contrasting models resonate in the problems discussed earlier and in the solutions suggested in the following.

SENTENCING

Our federal and state sentencing policy in the past quarter century has moved from indeterminacy to definiteness, from open to closed maximums, from rehabilitation to just deserts, becoming more punitive, less proportionate to culpability, and more generic. The movement reveals positivist ideology more than a magisterial policy.

In the magisterial ideal, punishment in general and sentencing in particular necessarily see retribution as more basic than other penal justifications. The offender stands before the court not as an instrument for the future utilitarian purposes of incapacitation, deterrence, or rehabilitation but fundamentally and only because of having previously broken a law. Culpability both justifies presence at sentencing and measures the fitting degree of punishment for moral restoration. Retribution, in this classic Kantian sense, is thus the most fundamental explanatory and limiting justification for sentencing, reflecting why the offender merits any deprivation, to what extent, and for what purpose.

Retribution explains only accountability; it does not dictate any future utilitarian goals. Liability and punishment based on retribution maximize the system's moral credibility and harness powerful reformative forces that influence an individual's conduct more so than the threat of punishment. Such a retributive distribution entails subsequent deterrent and incapacitation effects. But, for moral credibility, the amount of punishment necessarily reflects what the offender morally deserves because of the offense. Once this limiting norm is accepted, the conflict among sentencing purposes dissipates.[6]

Theoretical disputes about abstract penal purposes dissolve in a distinction between a general justice goal for all offenders (retribution) and particular utilitarian goals for an individual offender. As Tonry puts it, sentencing could be seen, analogously, somewhat like a cafeteria. It could offer a complete menu of all goals and then choose the most fitting for specific offenders. Retribution undergirds, rather than dictates, this choice. In a burglary involving three offenders, for example, the ringleader with a lengthy prior burglary record may deserve long incapacitation in prison. His companion, a first offender needing drug money, may need mandatory drug treatment. The remaining offender with education, no drugs, and a supportive family might deserve a fine coupled with utilitarian community service and a confessional lecture tour.

The overriding sentencing principles are that (1) the system, rooted in retribution, should offer a wide array of all utilitarian purposes and that (2) individual offenders, even those committing the same crime, should fit into only the one or two future utilities shaped by their unique circumstances, to avoid the faceless positivism of sentencing all those guilty of the same crime to the same sentence.[7]

A Common Law of Sentencing?

A recent book critical of federal sentencing guidelines suggests that the remedy for their mathematical computations is to return to a common law of judge-made sentencing.[8]

To be sure, a common law of sentencing would be simpler than codified guidelines that, like the tax code, quantify all contingencies. But simplicity risks disparity. Different judges could well impose radically different sentences for identical crimes. Without general boundaries a judge imposing a common-law sentence has nothing to apply but gut feelings. Different judges, of course, view sentencing differently. A wide divergence of sentences is inevitable without some legislative parameters. This unfettered judicial discretion prompted the Frankel call for legislative standards in

1972. To return to unstructured common-law sentencing would resurrect rampant sentence disparity.

Mandatory Sentencing

Practical nuts-and-bolts changes are needed in sentencing legislation. One of the first involves abolishing mandatory sentences.

Prior to the 1970s, a judge would set a minimum and maximum sentence and allow a parole board to determine release. Although this system provides incentives for inmates to improve during incarceration, too much discretion given to corrections and parole officials generates release disparities based on race, sex, and other factors. Determinate systems face the opposite problem of treating all offenders with similar offense histories as fungible look-alikes despite different circumstances. This problem reaches its positivist apogee with mandatory sentencing where judicial discretion yields to generic sentencing by crime category. Mandatory sentence policy falsely assumes that all criminals committing the same crime deserve the same punishment and thereby betrays the ideal of punishment proportioned to individual circumstances and, in the process, eviscerates any real claim to giving the offender a "just" desert.

The conclusion offered by Assistant Attorney General Brownsberger about the counterproductivity of mandatory drug sentences applies equally well to all mandatory sentences:

When incarceration becomes routine, it cannot deter crime and may even be seen as a positive rite of passage. . . . Mandatory penalties for drug offenses lead to the inflexible over-application of harsh punishment, further diminishing its deterrence value, misallocating scarce resources and exacerbating high incarceration rates. Our main conclusion from this report is that we need to moderate our mandatory drug sentencing policies.[9]

Rigid state sentencing guidelines pose similar problems. While they guide judicial discretion and control correctional resources, unless they allow flexibility for individual differences, they contribute to the same cookie-cutter inequities of "one size fits all" that mandatory minimums create.[10] By reducing the severity of mandatories, lawmakers would take an important step toward the goals of consistency and proportionality.

Presumptive Mandatories

Much of what legislators expect from mandatory sentencing would result from making sentences presumptive, with judges authorized to vary them, within limits, for aggravating or mitigating reasons. Converting mandatory

penalties to presumptive sacrifices few of the positivist values of mandatories but avoids the fungibility of preset, cookie-cutter dispositions.

In a flexible presumptive approach, judges could take account of mitigating or aggravating circumstances without subterfuge. Sentencing grids
could adopt an elastic presumptive format, and sentencing could address
the convicted offense without, however, any consideration of acquitted or
noncharged offenses. Aggravating and mitigating factors would permit an
articulated departure from the norm and, in the process, lessen the impetus
for covert plea bargaining to reach a fair penalty. The gain, in the end,
would be both punishment that fits the crime and fidelity to sentencing
statutes.

Nonlegislative Sentencing Commissions

Mandatory statutory punishments are irresistible targets for positivist
politicians who progressively increase penalties to enhance their authoritarian image. These sentencing policies succumb to ever-increasing penal
escalations because lawmakers focus on toughness to the exclusion of empirical data about sentence effectiveness and individual differences.

The time is overdue to remove sentencing from these political devices. In
lieu of legislative control, a sentencing agency constituted by law professors,
sociologists, and especially criminologists should set and amend sentence
lengths based exclusively on empirical data. This sentencing commission
could also monitor adherence to sentencing guidelines. The sentencing
lengths would be presumptive, neither merely voluntary nor mandatory,
and immune from reflexive "drive-by sentencing" by lawmakers.[11]

Sentencing laws would then be structured by this commission to mandate
educational or substance abuse programs based on specific offender needs
and to allow a preset reduction of sentence upon completion of an educational or substance abuse program. If the justice system wants to prevent
recidivism, prisoners need sentencing incentives to participate in such tailored programs, which need to be risk-specific in design and beyond the
reach of political tampering.

PLEA BARGAINING

Unlike evicting the money changers from the temple, plea bargaining is
unlikely ever to be evicted from the courthouse. It is our justice system's
embarrassing centerpiece, which, like a loveless marriage, can only be en-
dured. But the bleakness of this assessment need not prevent reform in how
it operates. Plea bargaining now is but another name for sentencing. The
most effective defense counsel and prosecutor are not those who can best
litigate but who can obtain the best "deal."

Our justice system now processes 95 percent of all cases through negotiable justice. We routinely reach condemnation without adjudication, and when adjudication appears on the horizon, prosecutors and sentencing mandates threaten a greater sanction to discourage it. Our justice system thus becomes a vice: the system favors a plea and penalizes the constitutional right to a trial. Practical pressures toward bargaining result in the de facto diminution of the constitutional right to a trial for most defendants.

From a positivist viewpoint, plea bargaining is a necessity not for any reason inherent in case facts but for lawyers' caseloads. Most defense attorneys, excepting those few known as true trial attorneys, depend on plea agreements to make their fees and move cases. Trials fall like a wrench in this turnstile, which impedes a trial even more when defendants face a draconian mandatory sentence. The posttrial sentence is almost always more severe than it would be under a plea agreement.

The plea bargaining dialectic reinforces an attitude of manipulation. The least sophisticated defendants understand that this positivist bazaar operates by threat, bluster, and push-pull gymnastics matching their criminal wiles. Instead of standing for principle, the courts thereby echo manipulative attitudes similar to those of the criminal. Rehabilitation is thus seriously compromised from the start because the system reinforces the very manipulative mentality it seeks to eradicate.

Another of bargaining's negative impacts is its deviation from the uniformity desired in fixed sentencing standards. Plea bargaining regularly circumvents federal sentencing guidelines in at least 30 percent of all cases; deviation from state mandatories is probably higher. Precisely because of their preset severity, rigid sentencing mandates increase the impetus for plea bargaining. Bargaining also shifts sentencing from judges to prosecutors and drives prosecutorial discretion more deeply underground. These circumventing practices are as statutorily dishonest as they are covert.

Neither attorneys nor judges announce their willful evasion of legislated penalties, of course, so bargaining occurs secretly in the bowels of the court, far from public scrutiny. Judges who find that downward departure mechanisms do not provide an adequate vehicle to individualize the sentence welcome low-visibility departures from the guidelines. By far the most important vehicle for evasion is charge bargaining, which leads to the dismissal of readily provable counts. This tactic includes "horizontal" charge bargaining and the use of superseding indictments to replace charges with an offense having a lower statutory maximum.

A number of ideas exist for altering this positivist culture of surreptitious bargaining. One is simply to provide a preset discount for defendants who plead guilty. The federal sentencing commission tries to do this by allowing a sentence reduction for "acceptance of responsibility," but the flip side of this same incentive punishes exercise of the right to trial.

In contrast to positivist reinforcement of an offender's manipulative worldview, a magisterial approach to plea bargaining would impose some standards reflecting the true severity of the crime and limiting the scope of charge and sentence reductions.

One way to take some manipulation out of the bargaining process is by taking the fixing of the criminal charge out of the lawyers' hands. An effective, systemic way to achieve this end is by revitalizing the preliminary hearing procedure with judicial amendment powers. At the preliminary hearing the prosecutor would propose a charge and present evidence to support it. The magistrate would then define the true charge based on the evidence presented, amending inflated charges to conform to the evidence. When preliminary hearings terminate in charges that accurately reflect the true state of the evidence, the prosecutor's compelling incentive to overcharge is counterbalanced, and, as a result, a stable system of bargaining becomes possible. To ensure some uniformity, both the prosecution and defense could appeal the magistrate's setting of the charge to an appellate court, as occurs in France, where the French Court of Appeals can review the magistrate's charge.

In addition to judicial review of the original charge, control could also appear at the charging and sentencing ends of the bargaining process. A magisterial approach would impose limits to unfettered discretion both to and overcharge and overreduce. Legislation could prohibit prosecutors from reducing either a charge or a sentence more than one level or class below its original status. Prohibiting charge and sentence reduction beyond one level would ensure equality of bargaining across the defendant population and reduce the unseemly message that charges can be drastically reduced at the total whim of prosecutors.

Finally, to ensure their impartiality, judges who participate in unsuccessful plea negotiations need to be disqualified by rule from conducting any trial of that defendant. To do so after hearing the defendant's abortive admission of guilt belies any notion of judicial impartiality.

THE DEATH PENALTY

Capital punishment is positivism at its apogee. The present sound-bite symbolism of the death penalty serves only vote-hungry politicians. As the regrettable Texas example shows, the death penalty is the great vote-getter, premised on fanning and appeasing the cries of a redneck electorate for a public executioner: retribution plus revenge plus retaliation equal reelection. To disregard that political chicanery is to follow Governors Dukakis and Cuomo and other politicians down the fatal path of appearing soft on crime. Setting out a firm crime policy that doesn't include the death penalty requires unusual patience for long-range change tied to persistence and courage, the latter difficult to come by these days. Many prosecutors and judges say privately that they're against the death penalty, yet in the court-room and city square no one is willing to mount the podium and say that the executioner wears no clothes.

The state's example of taking life in order to emphasize the value of life teaches the exact opposite of what it intends. French philosopher Michel Foucault observes that the rampant abuse of power in state executions itself creates crime. Excessive and arbitrary executions incited people at the end of the eighteenth century to violence: the terror of the public execution created its own illegality. On execution days, work stopped, the taverns were full, the authorities were abused, insults or stones were thrown at the executioner, fights broke out, and there was no better prey for thieves than the curious throng around the scaffold. People taught by this positivist system that imposed lethal violence copied the violence themselves. This phenomenon generated the monastic prison, private executions, and a more bureaucratic form of punishment deservedly hidden from public view.

Foucault's ideas apply to the transmission of all penal norms. Like any other law, but more emphatically, capital punishment shows government power teaching its truth via the principle of transmission, which is the legal system. The positivist teaching of our present death ethic is not subtle: if you have power, you may kill those who threaten that power. This axiom exactly matches the ethic of most capital offenders. Recent research amply supports this brutalization lesson: the example of an official execution, in-stead of deterring killings, actually prompts some power-addicted persons to follow the government's lethal example.[12]

From a magisterial perspective, capital punishment is offensive on both moral and technical grounds even apart from politicians' noxious swooning over it. For those who do not or cannot address the moral issues, there remain the disturbing facts, supported by national and international data, that our capital punishment falls disproportionately on minorities, espe-cially blacks and Hispanics. It also sweeps some innocent defendants in its wide nets, such as the seventy-three wrongfully convicted, wholly innocent death row survivors invited to an October 1998 death penalty conference at Northwestern University, living testimonials to the high rate of capital error.

These considerations, among other embarrassments of our death ma-chine, have prompted the United Nations, Amnesty International, and the American Bar Association to condemn our nation's burgeoning death prac-tice and to call for a moratorium on its use. A moratorium alone can hardly redress the moral and human shortcomings of our capital punishment. Nor can judicial or legislative control correct untrammeled prosecutorial discre-tion to charge, to seek the death penalty, and to plea-bargain around it at total whim—an ocean of discretion that still squarely violates the stan-dardization mandated in *Furman v. Georgia*.[13] The only realistic magiste-rial option is outright abolition.

If politicians lack the courage to confront capital punishment's counter-productivity head-on, there still remain modest, but necessary, improvements for the existing positivism. The embarrassing slaughterhouse practices of Texas suggest, instead, that capital defendants need to have truly expert legal counsel at public expense at all court stages. Furthermore, politician judges and prosecutors who campaign on promises to liberally impose the death penalty ought to be disqualified by law and ethical rule from trial or appellate involvement in any capital case, simply because their electoral pandering eviscerates any plausible remnant of impartiality. Rogue states like Texas need to adhere to the Anti-Terrorism and Effective Death Penalty Act of 1996, whose modest saving feature is to impose on state courts the burden of impartial confirmation that death penalties are truly constitutional, by providing reasons for judicial and parole board decisions.[14]

FELONY MURDER

Positivism's fifth principle finds a deserved home in the felony-murder rule, which shows from a rule-making perspective how our justice system disregards principle for those who act in unprincipled ways.

This positivist rule certainly is not an indispensable ingredient for any system of justice. It is now unknown in continental Europe and its nation of origin, England. Even in its limited formulations it is still objectionable. It is unsound principle to convert an accidental, negligent, or reckless death into a murder simply because it occurred during the time boundaries of a felony. Engaging in a felony, of course, may show enough recklessness to establish manslaughter or intent sufficient to establish murder, but such findings are independent determinations in each case. The ratio of homicides during felonies to the total number of felonies hardly justifies a universal presumption of homicide culpability sufficient to establish murder. No logic in the rule can presume culpability sufficient to establish first-degree murder universally.

To the Model Penal Code, the rule is so contrary to basic criminal and civil principles that it should be abandoned as an independent basis for homicide.[15] Some states that lack the political courage to abolish it have at least limited it, but even enlightened limitations do not resolve its essential illogic. Our law does not otherwise predicate liability automatically on conduct causing death. Apart from felony murder, punishment for homicide occurs only for conduct committed with an actual homicidal state of mind that makes the result reprehensible, not merely unfortunate. A murder conviction should result only from premeditative forethought, the very mental state lacking from capital felony murder.

In a magisterial view, criminal liability attaches to individuals rather than to generalities. It is no effective positivist rejoinder to these complaints to say that some felony murderers deserve this dire verdict. Some may, but others may not. Felony murder should rest on more than a generalized imposition of homicidal guilt on all unlucky felons.

Requiring that the underlying felony create a foreseeable risk to life limits felony murder to cases of negligent homicide, a crime that adequately covers all deaths during a felony. This worthwhile reform limits extreme applications of the rule and preserves mental state differences. First-degree murder and negligent homicide, after all, carry vastly different sanctions that reflect differing mental states. Punishment for the greater offense on proof only of the lesser mental state wreaks the same violence to standard principles of culpability as does the unqualified rule.

Most principled criminal codifications in states retaining the rule limit it to felonies of inherent violence. Some jurisdictions have enacted affirmative defenses when death is not a reasonably foreseeable consequence of the felony, in order to avoid a murder conviction where an actor lacks culpability for the homicidal behavior of an accomplice. Some states reduce the grade of the offense to a degree less than first-degree murder, such as manslaughter.

What does a magisterial perspective suggest? If principles such as *mens rea*, proportional punishment, congruity with civil law and, indeed, with the rest of criminal law itself are truly valued, a magisterial homicide law would proclaim those values to those whose behavior is unprincipled, precisely those who most need to learn principle.

Ultimately, the only honest remedy is to abolish the rule just as the more principled English and commonwealth legal systems did long ago. England has not moaned loss of the rule it created. The result is not a statutory vacuum. Prosecution under some less inflated degree of homicide such as reckless manslaughter or negligent homicide could still occur. A judgment and sentence consonant with the felon's true mental state would result. The law would regain the fairness lost via its descent into the unprincipled fiction that all felons deserve to be treated as killers just because they are unlucky. A magisterial system thereby would exemplify an insight from the common law lost in our current politicized penology, namely, that the universal principles of culpability should apply as much to felons as to other players in the justice system.

MARIJUANA

After alcohol and tobacco, pot is America's number one drug choice, offering a transient, introspective high that at one extreme can cure nausea or, at the other, make the evening sitcoms look like devastating wit. Its prohibition establishes a baseline cultural dishonesty that we cannot escape: President Clinton smoked pot but, wisely, "didn't inhale." Our positivist pot law continues to pursue a failed, arbitrary policy that needlessly ruins lives in order only to appear tough.

A society that punishes marijuana more severely than violent crimes reflects, if not a deep psychosis, at least racial prejudice and cultural fear. Pot laws reflect the positivist principle that empirical medical data about health effects are irrelevant to political authority. Our marijuana policy thus becomes a prohibition in search of a rationale, a desperate search to find some medical reason to validate a prior culturally inspired prohibition.

The claims made in the 1970s and 1980s about the effect of marijuana— that it causes brain damage, chromosome damage, sterility, infertility, and even homosexuality—have never been proven and likely never will. Marijuana may pose dangers still unknown, but apart from pot, we do not criminalize the unknown. The British medical journal *The Lancet*, in a recent editorial calling for decriminalization of marijuana, felt confident enough to declare that smoking cannabis, even long-term, is not harmful to health.[16]

Although heavy marijuana use does harm the respiratory system just as does tobacco, marijuana remains one of the least toxic therapeutic substances known. No fatal dose of the drug has appeared despite more than 5,000 years of recorded use. Pot is less toxic than many common foods and legal drugs. Denying cancer patients, AIDS patients, and paraplegics a useful medicine, safer than most legally prescribed drugs, is inhumane. Dronabinol, a drug that contains the same active ingredient, THC, as in marijuana, has been available by prescription for more than a decade.

A federal policy that prohibits physicians from alleviating suffering via marijuana is misguided. It is also hypocritical to forbid physicians to prescribe marijuana while permitting them to prescribe more dangerous morphine and meperidine to relieve dyspnea and pain. With both these drugs the difference between the dose that relieves pain and hastens death is very narrow. By contrast, there is no risk at all of death from marijuana. To demand evidence of therapeutic purity is equally hypocritical; we certainly don't make this demand for tobacco or alcohol. What really counts is whether a seriously ill patient feels relief as a result of pot's intervention, not whether a controlled trial proves its efficacy.

When the law is out of step with society's norms and labels ordinary citizens lawbreakers, its ability to shape the behavior of that community is seriously compromised. Public scorn results. In the watering holes of our youth, pot laws have created a subculture of lawbreakers with disdain for all law, an attitude that only induces more pot use and more disrespect for law and, indeed, for the adult world generally. Studies that show, falsely, that marijuana and alcohol lead to hard drugs get the question backward. The legal system, by branding potheads with a criminal label, reduces the cost of being so labeled a second time.

Whatever their reasons, authoritarian lawmakers are out of step with the public as well as with empirical data. Polls consistently show that the public favors marijuana for health purposes. Federal authorities could begin by rescinding the prohibition on medical marijuana for ill patients and eliminating marijuana's status as a schedule 1 drug.

We should go further. The conclusions of Presidents Nixon's and Reagan's many independent drug commissions are as valid today as they were decades ago: we should decriminalize marijuana. Decriminalization could be the first step toward a rational national policy. The benefits would be immediate. Law enforcement resources would shift from the apprehension and imprisonment of marijuana offenders to the prevention of truly serious crimes.

Human benefits would also accrue. The human cost of the pot war far exceeds financial cost. In 1997, 695,201 Americans (double the 1992 figure) were arrested for possession of marijuana, giving these mostly young people a permanent criminal record for use of a drug as accepted in their culture as alcohol in the adult culture. Many thousands of youngsters are serving long terms in prison for a first, nonviolent pot offense while being supervised by tobacco and alcohol addicts acting as guards. The inconsistency and hypocrisy of these policies undermine respect for law generally.

The time has come for a magisterial marijuana policy calmly based on facts. We could begin a step-by-step process by legalizing medical marijuana and then move gradually to the legalization of small amounts for personal use, moving to a policy that has worked well in the Netherlands: allowing pot to be bought and used in licensed coffeehouses. If, as expected, no disasters result in any of these stages, outright legalization is in order to put pot in the same broad category as our far more detrimental but legal drugs, alcohol and tobacco. In the process we would abandon the upside-down process of first prohibiting a drug and then trying to discover a reason for doing so.

HARD DRUGS

In the 1980s, organized parent groups vigorously demanded that something be done about hard drugs. Politicians, typically, responded by demanding increased punishment. That positivist approach is strikingly effective not in solving the problem but in alleviating the political pressure to do something. The public generally accepts that approach to almost all criminal problems without questioning whether more punishment really solves the problem.

This political posturing generates a succession of escalating drug cycles. Public demand leads to intensified efforts to attack the drug trade. That doesn't have much effect, so the efforts are intensified. Many states, as a result, have so inflated their mandatory-minimum sentences for drug dealing that they have made them comparable to the sentences for homicide, leading to dramatic growth in the number of drug arrests and filling prisons with many nonviolent drug offenders.

The frustration felt by politicians and law enforcement officers over their inability to kill the hydra-headed drug monster makes this positivist temptation strong. Prison camps for users and gallows for dealers sound good on the campaign trail but are ill suited for solving the drug problem or sending a respect-the-law message. Our government got into this drug war taffy pull in the first place less because of lapses in rational policy than because of the political seductions of drug control. Like plea bargaining, this war provides shiny badges of political empire-building opportunities at home and abroad: the rhetoric of the War on Drugs, like that of being tough on crime, increases jobs and brings out the vote.

Blanket prohibition itself is at the core of the drug problem. The diversion of substantial police, judicial, and prison resources to arresting, prosecuting, and incarcerating millions of drug users and dealers, at an annual cost of tens of billions of tax dollars and untold human lives, is not simply a drug problem but a drug prohibition problem. When drug dealers kill one another and innocent bystanders, that's a prohibition problem. When drug addicts steal or prostitute themselves to support drug habits made more expensive by the black market, that's also a prohibition problem. When addicts spread the HIV virus because sterile syringes are not legally and readily available, that, too, is a direct result of prohibition.

Our drug war has achieved a self-perpetuating life of its own, fueled by the fruits of seizures and forfeitures that have made drug policing profitable and acquisitive. However irrational as a policy, it is fully rational as a bureaucratic, empire-building strategy for enforcers. Like addicts, drug war politicians are in denial. The debate about hard drugs will go nowhere if it remains a choice between waging a scorched-earth war as though defeat were impossible or surrendering completely to legalization. So long as the question is structured in bleak extremes, we will continue to turn our prison empires into the most expensive and least effective drug treatment centers in the world.

Contrasted to American policy, other Western countries follow a principle of harm reduction: they hope to minimize the injury drugs do rather than stamp them out. They do not, as we do, expect to make their country drug-free, and they do not rely, as we do, on the punitive criminal law as the first line of defense. In our nation, where both major political parties accept millions of dollars from alcohol and tobacco lobbyists, demand for "zero-tolerance" and blanket condemnations of hard drugs ring hollow. Tobacco and alcohol, not heroin or cocaine, are the most widely abused and deadly drugs ingested by teenagers. Eighth graders in America today drink alcohol at least three times as often as they use hard drugs. Drug education should promote drug-free lives without scare tactics, lies, and hypocrisy to suggest, falsely, that drug abuse is worse than alcoholism or nicotine addiction.

Drug researcher Joseph Califano has observed that our national drug policy of using blanket imprisonment for all drug users wastes public funds, endangers public safety, supports the illegal drug market, defies common sense, and offends compassion.[17] The most common denominator among prison inmates is not race or ethnic background; it is addiction, and alcohol is the addiction greater than drugs.[18]

Politicians spouting tough, but unfounded, rhetoric have led us to believe (1) that prisons are full of incorrigible psychopaths, (2) that treatment does not work, and (3) that addiction is a moral weakness that any individual can correct by willpower. The truth is that prisons are, wall-to-wall, full of addicts and abusers; that alcohol is more criminogenic than hard drugs; that treatment works better than many long-shot cancer therapies; and that, like diabetes or hypertension, drug addiction is a chronic disease that requires continuing treatment.

Our drug policy needs to call an armistice, to seek a realistic accommodation, to discourage Rambo misadventures that have proven ineffective. It might be less threatening to our expanding narcomilitary empire if we spoke in terms of getting smart instead of merely getting tough.

Treatment

A federal study in 1998 finds 21 percent fewer drug abusers regularly using illicit drugs five years after they leave treatment, a success rate that translates into more than 150,000 fewer drug users on the streets.[19]

The study tracked drug use and criminal behavior of 1,799 clients discharged from ninety-nine drug treatment facilities in 1990. It found that the percentage using cocaine five years after treatment declines by 45 percent, marijuana by 28 percent, crack cocaine by 17 percent, and heroin by 14 percent. Those who continued using drugs generally used less than before their treatment. The study also found that thefts and burglaries committed by former patients declined by as much as 38 percent, prostitution by 23 percent, and car thefts by 56 percent compared with the five years before they entered treatment. Recent research has again shown the efficacy of the drug treatment approach even in the Nixon era, by comparison with our present punitive approach.[20] Yet, despite these repeated treatment successes, only 17 percent of drug users needing treatment receive it.

Arizona, the first state to begin treating all its nonviolent drug offenders rather than locking them up, reported in April 1999 that its policy of diverting personal possessors and users from prison into mandatory treatment saved $2.5 million in tax money, most of which otherwise would have gone simply to build more prison cells. Furthermore, of the 2,622 people on probation diverted into treatment, 77.5 percent tested free of drugs after one year, a rate significantly higher than for offenders on probation in most other states. Arizona sentences drug offenders to mandatory treatment once they have been convicted and tailors the treatment regimen to the particular drug dependency.

Drug Courts

In response to growing prison numbers, many jurisdictions have created drug courts based on an aggressive intervention model that focuses on treatment as an alternative to prison. Treatment-oriented courts feature outpatient treatment under close court supervision. A drug treatment court represents a collaborative effort of every segment of the justice community, including the court, prosecutor, defense attorney, probation officer, and treatment provider. Eligible drug users identified early in the process are assessed for treatment needs and directed toward tailored treatment programs rather than prisons. All this typically occurs within one to three days of arrest.

Besides front-loading treatment upon entry into the system, rather than back-loading it after adjudication, the most distinguishing characteristic of a drug treatment court is continuous judicial supervision throughout the individual's contact with the justice system by regular, biweekly court appearances and testing for review of compliance with the treatment program.[21]

Methadone

In the fall of 1998, when President Clinton's drug czar, Gen. Barry McCaffrey, announced that he wanted to make methadone more widely available, one of the first to attack the plan ("replacing one drug with another") was New York mayor Rudy Giuliani, who proclaimed that the goal, instead, should be "to make America drug free." This former prosecutor somehow failed to imagine how New York's 30,000 addicts on methadone would finance their habits if the government took their free methadone away. We thus have a mayor who prides himself as a crime fighter opposing the one drug strategy proven to fight drug-related crime.

The efficacy of methadone in the treatment of drug addiction is well documented. Regular doses break the user's wild swings between euphoria and withdrawal by stabilizing the level of opiates in the bloodstream. Methadone does not generate the euphoria of an opiate but reduces withdrawal symptoms and blunts the craving for heroin. Addicts in methadone maintenance programs show decreased drug use, lower crime rates, better social functioning, and reduced likelihood of transmitting AIDS and hepatitis.

These outcomes have caused panels of the National Institutes of Health and the Institute of Medicine at the National Academy of Sciences to recommend expanding access to methadone maintenance.

Methadone needs to be available in drug-infested neighborhoods on a walk-in basis. We need to create more intensive residential treatment slots for hard-core addicts. Methadone programs cost $3,000 a year in 1999 dollars; residential programs cost upward of $20,000. Moreover, Medicaid doesn't pay for residential programs, but it does pay for methadone, even when patients don't give up their other drugs.

Severity

Our drug sentences are too punitive, often more so than our violent-crime penalties. We could mitigate the harshness of these policies with little risk of expansion of drug use to give shorter sentences to retail drug sellers; to de-emphasize the arrest of users for simple possession; and to shift drug resources from prison into prevention and treatment. Fairness, penal efficiency, and less plea bargain pressure would result.

The political fear of appearing soft on drugs has contaminated our public drug debate. Drug crimes are not part and parcel of a univocal category of crime. Drug enforcement differs from other kinds of law enforcement in that locking up a burglar might lessen that crime, whereas locking up one drug dealer simply leaves the same customers for new dealers, just as with prostitution. The prostitution analogy is apt. Do we really want to pursue a policy of targeting replaceable street-level dealers for mandatory sentences that impose great costs on vulnerable minorities while accomplishing little, if any, objective deterrence? It is too high a price to pay to provide politicians with a halo regarding a problem that, at its root, lies in the consumption habits of impoverished, urban youth.

If we harbored a less bellicose frame of mind, we might devise a workable hard-drug strategy with less polarity. Let us tolerate some mild drugs such as marijuana, which consumes enormous justice resources but creates far less evil than tobacco or alcohol. At the same time we could use high taxation and personal licensing to reduce alcohol and tobacco use and even prohibit tobacco sales except to registered nicotine addicts indifferent to their death wish. For everyone who dies from cocaine poisoning, fifteen die from alcohol and sixty from tobacco-related illnesses. The mortality rate of tobacco users because of tobacco is more than 100 times greater than the rate for cocaine users. We could begin by ranking these health risks and treating them proportionate to their severity.

Whatever the statutory scheme, our law needs to treat addicts alike. Lower-class addicts, tuxedoed millionaire addicts, and addicts in sports uniforms need to be treated in an evenhanded manner without special exemptions. An antidrug commercial from a convicted sports addict from one of our drug-infested pro teams might well exceed the credibility of endorsements for tennis shoes, especially if the commercial is delivered from behind bars.

Interdiction

Our whole narcomilitary drug interdiction policy needs rationale, if any can be found. General McCaffrey has stated on several occasions that he doesn't think our country can do much to stop the flow of drugs across the borders. By his own admission, our border inspectors searched more than a million trucks and railway cars entering our country from Mexico in 1997 and found drugs stashed inside on only six occasions. Nonetheless, he has funneled millions of dollars to tighten the border anyway because, as he also has said, if smugglers are forced out to sea, "there'll be less murder and corruption of democratic institutions in Mexico and the United States."[22] We thus have the incoherence of our drug czar practicing an interdiction policy he admits is ineffective. Its continuation suggests a narcomilitary interest behind his back promoting that practice for empire-building reasons, often hurting our relations with other countries.

One place to begin on the enforcement side is to treat hard-drug usage in private homes the same way we treat pornography: without legalizing it, we could adopt an enforcement strategy not to disturb personal use in a home. We could concentrate enforcement on major manufacturers and distributors and downplay or even ignore casual public street sales and use. This policy would shift attention away from racial minorities on inner-city streets to those higher in the marketing chain. Then we could adopt more magisterial policies oriented toward efficacy rather than raw power: no imprisonment for possessing drugs unless the amount possessed clearly indicates a substantial business investment directed toward sales; drug treatment available for all addicts, including residential treatment backed by the threat of imprisonment; and no incarceration for dirty urine when under treatment (only if repeated tests reveal rejection of treatment). This approach would retain the illegality of drugs but treat drugs and addiction generally with more rationality.

PRISONS

The federal Bureau of Justice Statistics suggests that the United States will house about 2 million inmates by the year 2000. These grim statistics set our penal policy apart from the rest of the world and from our own history. At our millennium we lock up people at a higher rate than any country except Russia, at six to ten times the rate in most industrialized nations. Our prison population has quintupled since 1973.

During the same quarter century in which prison populations increased so dramatically, crime rates both rose and fell. Overall, the National Crime Victimization Survey showed a decrease in property crimes and little change in violent crimes. The Federal Bureau of Investigation's (FBI) Uniform Crime Reports, which showed an overall increase in both property and violent crimes, indicate that crime rose and fell in three cycles during this period. Those cycles cast doubt on the claimed causal effect of this incarceration policy on crime rates. Our recidivism rates are nearly identical for prisoners whether they serve one year or five years in prison.[23]

By all accounts, dramatic declines in violent crime (apart from homicide) have occurred in most states since 1994. But not even hard-liners credit incarceration as the prime reason. The crime decline of the 1990s is more likely related to demographics, a smaller juvenile population, a flourishing economy, and better policing.

Nonetheless, our national penology still reflects a pre-Galileo, prison-centric universe, where our positivist conceptions of justice envision punishment as only incarceration in a prison. We have embarked on a vast positivist experiment to imprison our population to achieve civic harmony. Prison has become the universal answer to any crime question. We have the highest reliance on incarceration of any Western nation. In Sweden, less than a quarter of prison sentences are to terms of six months or longer. In the Netherlands less than 15 percent are for a year or longer. Half or more offenders convicted of violent crimes in Sweden, Germany, and England are sentenced only to fines. Equivalent crimes in the United States are punished by terms measured in many years.

Without entering endless statistical wars, one can conclude from our present draconian sentencing scene that (1) severe prison terms have not reduced crime rates, (2) the headlong drive to build more and bigger prisons diverts enormous resources from cheaper front-end crime prevention efforts like education and job training, and (3) imprisonment as the norm for the mass of criminals cannot be considered successful as long as 60 percent of released young prisoners recidivate.

We need to replace the knee-jerk instinct to put prison bars around the Grand Canyon with more enlightened, less costly, up-front prevention techniques aimed at young people before they commit crime. Within prison, similar steps are needed, because almost all who do go to prison will eventually return to this same society. Their access to job training and family support should be strengthened in prison rather than severed so that when they return to the community, they can survive other than by crime or welfare, the only two careers our prisons now successfully promote.

Underlying these reflections comes a sobering recognition about the limited deterrence of the prison sanction. Little, if any, street crime stems from a reflective, calculated balancing of success versus capture. Instead, most crime reflects an impulsive, ill-thought-out reaction to a fleeting opportunity of the moment. The potential for deterrence via the message of lengthy prison terms is illusory. It is our own illusion if we think this message of severity gets across. We entertain a similar illusion if we think that courts or prisons are much more than bandaids; the "more courts and prisons" mind-set is akin to building more hospices in order to cure AIDS.

We know at least this much: as incarceration rates have skyrocketed, our prisons are increasingly filled with nonviolent offenders. Their presence forces violent offenders serving indeterminate sentences out the prison's back door. For the short term, we do need to imprison those expected to continue to act violently. We need to make more room for those for whom prison is most appropriate: those prone to violence. But sentencing non-violent offenders, including recidivists and drug addicts and older offenders past the crime-prone years of sixteen to twenty-four, to very long prison sentences expresses our frustrations in a very expensive and counterproductive way. We are now building prisons not to house violent criminals but rather to accommodate a tidal wave of nonviolent inmates, especially drug users and sellers, who take up a third to a half of valuable space needed for truly violent offenders. The Bureau of Justice Statistics concludes that, because of nonviolent crowding, violent offenders, such as murderers and rapists, serve only 48 percent of the imposed sentence.[24] Our desire to impose strict prison sentences on every offender means that we impose less-than-optimal sentences on violent offenders simply because we have to free up space.

Our penchant for mandatory prison sentences has become our Achilles' heel. As an all-too-typical example, more than 84 percent of those serving mandatory prison sentences in Massachusetts are first-time offenders doing an average of five years in their first prison sentence, a year longer than the average state sentence for a violent crime. The federal system shows the same topsy-turvy process: a 1992 analysis, the latest available, finds that 55 percent of all imprisoned drug offenders were "low-level," that is, either street dealers or mules, and only 11 percent were high-level dealers, supporting Chief Justice Rehnquist's observation that mandatory prison sentences "impose unduly harsh punishment for first-time offenders, particularly for mules who played only a minor role in a drug distribution scheme."[25]

The Prison-Industrial Complex

The imprisonment mania in this country is propelled not only by politicians but also by one of their expanding offspring, the private prison companies for whom burgeoning prison expansion is a lucrative market. Corporate prison-industrial allies now replace the ideal of public service with the lure of pure profits, achieved, of course, by increasing inmates and by encouraging legislative votes for still more prisons, all under a philosophy of "if we build it, they will come."

Privatization may have its place, but for-profit companies whose own growth depends on growing prisoners should be viewed with great suspicion for conflicts of interest and subjected to legislative restraints on profit-taking, not to mention their all-too-frequent abuse of inmates by cost-cutting and outright brutality. We might well consider the possibility that "if we dismantle it, they will go."[26]

Sunset Sentences

Little public harm would accrue and considerable private benefit would obtain if correctional authorities acquired discretion to release prisoners serving long mandatory terms after some decent interval. Increasing numbers of prisoners are now being held under ten-, twenty-, and thirty-year mandatory-minimum terms or under sentences of life without parole. The steady accumulation of these prisoners promises sizable increases in prison populations and budgets for prisoners held long after their crime threat has subsided. In most states such prisoners can be released only by pardon or commutation, powers seldom exercised because they expose politicians to soft-on-crime attacks. The magisterial and humane approach would be selective release of long-termers, a power best vested in correctional or parole administrators who need not pander to the public.

Aged Release

Federal and state governments can also similarly reduce prison spending if they could put hundreds, perhaps thousands, of aged convicts back in society. Upward of forty states' prison systems are under court orders to rectify overcrowding, which is partly caused by senior inmates. Some states' prisons even have a zero-sum status: the addition of a new inmate requires the release of an existing one: public safety at the mercy of arithmetic.

The practical question is not whether but which aged prisoners to release. Youth by far is a surer predictor of recidivism than age. States can reap sizable savings by designating some older prisoners for minimum-security facilities for geriatrics—essentially, nursing homes—or assigning them to live at large but wearing electronic bracelets for monitoring. Prisons designed for violent young predators now are being occupied by decreasingly dangerous individuals. We could make more effective use of this space by an aged release policy.

Three-Strikes Laws

Three-strikes laws make sense, if at all, only if the offenses defined as strikes are limited to the most seriously violent felonies. One of the problems with three-strikes laws is that the list of offenses included as strikes expands, under legislative pressure, over time, so that three-strikes laws become a platform onto which other offenses congregate, as happens when a particularly sensational offense hits the news and legislators rush to be the first to introduce a bill adding that offense to the list. Once that proposal gets to the floor, no one can oppose it for fear of being labeled soft on crime in the next election, with the ultimate result that the strikes become pregnant with many nonviolent offenses undeserving of prison at all. The solution is to limit strikes narrowly to only the most violent felonies.[27]

Disfranchisement of Inmates

As of 1999, 3.9 million Americans, or one in fifty adults, have lost their voting rights as a result of a felony conviction and imprisonment. Fully 1.4 million of these citizens are ex-offenders who have completed their sentences and returned to their communities. In seven states one in four black men is permanently disfranchised.

These sober statistics serve no one's interests, not the interests of the ex-offenders who would like to vote nor those of a country suffering from nationwide chronic low voter turnout. From a magisterial viewpoint, this disfranchisement policy incapacitates offenders from doing what they and the justice system most want: to become responsible participants in civic life. We could begin by modeling the civic lessons of voting to released offenders.

Intermediate Sanctions

To positivist policymakers imprisonment remains the only real penal option. Our current myopic penology polarizes probation and imprisonment as the only alternatives. A magisterial view would make room for an expanded middle range of sanctions between these extremes: fines, community service, home arrest, work furlough, electronic monitoring, and so on, which allow more individual tailoring than imprisonment and almost always drain less from the public treasury without any loss of deterrence. A judicial sentencer should prefer intermediate sanctions to confinement, and among intermediate sanctions the least restrictive and intrusive among those authorized should be chosen.

Research on intensive supervision probation, house arrest, fines, and community service consistently shows that offenders sentenced to those sanctions have no worse recidivism rates than comparable offenders sentenced to prison, and at much less cost to the public treasury. In many countries, including Germany and the Netherlands, fines are the most frequent sentence, regularly imposed for crimes that result in our country in long prison sentences. In England, Scotland, and the Netherlands, community service orders exist as a sentence more severe than probation, imposed for crimes that in our country result in expensive prison sentences. Unfortunately, comparatively few intermediate sanctions are adequately funded in our country. A serious crime control policy would also spend its resources on crime prevention by strengthening far more universal, earlier, and more lasting deterrents: a healthy family, school discipline standards, anti-idleness programs, and a justice system whose procedures model the fairness it expects the public to adopt.[28]

Modest expectations are also in order. Our prison system cannot be the principal force in reducing crime anymore than cemeteries can diminish death. While confinement has some impact in reducing crime, far more important "up front" societal factors work to prevent crime—education, shared moral and religious codes of conduct, family structure, and viable opportunities for employment and upward mobility.

POLITICIANS AND CRIME

Norval Morris tells the story of a medieval monk who said the word "mumpsimus" in the mass instead of the correct "sumpsimus" ("we consume"). When his superiors corrected him, he responded by saying, "I don't care what is correct; You take your sumpsimus, and I will stick to my mumpsimus no matter what is right." The medieval monk and today's positivist politician have "mumpsimus" in common: a preference for doing things their own way coupled with dogged disregard of contrary, correct data.

The past twenty-five years have linked political success to a tough-on-crime image that translates, first and foremost, into the emphasis on the absolute severity of punishment, which, in turn, translates into prison as the paradigm of severity. This political penchant for severe prison sentences at all costs, including taxes and human lives, stands in the way of more realistic, less expensive, more effective crime policies.

The politicians who establish high-sanction policies may understand the limitations of their policies but need some means to respond to the public pressure to "do something." Lacking any better alternative, they continually increase sanctions not so much because they think they will work but because increasing sanctions seems an effective way to relieve political pressure. A companion folly of current crime policies is lawmakers' rampant ignorance of, or indifference to, empirical crime data. Lawmakers either cannot or will not respond to criminological research or even anecdotal judicial input or reports from experienced workers in the trenches.

The result is a vast chasm between what lawmakers enact and what criminological and social science data suggest. The political and empirical positions are rarely consonant and seldom the subject of dialogue. Judges find themselves squarely pitched into the depths between the two, usually remaining quiet about the dire consequences of inept penal inflation. Criminologists, too, have allowed themselves the comfort of speaking and writing about sensible crime policies in academic forums far removed from legislative comprehension. Like judges, social science researchers need to confront lawmakers about crime policy in any way likely to get a hearing—by testifying, helping draft legislation, or offering their research services.

Of all these groups, the prime culprit is the collective "mumpsimus" political mentality at both federal and state levels, which panders to the electorate with increasing hysteria about toughness on crime in order to seduce the public's votes. Pandering to public fear usurps public leadership and education on effective crime policy. When "mumpsimus" judges and lawmakers consider relevant empirical data, they usually turn their backs on them because they may tarnish their image of toughness.

The prospect of turning "mumpsimus" politicians into careful followers of social science data is bleak; espousing the topics in these pages would ruin many careers. Some decisions present such excruciating demands for courage for elected officials that it is better to eliminate their need to make them. The question, then, becomes how best to introduce magisteriality into positivist penal policy and to separate it from a political environment where concern over toughness silences well-researched contrary positions.

The nation needs another forum to manage our penal system rationally, a group beyond political vulnerability, to bring empirical research to bear on crime and to highlight where current policies behave irrationally. Ultimately, the best interests of lawmakers themselves suggest that they shed control over the justice system. Given its interest in federalizing criminal law, Congress might well divest itself and state legislatures as well from any direct control over tinkering with crime definitions and punishments and replace our national patchwork penology with a standing national commission, perhaps in the Department of Justice, composed of a few lawmakers, many justice system practitioners, and mostly top-ranking criminologists of national and international reputation. This body could establish a new justice system from scratch, with new nationwide crime definitions, punishments, and policies, uniform from coast to coast and based on the Model Penal Code and on the best empirical data and principles, with enforcement, sentencing, and corrections remaining at the local level.

Such a national body could take a realistic look at current checkerboard criminal policies and do a cost-benefit analysis to highlight those whose costs exceed utilitarian benefits. The commission would enact enlightened, nationwide, uniform policies to counter our present knee-jerk fiefdom forays. Precedent exists for such a body: in addition to the Federal Sentencing Commission, state and federal salary commissions also exist, in part, to remove lawmakers from quicksand-type dilemmas. We could follow and expand those models in the important work of crafting anew a professionally managed, uniform, apolitical, data-based justice system worthy of its name, which practices the justice it preaches.

NOTES

1. T. Tyler, *Why People Obey the Law* (New Haven, CT: Yale University Press, 1990), 22–23 (hereafter, Tyler). A related discussion of the allied "broken windows" concept appears in M. Massing, "The Blue Revolution," *New York Review of Books*, No. 18, 32 (Nov. 19, 1998), dealing in part with the pedagogical message given the public by official indifference to squalor. See also *The Sociology of Georg Simmel*, trans., Wolff (New York: Free Press, 1950), 186–189.

2. N. Morris, "Teenage Violence and Drug Use," 31 *Valpo. L.R.*, 547 (1997).

3. Massing, "The Blue Revolution," 32–33.

4. Tyler, *Why We Obey*, 110, 165, 178.

5. Paul H. Robinson and John M. Darley, *Justice, Liability and Blame* (Boulder: Westview Press, 1995), 201.

6. P. Robinson, "Introduction," 91 *N.W. L.R.* 1231, 1243 (1997).

7. M. Tonry, *Sentencing Matters* (New York: Oxford University Press, 1996), 139 (hereafter, Tonry).

8. K. Stith and Jose Cabranes, *Fear of Justice* (Chicago: University of Chicago Press, 1998), which insightfully and effectively criticizes the amoral mathematics of federal guideline sentencing.

9. W. Brownsberger, *Mandatory Drug Sentences* (Cambridge: Robert W. Johnson Research Foundation, 1997), 5.

10. Tonry, 195. On December 16, 1998, the *New York Times* reported that federal district court Judge Nancy Gertner in Boston, in the course of explaining a reduced sentence, found that federal sentencing guidelines focus "entirely on the sentences received for prior convictions" without distinguishing the kind of offenses and that under the guidelines' arcane mathematical structure, an 18-month sentence computes just as a sentence of 18 *years*. See F. Butterfield, "Bias Cited in Reducing Sentence," *New York Times*, A12 (Dec. 16, 1998).

11. Tonry, *Sentencing Matters*, 193.

12. E. Thomson, "Deterrence versus Brutalization," 1 *Homicide Studies*, 110–128 (May, 1997) cites a number of studies like the author's showing that executions prompt some homicidally inclined persons to follow the government's example, a finding consistent with the "broken windows" concept that government attitudes toward crime and law teach consonant attitudes to the citizenry. See also J. Rauch, "Death by Mistake," *National Journal*, 1224 (May 30, 1998). Cf. also the 1998 Amnesty International Report condemning the U.S. death penalty as arbitrary, vengeful, and driven by political ambition.

13. 408 U.S. 238 (1972). *Furman* held the death penalty as applied at the time unconstitutional because of its lack of standards, the same failing still prevalent in prosecutorial choices to seek or not the death penalty, to charge capital or non-capital homicide, to offer or not plea bargains which may or may not allow escape from that penalty.

14. In Texas, a man was executed even though his lawyer's entire closing argument at sentencing was: "You are an extremely intelligent jury. You've got that man's life in your hands. You can take it or not. That's all I have to say." In Houston, at least three capital sentences have been upheld in recent years (and one has been carried out) even though the defendant's court-appointed lawyers slept

through large portions of the trials. "His mouth kept falling open and his head lolled back on his shoulders," reported the *Houston Chronicle* of the lawyer in one such case. "Every time he opened his eyes, a different prosecution witness was on the stand." See J. Rauch, "Death by Mistake," *National Journal*, 1224–1228 (May 30, 1998). Data compiled by Richard Fowles of the University of Utah show that the national homicide rate increases 5.6 for every 1 percent increase in the unemployment rate, suggesting that employment is a far greater deterrent to homicide than is the death penalty.

15. Model Penal Code § 210.2, comment 6, at 30 (Philadelphia: American Law Institute, 1980).

16. The popular press reported on December 25, 1998, that Prince Charles of England recommended that a multiple sclerosis patient take marijuana to ease her pain. See *Arizona Republic*, A14 (Dec. 25, 1998).

17. J. Califano, "A Punishment-Only Prison Policy," *America*, 14 (Feb. 22, 1998).

18. Id.

19. As reported in the *Arizona Republic* (Sept. 10, 1998).

20. M. Massing, *The Fix* (New York: Simon and Schuster, 1998). Massing advocates Jaffe's "code," a set of principles that sum up his approach to drug use: "chronic drug users are at the heart of the nation's drug problem; a diverse array of services is required; Government must assure their availability and efficacy; law enforcement is an adjunct to rehabilitation and, always, reducing demand for drugs through education and treatment must take precedence over law enforcement efforts to reduce the supply of drugs." Massing says the Nixon administration, following the Jaffe prescription, managed to bring a "serious heroin epidemic" under control "in a few short years."

21. 82 *Judicature*, 8–10. (July–Aug. 1998).

22. Massing, *The Fix*, 224. See also D. Musto, "Just Saying 'No' Is Not Enough," *New York Times Book Review*, 12 (Oct. 18, 1998).

23. A. Beck, "Recidivism of Prisoners," Bureau of Justice Statistics (Apr. 1989). See also press release, "The Sentencing Project," 1 (Dec. 1998).

24. Department of Justice, Bureau of Justice Statistics (1997), 23.

25. "A Big Time Bust," *Boston Globe*, D1 (Nov. 8, 1998).

26. E. Schlosser, "The Prison-Industrial Complex," *The Atlantic Monthly*, 51–54 (Dec. 1998):

Three decades after the war on crime began, the United States has developed a prison-industrial complex—a set of bureaucratic, political, and economic interests that encourage increased spending on imprisonment, regardless of the actual need. The prison-industrial complex is not a conspiracy, guiding the nation's criminal-justice policy behind closed doors. It is a confluence of special interests that has given prison construction in the United States a seemingly unstoppable momentum. It is composed of politicians, both liberal and conservative, who have used the fear of crime to gain votes; impoverished rural areas where prisons have become a cornerstone of economic development.

27. Professor Walter Dickey of the University of Wisconsin Law School and his research assistant, attorney Pam Stiebs Hollenhorst, have looked at the five years since the three-strikes laws went into effect and, as of 1998, found that Alaska,

Connecticut, and New Mexico have each had one conviction under their three-strikes law; Tennessee has three, but Georgia has had 2,000, and California, 40,511. The study, released November 14, 1998, claims that three-strikes laws are not cost-efficient. By the time the offenders commit their third felony and are sentenced to life, they've usually reached an age—their early to mid-thirties—at which their criminal activity is ending. Lawrence W. Sherman, chairman of the Criminal Justice Department at the University of Maryland, says "For every piranha we're getting off the street, we're getting a lot of tuna . . . and may be turning them into piranhas." See *National Law Journal*, A8 (Dec. 7, 1998).

28. Tonry, 163. The Rand Corporation finds that the number of serious crimes prevented by every $1 million spent incarcerating repeat felons is 61; the number prevented by the same amount spent on high school graduation incentives is 258. Harpers Index, *Harpers*, 13 (June 1998).

BIBLIOGRAPHY

CHAPTER 1

Books

Aristole. *Nicomachean Ethics: The Complete Works of Aristotle.* Jonathan Barnes, ed. Princeton: Princeton University Press, 1984.

Blumstein, A. "Prisons." In *Thinking About Crime.* J. Q. Wilson, ed. New York: Basic Books, 1994.

Brownsberger, W. *Profile of Anti-Drug Enforcement in Urban Poverty Areas of Massachusetts.* Cambridge: Robert W. Johnson Research Foundation, 1997.

Caulkins, J., C. Rydell, W. Schwabe, and J. Chiesa. *Mandatory Minimum Drug Sentences: Throwing Away the Key or the Taxpayers' Money?* Santa Monica: Rand Corporation, 1997.

Davis, K. *Discretionary Justice: A Preliminary Inquiry.* Baton Rouge: Louisiana State University Press, 1969.

Estrich, S. *Getting Away with Murder.* Cambridge: Harvard University Press, 1998.

Frankel, M. *Criminal Sentences: Law without Order.* New York: Hill and Wang, 1972.

Joint Committee on New York Drug Law Evaluation. *The Nation's Toughest Drug Law: Evaluating the New York Experience.* New York: New York Bar Association and Drug Abuse Council, 1978.

Lipton, D., R. Martinson, and J. Wilks. *The Effectiveness of Correctional Treatment: A Survey of Treatment Evaluation Studies.* New York: Praeger, 1975.

Morris, N. *The Future of Imprisonment.* Chicago: University of Chicago Press, 1974.

Reiss, A. and J. Roth. *Understanding and Controlling Violence.* Washington, D.C.: National Academy Press, 1993.

Tonry, M. *Sentencing Matters*. New York: Oxford University Press, 1996.
U.S. Sentencing Commission. *Sentencing Commission Guidelines Manual*. St. Paul, Minn.: West, 1994.
U.S. Sentencing Commission. *The Federal Sentencing Guidelines: A Report on the Operation of the Guidelines System and Short-Term Impacts on Disparity in Sentencing, Use of Incarceration, and Prosecutorial Discretion and Plea Bargaining*. 1991.
Zimring, F. and G. Hawkins. *Incapacitation: Penal Confinement and the Restraint of Crime*. New York: Oxford University Press, 1995.

Articles

Flaherty, M. and J. Diskupic. "Despite Overhaul, Federal Sentencing Still Misfires." *Washington Post*, A1 (Oct. 6, 1996).
Frase, R. "Sentencing Guidelines in the States: Still Going Strong." 78 *Judicature*, 173 (1995).
Massing, M. "The Blue Revolution." *N.Y. Review of Books* (Nov. 19, 1998).
Messinger, R. and B. Johnson. "California's Determinate Sentencing Laws." In *Determinate Sentencing: Reform or Regression*. Washington, D.C.: U.S. Government Printing Office, 1978
Mitva, A. "Justice Reform." 43 *Cleveland S.L.R.* 5 (1997).
Nagel, I. and S. Schulhofer. "A Tale of Three Cities: An Empirical Study of Charging and Bargaining Practices under the Federal Sentencing Guidelines." 66 *So. Cal. L.R.* 501–566 (1992).
Nagin, D. "General Deterrence: A Review of the Empirical Evidence." In *Deterrence and Incapacitation*. A. Blumstein, ed. Washington, D.C.: National Academy Press, 1978.
Robinson, P. "Sentencing Reform." 8 *Crim. Law Forum* 12 (1997).
Slater, E. "Pizza Thief Receives Sentence of 25 Years to Life in Prison." *L.A. Times* (Mar. 3, 1995).
Stith, K. and J. Cabranes. "Judging under the Federal Sentencing Guidelines." 91 *N W L.R.* 1247 (1997).
U.S. Department of Justice. "An Analysis of Non-Violent Drug Offenders" (1994).
Wesson, M. "Sentencing Reform in Colorado: Many Changes, Little Progress." 4 *Overcrowded Times* 14 (1993).

Cases

Mistretta v. United States. 488 U.S. 361, 412 (1989).
Olson v. Walker. 162 Ariz. 174, 781 P.2d. 1015 (1989).

Statutes

The Sentencing Reform Act of 1984. Pub. L. No. 98–473, 98 Stat. 1837 (1984) (codified at 18 U.S.C. §§ 3551–3586, 3621–3625, U.S.C.).

CHAPTER 2

Books

Black's Law Dictionary, 6th ed. St. Paul, Minn.: West, 1990.

Articles

Alschuler, A. "An Exchange of Concessions." 142 *New L.J.* 937 (1992).

Brunk, C. "The Problem of Voluntariness and Coercion in the Negotiated Plea." 13 *Law and Soc.* 528–529 (1979).

Easterbrook, F. "Criminal Procedure as a Market System." 12 *J. Legal Stud.* 289 (1983).

Easterbrook, F. "Plea Bargaining as Compromise." 101 *Yale L.J.* 1969 (1992).

Gerber, R. "A Judicial Perspective on Plea Bargaining." *Ariz. Atty.* 38, 39 (Sept. 1, 1998).

Goldstein, A. "Criminal Justice Systems: Guilty Pleas and the Public Interest." 49 *SMU L.R.* 567 (1996).

Lowenthal, G. "Mandatory Sentencing Laws." 81 *Cal. L.R.* 61 (1993).

Schulhofer, S. "Plea Bargaining as Disaster." 101 *Yale L.J.* 1979 (1992).

Schulhofer, S. "A Wake-Up Call from the Plea Bargaining Trenches." 19 *Law and Soc. Inquiry* 135 (1994).

Scott, R. and W. Stuntz. "Plea Bargaining as Contract." 101 *Yale L.J.* 1909 (1992).

Cases

Bordenkircher v. Hayes, 434 U.S. 357 (1978).
Santobello v. New York, 404 U.S. 257 (1971).

CHAPTER 3

Books

Amnesty International. *When the State Kills: The Death Penalty: A Human Rights Issue.* New York: Amnesty International, 1989.

Andenaes, J. *Punishment and Deterrence.* Ann Arbor: University of Michigan Press, 1974.

Bedau, H. *Capital Punishment in the U.S.* New York: Oxford University Press, 1976.

Bedau, H. *The Death Penalty in America.* New York: Oxford University Press, 1982.

Bentham, J. *The Rationale of Punishment.* London: Verso, 1830.

Berns, W. *For Capital Punishment.* New York: Basic Books, 1979.

Black, C. *Capital Punishment: The Inevitability of Caprice and Mistake.* New York: W. W. Norton, 1981.

Blackstone, W. *Commentaries on the Laws of England.* Chicago: University of Chicago Press, 1979.

Blumberg, A. and E. Niederhoffer, eds. *The Ambivalent Force: Perspectives on the Police*. New York: Holt, 1985.

Blumstein, A., J. Cohen, and D. Nagin. *Deterrence and Incapacitation*. Washington, D.C.: National Academy of Sciences, 1978.

Bowers, W., G. Pierce and J. McDevitt. *Legal Homicide: Death as Punishment in America. 1864–1982*. Boston: Northeastern University Press, 1984.

Camus, A. "Reflections on the Guillotine." In *Resistance, Rebellion, and Death*. J. O'Brien, trans. 1961, 175.

Hart, H.L.A. *Law, Liberty, and Morality*. Stanford: Stanford University Press, 1963.

Hass, R. and J. A. Incardi, eds. *Challenging Capital Punishment: Legal and Social Science Approaches*. Newbury Park, CA: Sage Publications, 1988.

Jamieson, K. and T. Flanagan. *Sourcebook of Criminal Justice Statistics*. Albany: Hindelang Cr. Justice Research Center, 1989.

Kaminer, W. *It's All the Rage*. New York: Addison-Wesley, 1995.

Kappeler, V., M. Blumberg, and G. Potter. *The Mythology of Crime and Criminal Justice*. Prospect Heights, IL: Waveland Press, 1993.

Maguire, K. and T. Flanagan. *Sourcebook of Criminal Justice Statistics*. Albany: Hindelang Cr. Justice Research Center, 1991.

Radlet, Michael L., Hugo A. Bedau, and Constance E. Putnam. *In Spite of Innocence*. Boston: Northeastern University Press, 1992.

Scott, G. *History of Capital Punishment*. New York: AMS Press, 1950.

Sellin, T. *The Death Penalty*. Philadelphia: American Law Institute, 1959, 1982.

Sellin, T. *The Penalty of Death*. Ann Arbor, MI: Sage Publications, 1980.

Short, J. and M. Wolfgang, eds. *Collective Violence*. New York: American Academy of Politics and Social Science, 1972.

Streib, V. *Death Penalty for Juveniles*. Bloomington: Indiana University Press, 1987.

Voltaire. *A Commentary*. Appended to C. Beccaria, *An Essay on Crimes and Punishments*. Ingraham, trans. London: Verso, 1819.

Zeisel, H. "The Deterrent Effect of the Death Penalty." *The Supreme Court Review 1976*. Philip Kurland, ed. Chicago: University of Chicago Press, 1977.

Zimring, F. and G. Hawkins. *Capital Punishment and the American Agenda*. Cambridge: Cambridge University Press, 1986.

Zimring, F. and G. Hawkins. *Deterrence*. Chicago: University of Chicago Press, 1973.

Articles

Bailey, W. and R. Peterson. "Police Killings and Capital Punishment: The Post Furman Period." 25 *Criminology* 1 (1987).

Baldus, D. and J. Cole. "A Comparison of the Work of Thorsten Sellin and Isaac Ehrlich on the Deterrent Effect of Capital Punishment." 85 *Yale L.J.* 170 (1975).

Brennan, W. "Foreword," 8. *Notre Dame J. Law, Ethics and Public Policy* 4 (An Issue Devoted to the Death Penalty) (1994).

Bright, S. and P. Keenan. "Judges and the Politics of Death." 75 *B.U.L.R.* 759 (1995).

Browning, J. "The New Death Penalty Statutes: Perpetuating a Costly Myth." 9 *Gonz. L. Rev.* 651, 660 (1974).

Cardarelli, A. "An Analysis of Police Killed in Criminal Action." 59 *J. Crim. L. Crim. Pol. Sc.* 447 (1968).

Cohn, D. "The Penology of the Talmud." 5 *Israel L. Rev.* 53, 66 (1970).

Dann, R. "The Deterrent Effect of Capital Punishment." *Friends Social Service* series (1935).

Ehrlich, I. "Capital Punishment and Deterrence." 85 *J. Pol. Econ.* 741 (1977).

Ehrlich, I. "The Deterrent Effect of Capital Punishment: A Question of Life and Death." 64 *Am. Ec. R.* 397–417 (1975).

Godfrey, M. and V. Schiraldi. "How Have Homicide Rates Been Affected by California's Death Penalty?" *In Brief* (San Francisco: Center for Juvenile and Criminal Justice: Apr. 1995).

Graves, W. "A Doctor Looks at Capital Punishment." 10 (4) *Journal of the Loma Linda University School of Medicine* 137 (1956).

Lehtinen, M. "The Voice of Life: An Argument for the Death Penalty." 23 *Crime and Delinquency* 237 (1977).

Lempert, R. "The Effect of Executions on Homicides: A New Look in an Old Light." 29 *Crime and Delinq.* 88 (1983).

Marquart, J. and J. Sorenson. "Institutional and Post-Release Behavior of *Furman*—Commuted Inmates in Texas." 26 *Criminology* 677 (1988).

Pascucci, R. "Special Project, Capital Punishment in 1984: Abandoning the Pursuit of Fairness and Consistency." 69 *Cornell Law Rev.* 1129 (1984).

Peterson, R. and W. Bailey. "Murder and Capital Punishment: The Post-Furman Era." 66 *Soc. Forces* 774 (1988).

Peterson, R. and W. Bailey. "Police Killings and Capital Punishment." 25 *Criminology* 1 (1987).

Radelet, M. "Persistent Flaws in Econometric Studies of the Deterrent Effect of the Death Penalty." 23 *Loy. L.A. L. Rev.* 29 (1989).

Rosenberg, T. "The Deadliest D.A." *N.Y. Times Magazine* (July 16, 1995).

Stack, S. "Publicized Executions and Homicide." 52 *Am. Soc. Rev.* 532 (1987).

Steiker, J. "The Long Road from Barbarism." 71 *Tx. L.R.* 1131 (1933).

Tabak, R. and J. Lane. "The Execution of Injustice: A Cost and Lack of Benefit Analysis of the Death Penalty." 23 *Loy. of L.A. L.R.* 136 (1989).

Thomson, E. "Deterrence vs. Brutalization." 1 *Homicide Studies* 110 (1997).

van den Haag, E. "In Defense of the Death Penalty." 14 *Cr. L. Bul.* 51–68 (1978).

Vito, G., P. Koester, and D. Wilson. "Return of the Dead: An Update on the Status of Furman-Commuted Death Row Inmates." In *The Death Penalty in America: Current Research*, R. Bohm (ed.). Cincinnati: Anderson, 1991.

Wilkes, J. "Murder in Mind." *Psychology Today* (June 1987).

Newspapers and Periodicals

ABA Journal (Feb. 1997).

Arizona Republic (Feb. 18, 1997; Aug. 9, 1997; Oct. 5, 1997).

Harpers Index (June 1998).

National Law Journal (June 11, 1990).

New York Times (Jan. 11, 1998).

San Francisco Daily Banner Journal (Feb. 4, 1988).

Time (Jan. 15, 1996; Nov. 11, 1996; Jan. 19, 1998).
Wall Street Journal (Jan. 16, 1998).

Cases

Trop v. Dulles, 356 U.S. 86, 102 (1958).
Furman v. Georgia, 408 U.S. 238 (1972).
Gregg v. Georgia, 428 U.S. 158 and 169 (1976).
Coker v. Georgia, 433 U.S. 584, 596 n. 10 (1977).
Enmund v. Florida, 458 U.S. 782, 796–97. n.22 (1982).
Tison v. Arizona, 481 U.S. 137, 157–58 (1987).
Stanford v. Kentucky, 492 U.S. 361, 369 n. 1 (1989).
Case of Soering, 162 Eur. Ct, H.R. ser.A. (1989) reprinted in 28 I.L.M. 1063 (1989).
Penny v. Lynaugh, 492 U.S. 302 (1989).

Legislation

Arizona Revised Statutes 13–1101.
G.A. Res. 28/57 U.M. GAOR, 26th Sess., Supp. No. 29, para. 3, U.M. Doc. A/ 8429 (1972); G.A. Res. 32/61, U.M. GAOR, 32d Sess., Supp. No. 45, para. 1, U.M. Doc. A/3245 (1978).
International Covenant on Civil and Political Rights. Art. 6, 999 U.N.T.S. 171 (Dec. 16, 1966).
Nov. 4, 1950, Protocol No. 6, art. 1, 213. U.N.T.S
Senate Comm. on Foreign Relations, Report on the International Covenant on Civil and Political Rights. S. Doc. No. 102–23 102d Cong., 2d Sess. 6 (1992), reprinted in 31 I.L.M. 645, 649 (1992).
U.M. Dept. of Economic and Social Affairs. Capital Punishment, 1968, at 40. N. Doc. ST/SOA/SD/9–10, U.M. Sales No. 62 IV.2 (1968).
Violent Crime Control and Law Enforcement Act of 1994. Pub. L. No. 103–322, codified at 18 USC 924.

CHAPTER 4

Books

Blackstone, W. *Commentaries on the Laws of England* 947. George Chase, ed. 4th ed. Chicago: University of Chicago Press, 1938.
Dressler, J. *Understanding Criminal Law*. New York: McGraw-Hill, 1987.
Fletcher, G. *Rethinking Criminal Law*. Boston: Little, Brown, 1978.
Hall, J. *General Principles of Criminal Law*. Albany: Lexis Law Publications, 1981.
LaFave, W. and A. Scott. *Substantive Criminal Law*. St. Paul, Minn.: West, 1986.
Model Penal Code. Philadelphia: American Law Institute, 1980.
Stephen, J. *A History of the Criminal Law of England*. Cambridge: Cambridge University Press, 1883.

Torcia, C. (ed.) *Wharton's Criminal Law*. 15th ed. New York: Fred Rothman, 1994.

Articles

Baier, D. "Arizona Felony Murder Rule; Let the Punishment Fit the Crime." Note 36 *Ariz. L. Rev.* 701, 707 (1994).

"Felony Murder: A Tort Law Reconceptualization." Note 99. *Harv. L.R.* 1918 (1986).

Fletcher, G. "Reflections on Felony-Murder." 12 *Sw.U.L. Rev.* 413, 421 (1980).

"The Merger Doctrine as a Limitation on the Felony-Murder Rule: A Balance of Criminal Law Principles." Note 13. *Wake Forest L. Rev.* 369 (1977).

Roth, N. and S. Sundby. "The Felony Murder Rule: A Doctrine at Constitutional Crossroads." 70 *Cornell L.R.* 446, 450 (1985).

Tomkovicz, J. "The Endurance of the Felony-Murder Rule." 51 *Wash. and Lee L. Rev.* 1429 (1994).

Cases

Edmund v. Florida, 458 U.S. 782 (1982).

Fisher v. United States, 328 U.S. 463 (1946).

Gregg v. Georgia, 428 U.S. 153 (1976).

Griffith v. State, 171 So. 2d. 597, 597 (Fla. Dist. Ct. App. 1965).

Morrissette v. United States, 342 U.S. 246 (1952).

People v. Aaron, 299 N.W. 2d. 315 (Mich., 1980).

People v. Dillon, 34 Cal. 3d at 477, 668 P. 2d. at 719, 194 Cal.

People v. Pavlic, 227 Mich. 562, 199 N.W. 373 (1924).

People v. Stamp, 2 Cal. App. 3d. 203, 209–11, 82 cal. Rptr. 598, 602–03 (1969), cert. denied, 400 U.S. 819 (1970).

State v. Dixon, 109 Ariz. 441, 511 P. 2d 623 (1973).

State v. Lopez, 173 Ariz. 552, 845 P. 2d 478 (1992).

State v. Medina, 172 Ariz. 287, 836 P. 2d. 997 (Ct. App. 1992).

White v. Digger, 483 U.S. 1045 (1987).

Woodson v. North Carolina, 428 U.S. 280 (1976).

Zant v. Stephens, 462 U.S. 862, 877 (1983).

Statutes

Arizona Revised Statutes, 13–1603.

CHAPTER 5

Books

Grinspoon, L. *Marijuana, the Forbidden Medicine*. New Haven, CT: Yale University Press, 1993.

Massing, M. *The Fix*. New York: Simon and Schuster, 1998.

Report, U.S. Sentencing Commission. Washington, D.C., 1998.

Zimmer, L. and J. Morgan. *Marijuana Myths, Marijuana Facts: A Review of the Scientific Evidence.* New York: Open Society Institute, 1997.

Articles

Editorial, 273 *Journal of the American Medical Association* 1875 (June 21, 1995).

Nadelmann, E. "Commonsense Drug Policy." 77 *Foreign Affairs* 111 (Jan.–Feb. 1998).

Office of National Drug Control Policy. "Drugs and Crime Data, Drug Use Trends" (June 1995).

Schlosser, E. "More Reefer Madness." *Atlantic Monthly* (Apr. 1997).

Schlosser, E. "Reefer Madness." *Atlantic Monthly* 45–63 (Aug. 1994).

Stempsey, W. "The Battle for Medical Marijuana." *America* 14–16 (April 11, 1998).

Toruella, J. "One Judge's Attempt at a Rational Discussion of the So-Called War on Drugs." 6 *Public Interest Law Journal* (Jan. 1996).

Television Documentary

Moyers, W. "America's War on Marijuana." *Front-Line*, PBS. Apr. 28, 1998.

Newspapers and Periodicals

Arizona Republic (Nov. 13, 1995; Dec. 22, 1996; Aug. 10, 1997; Oct. 27, 1997; Apr. 19, 1998; July 1, 1998; July 3, 1998).

New York Times (Dec. 20, 1996; Apr. 20, 1997; Oct. 26, 1997).

Esquire (Oct. 1997).

Time (Dec. 9, 1996; Apr. 6, 1998).

Statutes

Ariz. Rev. Statutes 13–1105.

CHAPTER 6

Books

Bar of the City of New York. *A Wiser Course: Ending Drug Prohibition.* New York: Association of the Bar of New York City, 1994.

Bennett, W. *Body Count.* New York: Simon and Schuster, 1996.

Carnegie Foundation. *Keeping Score: What We Are Getting from Our Federal Drug Control Dollars.* 1995.

Currie, E. *Crime and Punishment in America.* New York: Holt, 1998.

Federal Bureau of Investigation. *Crime in the United States.* Washington, D.C.: Government Printing Office, 1991.

Lyman, M. and G. Potter. *Drugs in Society.* Cincinnati: Anderson, 1991.

Massing, M. *The Fix.* New York: Simon and Schuster, 1998.

Packer, H. *The Limits of the Criminal Sanction.* Stanford: Stanford University Press, 1968.

Pennsylvania Crime Commission. *Annual Report.* Philadelphia: 1987.

Reuter, P., G. Crawford, and J. Case. *Sealing the Borders.* Santa Monica: Rand Corp., 1998.

Rotella, S. *Underworlds and Politics at the Mexican Border.* New York: Norton, 1997.

Schaler, J., ed. *Drugs.* Amhurst, NY: Prometheus, 1998.

Tonry, M. *Malign Neglect: Race, Crime and Punishment in America.* New York: Oxford University Press, 1995.

Articles

Bertram, E. and K. Sharpe. "The Drug War's Phony Fix." *The Nation* (Apr. 28, 1997).

Bishop, K. "Front in Marijuana War: Business Records." *New York Times* (May 24, 1991).

Califano, J., Jr. "Battle Lines in the War on Drugs: No Fight Harder." *New York Times,* A27 (Dec. 15, 1993).

Califano, J., Jr. "A Punishment-Only Prison Policy." *America,* 3–6 (Feb. 21, 1978).

Courtwright, D. "Should We Legalize Drugs? History Answers No." 44 *Amer. Heritage* 41, 50 (1993).

Department of Justice Report: Two-Thirds of Non-Violent Offenders Serving Mandatory Minimum Sentences. *The Drug Policy Letter* (Spring 1994).

Drucker, E. and P. Arno. Letter to the Editor, "Put Drug War Price at $500 Billion." *New York Times* (July 1, 1992).

Grinspoon, L. and J. Bakalar. "The War on Drugs—A Peace Proposal." 330 *New Eng. J. Med.* 357 and n.2 (1994).

Inciardi, J. and W. Pottieger. "Kids, Crack and Crime." 21 *J. Drug Issues* 266, 266–67 (1991).

Jehl, D. "Clinton to Use Drug Plan to Fight Crime." *New York Times* (Feb. 10, 1994).

Kleber, H. "Our Current Approach to Drug Abuse—Progress, Problems, Proposals." 330 *New Eng. J. Med.* 361, 361 (1994).

Kleiman, M. "Reducing Dealing among Adolescents." 31 *Val. L.R.* 551, 556 (1997).

Kyl, J. "White House Drug Policy." *Arizona Republic,* B4 (May 29, 1998).

Meares, T. "It's a Question of Connections." 31 *Val. L.R.* 579, 589 (1997).

Morris, N. "Teenage Violence and Drug Use." 31 *Valpo. L.R.* 547, 548 (1997) (describing the "ready availability" of drugs within prisons).

Nadelmann, E. "Drug Prohibition in the U.S." 245 *Science* 940 (1989).

Ostrowski, J. "Thinking about Drug Legalization." Cato Institute Policy Analysis. No. 121 (May 25, 1989).

Rand Drug Policy Research Center. "Are Mandatory Minimum Sentences Cost Effective?" (1997).

Torruella, J. "One Judge's Attempt at a Rational Discussion of the So-Called War on Drugs." 6 *Pub. Int. L.J.* 1, 19 (1996).

Treaster, J. "Echos of Prohibition: 20 Years of War on Drugs, and No Victory Yet." *New York Times*, sec. 4, 7 (June 14, 1992).

Treaster, J. "Survey Finds Marijuana Use Is Up in High Schools." *New York Times* (Feb. 1, 1994).

Newspapers and Periodicals

Arizona Republic (Mar. 18, 1998).
Crime Control Digest (Apr. 3, 1998).
The Economist (May 21, 1994).
New York Times (Feb. 25, 1994; May 26, 1998).
New York Times Magazine (Mar. 22, 1998).
Wall Street Journal (Aug. 26, 1998).

Cases

Harmelin v. Michigan, 501 U.S. 957 (1991).

CHAPTER 7

Books

Anderson, D. *Sensible Justice*. New York: New Press, 1998.

Christie, N. *Crime Control as Industry*. New York: Routledge, 1994.

Currie, E. *Crime and Punishment in America*. New York: Holt, 1998.

Department of Justice, Bureau of Justice Statistics. *Annual Prison Report* 1997.

Donziger, S., ed. *The Real War on Crime*. New York: Harper, 1996.

Estrich, S. *Getting Away with Murder*. Cambridge: Harvard University Press, 1998.

Goins, T. *Institutional Research*. Richmond, Va., Branch Cabell, 1994.

Katz, B. *Justice Overruled*. New York: Warner Books, 1996.

Kozodoy, N., ed. *What to Do about Crime*. New York: Basic Books, 1990.

Lipton, R., R. Martinson, and J. Wilks. *The Effectiveness of Correctional Treatment*. New York: Praeger, 1975.

Morris, N. *The Future of Imprisonment*. New York: Oxford University Press, 1974.

Morris, N. and D. Rothman, eds. *The Oxford History of the Prison*. 2d ed. New York: Oxford University Press, 1998.

National Center on Addiction and Substance Abuse Press Release. *Behind Bars: Substance Abuse and America's Prison Population*. New York: Columbia University, 1998.

Wilson, J. *Moral Judgment*. New York: Basic Books, 1997.

Zimring, F. and G. Hawkins. *Crime Is Not the Problem*. New York: Oxford University Press, 1997.

Zimring, F. *Estimating the Effect of Increased Incarceration in California*. Berkeley: University of California Press, 1995.

Articles

Butterfield, F. "Punitive Damages." *New York Times*, sec. 4 (Sept. 28, 1997).
New Yorker (Feb. 28, 1998).
New York Times (March 7, 1997; Aug. 9, 1998).

Cases

State v. Michigan, 1 CA-CR. 94–0757 (May 2, 1996).

CHAPTER 8

Books

Currie, E. *Crime and Punishment in America*. New York: Holt, 1998.
Donziger, S. *The Real War on Crime*. New York: Harper, 1996.
Estrich, S. *Getting Away with Murder*. Cambridge: Harvard University Press, 1998.
Kappeler, V., M. Blumberg, and G. Potter. *Mythology of Crime and Criminal Justice*. Prospect Heights, IL: Waveland Press, 1993.
Parker, H. *The Limits of the Criminal Sanction*. Stanford: Stanford University Press, 1968.
Pepinsky, H. and P. Jesilow. *Myths That Cause Crime*. Cabin John, MD: Seven Locks Press, 1985.
Tonry, M. *Sentencing Matters*. New York: Oxford University Press, 1994.
Windlesham, Lord. *Politics, Punishment and Populism*. New York: Oxford University Press, 1998.

Articles

Blumstein, A. "Violence by Young People: Why the Deadly Nexus?" *Nat'l. Inst. Just. J*. 3 (Aug. 1995).
Blumstein, A. "Seeking the Connection between Crime and Punishment." 4 *Jobs and Capital* 23 (1995).
Bright, S. and P. Keenan. "Judges and the Politics of Death." 75 *B.U.L.R*. 759, 774 (1995).
Chernoff, H. et al. "The Politics of Crime." 33 *Harvard J. Legislation* 527, 537 (1996).
Rauch, J. "Death by Mistake." *National Journal*, 1225 (May 30, 1998).
Rothman, D. "The American Way of Jail." *New York Times Book Review* (March 1, 1998).

Newspapers and Periodicals

Arizona Republic, A1 (Apr. 3, 1998).
Boyd, S. "Bush Challenges Dukakis to Explain Stand on Crime." *New York Times*, A20 (June 19, 1988).

"Cuomo Takes Anti-Crime Stance." *Washington Post*, A9 (Jan. 6, 1994).
Gugliotta, G. "Crime Bill a Hostage of Politics." *Washington Post*, A1 (Aug. 5, 1992).
Time, 25 (Aug. 23, 1993).

Cases

Harris v. Alabama. 115 S. Ct. 1031, 1039. (Stevens, J. dissenting).

CONCLUSION

Books

Brownsberger, W. *Mandatory Drug Sentences*. Cambridge: Robert W. Johnson Research Foundation, 1997.
Massing, M. *The Fix*. New York: Simon and Schuster, 1998.
Model Penal Code. Philadelphia: American Law Institute, 1980.
Robinson, P. and J. Darley. *Justice, Liability and Blame*. Boulder: Westview Press, 1995.
Stith, K. and J. Cabranes. *Fear of Justice*. Chicago: University of Chicago Press, 1998.
Tonry, M. *Sentencing Matters*. New York: Oxford University Press, 1996.
Tyler, T. *Why People Obey the Law*. New Haven, CT: Yale University Press, 1990.

Articles

Beck, A. "Recidivism of Prisoners." *Bureau of Justice Statistics* (Apr. 1989).
Califano, J. "A Punishment-Only Prison Policy." *America* (Feb. 22, 1998).
Morris, N. "Teenage Violence and Drug Use." 31 *Valpo. L.R.* 547 (1997).
Robinson, P. "Introduction." 91 *N.W. L.R.* 1231, 1243 (1997).
Thomson, E. "Deterrence versus Brutalization." 1 *Homicide Studies* 110–128 (May 1997).

Newspapers and Periodicals

Arizona Republic (Sept. 10, 1998).
"A Big Time Bust." *Boston Globe*, D1 (Nov. 8, 1998).
82 *Judicature*, 8–10 (July–Aug. 1999).
Department of Justice, Bureau of Justice Statistics (1997).

Cases

Furman v. Georgia. 408 U.S. 238 (1972).

INDEX

About the Author

RUDOLPH J. GERBER is a Judge of the Arizona Court of Appeals.

ISBN 0-275-96475-2

HARDCOVER BAR CODE